CRACKING the Hard Class

Strategies for Managing the Harder than Average Class

CRACKING the Hard Class

Strategies for Managing the Harder than Average Class

Second Edition

Bill Rogers

P·C·P
Paul Chapman
Publishing

© Bill Rogers 2006
© Scholastic (Australia) Pty Limited 2006 Illustrations

First published in 1997 by Scholastic (Australia) Pty Limited
Re-issued in 2000 by Paul Chapman Publishing
This edition published in 2006 by Paul Chapman Publishing

Paul Chapman Publishing
A SAGE Publications Company
1 Oliver's Yard
55 City Road
London EC1Y 1SP

SAGE Publications Inc
2455 Teller Road
Thousand Oaks, California 91320

SAGE Publications India Pvt Ltd
B-42, Panchsheel Enclave
Post Box 4109
New Delhi 110 017

Library of Congress Control Number: 2006928220

A catalogue record for this book is available from the British
Library

ISBN-10 1-4129-2355-7   ISBN-13 978-1-4129-2355-2
ISBN-10 1-4129-2356-5   ISBN-13 978-1-4129-2356-9 (pbk)

Typeset by Dorwyn, Wells, Somerset
Printed in Great Britain by The Alden Press, Osney Mead,
Oxford
Printed on paper from sustainable resources

Contents

What reviewers said about
Cracking the Hard Class (first edition)

In **Cracking the Hard Class**, the undisputed master of behaviour management, Bill Rogers, shows us that being an effective teacher isn't a result of God-given gifts of charisma and presence, but can be developed through a series of specific skills and learned actions. It's one of the most useful books around for new teachers — *Geoff Barton, The Times Education Supplement*

'[Bill Rogers'] most recent books — both from Paul Chapman Publishing — are **Behaviour Management: A Whole-School Approach** and **Cracking the Hard Class**. Both are excellent and, if you can catch him live on one of his UK roadshows, you're in for a real treat. This practical approach from a writer who has clearly retained at least a notional foot in the classroom is the one that works best for me' — *Geoff Barton, Times Educational Supplement*

'It is rare to read a book about education that makes you laugh and cry. Members of our profession frequently adopt academic, ponderous or obscure writing styles. Here is a writer who has rejected the pulpit to reveal the human emotions in a teacher's work in an entertaining, thought provoking book. While light-hearted Bill is no lightweight, his work has a sound theoretical base but out of this we catch only a passing glimpse. He prefers to concentrate on practical strategies to help teachers cope' — *Books and Writing*

'This book would certainly be invaluable to colleagues in the school where some had done the course and others had learnt at second hand. It would have a place in the staffroom of most schools, especially in the secondary sector. Bill Rogers is clearly a charismatic teacher … what he offers is based on secure knowledge of child psychology, classroom dynamics and staffroom politics' — *Emotional & Behavioural Difficulties*

'Bill Rogers is the modern guru of discipline … I enjoyed both books and found **Cracking the Hard Class** especially interesting. Mind you, you can't go far wrong with a title like that' — *Times Educational Supplement*

'If you are a fan of Bill Rogers then this book will not disappoint. If you have never heard of him and want to know more about strategies for coping with discipline, then read this. An excellent book with many clear ideas and examples that will undoubtedly change the way you teach. This book covers all key stages but seems to edge slightly more towards secondary school. Buy it now!' — *Phil Burney-Cumming*

'This is an excellent book for teachers at any key stage who have one or more "difficult" pupils in their class, as well as those with the "hard class". It provides simple and effective behaviour management strategies and makes you realise you are not alone and that it's okay to have a bad day. It mainly discusses secondary education but does refer to primary. Many of the strategies are suitable for all levels anyway. An absolute must-have for teacher' — *Amazon Review*

Acknowledgements

Many thanks, appreciation and admiration to the many colleagues who have allowed me to take demonstration lessons and mentor-teaching lessons in difficult and challenging classes from Year 1 to Year 10, and a few in Year 11 as well. They didn't need much prompting; (I especially recall many difficult Year 8 and Year 9 classes in the past few years). This book is as much their story as mine. We learned together in our on-going teaching journey that the crucial feature in dealing with the hard class is the support of colleagues. I have seen teachers admit in front of their peers (sometimes with tears) how difficult or demanding *that* Year 1 or Year 8 class really is, and then show genuine and appropriate relief when other colleagues recount their struggles with that class or those students. This is the beginning of 'cracking the hard class'. The support of colleagues is the underlying theme of this book.

There are many case studies of challenging classes (and accounts of individual students with challenging behaviours) in this book. For reasons of ethical probity I have not named the schools (or students) noted in case studies.

My particular thanks go to David, Robin, Greg, Debbie, Ros, Peter, Joy, Colleen, Don, Denise, Roxanne, Jo, Jackie, Rachel and Toby. Thank you for letting me share your experience with hard-to-manage classes in this book.

My thanks to Linda Moorhouse and Felicia Schmidt, the ever-patient and efficient transmitters of scribbled biro into readable print. Scholastic has been continually supportive of this project – remember Shane, this was your idea. My thanks to Shane Armstrong and his team, to my first editor Valerie Marlborough, to Virginia Greig, Teacher Product Manager, and to Julian Gray and the team who enabled, and supported, this second edition.

Bill Rogers
Melbourne
First Edition March 1997
Second Edition August 2005

Introduction

He supposed that for a crowd of boys aged from eight to eighteen, for the moment not under the direct eye of authority, they looked docile enough, even perhaps verging on the well behaved? In this and in other ways they were quite unlike the boys in his favourite kind of school story. These fictional boys either behaved like men of forty or carried on like comic lunatics or were wasters, scapegraces, bounders.
Kingsley Amis (1996), *You Can't Do Both*

1995: Halfway through the year Tim was appointed as a maths/science teacher to the local high school. As a teacher new to the profession he was pleased he had a job; even if he was only covering a teacher who had gone on leave (little did he know she had gone off on stress leave).

Tim's timetable loading included several periods with a really challenging Year 8. It was clear within a week that he was really losing any sense of focus, control or direction with the group. There was constant calling out, butting in, aimless wandering, lateness to class, task avoidance (and some task-refusal) and boys in ritualistic silly play fights. As part of my consultancy I was asked to 'work with him' (three weeks down the track).

I thought I would visit a couple of his science classes – informally – and then set up some team teaching and mentoring. As I walked down the corridor I could hear the loud multitudinous voices of a class 'over the top'. I could also hear the teacher's high-pitched voice getting higher and louder with a mix of pleading and urgency. It sounded (as it was) chaotic. I walked in – a knock on the door wouldn't have been heard.

I saw, in an all-encompassing scan of the room, a student pushing another out of the window or at least it looked like that. I knew the boy who was doing the 'pushing' (thank goodness it was the ground floor); or was Robyn clutching him and coming back into the classroom via the window? Who knows? It was entertainment for the audience of their peers: a male and female student wrestling 'through' a window!

Justin, ectomorphic in build, with ripped jeans, huge gym shoes and a visually deafening rock T-shirt, was grappling with what looked like Robyn's diary.

Tim looked totally fazed. As I entered the classroom he gave me a look that said 'Help!' and 'I want out of here!' I tried to 'read' the situation quickly. I raised my voice: 'Justin, Justin!' The class looked around, unsure of what I would do. Justin turned. I repeated, 'Justin!' Lowering my voice as he returned eye contact, I directed Justin to leave the room. I turned to Robyn, 'Robyn – back to your table now. Justin, outside now! Now!' There are no guarantees when one gives unilateral commands. I don't use them often. Justin threw Robyn's diary on the floor, marched across the room, head-butted the light switch (literally) and followed me down the corridor, muttering and swearing as I 'led' him to the administration area and the deputy principal.

I found out later (on the internal grapevine) that Tim's timetable slots with 8C had been given purposefully. 'Oh well, he was there to cover the other teacher – and, well, he was the last teacher in the allocation.' I argued that Tim was a first-year teacher and new to that school. 'Yes, but we all had hard times when we were at our first schools.'

This was said in an off-hand way by the senior concerned. Implication? If you can't 'hack it' don't teach here.

Tim had received no emotional support – he'd been given the timetable, the curriculum materials and left to cope. Most of all there had been no preparation for the class, no structural or problem-solving support, and no clear direction about use of time-out or follow-up discipline strategies. At the staff meeting at the close of the day he stood up, fighting tears, explaining how he felt several weeks into the school year.

There was an embarrassed silence across the staff room.

We then, *then*, tried to salvage his early teaching career by setting up a considered support process. This process should have been set up from day one.

2004 Habituation

The teacher was trying hard to settle the class. This was her second lesson with this Year 8 class. The bell had 'gone' some minutes back. There were a number of students chatting away with distracting engagement as she sought to gain whole-class attention. Several students were turning around to chat with students behind them (they *seemed* to her to be ignoring her).

'*Come on now, please be quiet. Would you please listen and face this way? Michael and what's your name ... yes, you?*' She turned to face the lads chatting and looking out the window to their mates (some lads dawdling off to arrive late at another class).

'*What?*' Bilal turned, '*what did you say?*'

'*Your name, what's your name?*' Dianne was getting annoyed. Someone yelled out '*He's Bilal.*'

'*Look, you two, please stop talking and just face this way now! Alright?*'

'*We weren't the only ones talking.*' Michael leaned back heavily in his seat sighing.

'*Look, I don't care if you were, just do what I've asked alright? It's not difficult.*'

Someone chanted, '*Yes Michael, it's not difficult.*'

'*Who said that?!*' Dianne scanned the room. Michael was sulking, Bilal laughing along with several other boys. Dianne was getting annoyed. Why not? Slowly (ever so slowly it seemed to her) the class began to settle.

Several students were fiddling with their pencil cases. She ignored that. Several students called out, while she was trying to introduce the unit of work for that term. Sometimes she accepted 'the question', sometimes she seemed to ignore, other times she got annoyed – particularly if Michael or Bilal called out. '*Do you have to call out? Do you? Why can't you put your hand up?*'

Michael started – again – to argue '*Other people call out – it's not just me!*'

Already Dianne was getting more and more frustrated, even tense. Two lads walked in, five minutes late. They walked past her, seeming to ignore her. She had forgotten their names from the first session.

They hadn't knocked on the door, they walked in, past her, and started chatting to their mates *en route* to the back row, '*So, what's happening?*' Darren and Kosta were grinning away to their mates while Dianne stood there, at the front, ignored by these students (and their peer-audience). The lesson had only been underway five minutes and already she felt the class 'slipping away' ... It is one of the most uncomfortable feelings in our profession.

Yes; of course we can rein such a class back in to some sense of fair, focused, purposeful 'order'. But, we can all remember that feeling of half a dozen distracting behaviours all happening at once. Unfocused behaviour leadership can lead to patterns of habituation such as frequent calling out; the chatting; the inconsiderate (even arrogant) lateness (complete with grand entrance).

It is crucial to plan ahead for those critical first meetings; this is addressed later in ch. 5. What we do, and say, in those first meetings, day one, lesson one, has a significant impact on general behaviour in our classroom. The students will watch, listen, 'test'-out their relationship with us. This is par-for-the-course in *all* group settings where there is a leader responsible for establishing a sense of purpose, focus and reasonable social order. It is no mean feat; those outside the teaching profession have little idea of the demands of such a role.

Support – not blame

I have worked with many classes like Tim's and Dianne's. The first thing to say about such classes (and our colleagues' struggles with such classes) is that we do not invoke the easy, tempting, and simplistic notion of 'blame': either blaming the teacher or the class of students. It is never that simple.

There are many reasons why a class is (or becomes) hard to manage (p 11*f*). The overriding concern with such classes is to generate adequate (and early) colleague support. Such support will need to address both students' and teachers' behaviours. It will particularly need to address patterns of *group behaviour*. When we can thoughtfully work *with the group* (as well as individuals) to give them an adequate, and appropriate, 'voice', we can re-engage their co-operative goodwill. This requires conscious, willing, purposeful and planned effort by the teacher and the class group. That effort, though, will be more effectively *realised* when the teacher has on-going, non-judgemental, colleague support. That is the theme, and purpose, of this book.

Habituation and 'distribution of behaviour'

In every class I've ever taught (and worked with as a mentor-teacher) I make the conscious assumption that behaviour is distributed along the '60, 30, 10 principle'. On a broad 'distribution curve' of reasonable, co-operative and distracting, disruptive behaviours the picture looks something like this:

- 60% of students (more in some schools) are 'characteristically' co-operative; reasonable and considerate in their behaviour in classrooms.
- 30% of students behave in attentionally annoying ways: clowning or 'notice me' behaviours (rolling under tables, quacking like a duck, cawing like a crow or other silly voices); frequent calling out (often to 'get noticed'); butting-in; leaning back heavily, noisily, in their chairs; making 'silly' or inappropriate comments; overly noisy during on-task learning time; seat wandering; task avoidance, etc.
- 10% of students (or more in some schools I have taught) present with *frequent*, challenging behaviours: arguing with, or confronting their teachers; task refusal; defiance … Students who present with socio-emotional behaviour disorders can also present with diagnosed patterns of behaviour such as: attention

deficit disorder, or ADHD; Autism Spectrum Behaviour or Oppositional Defiance Disorder spectrum behaviour.

These children have diagnosed behaviour disorders and, consequently, have behaviour learning *needs*. They still, however, present with significant challenges to behaviour leadership for teachers in class (alongside the 30% of the class who present with the annoying, irritating, and frustrating attentional behaviours).

I have noticed in many hard to manage classes that some teachers see a rapid deterioration in *group behaviour* when those students in the '60% range' start to 'drift' – even collude – along with those distracting disruptive behaviours of those students in the '30% range'. A pattern starts to develop: group restlessness; inattention; calling out; lack of task focus and talking while the teacher is talking. The degree, and extent, of such behaviours are often related to how a teacher establishes the class group in those initial (and critical) first meetings with the new class group.

- Do the '60%–70%' of normally co-operative students perceive us as confident in our role as teacher-leader? (*Confident*, in contrast to that strident self-assurance that some teachers display.)
- Do they (the 60%–70%) perceive us as indecisive, unsure, non-assertive (when we need to evidence confident, respectful, assertion)?
- Are we able to convey some clear sense of why we (as a class) are here, together, in this place (our classroom) with this subject, this unit of work, this lesson?
- Are we able to convey (within our subject/classes) some reasonable enthusiasm, some engagement in our teaching?
- Above all do we evidence that respect towards *all* our students? This is essential in those classes where some students are not easy to *like*.

In those critical first meetings we need to establish ourselves as confident, respectful teacher-leaders particularly when we have to bring necessary discipline to bear within our teaching. The practices and skills of such discipline are developed in each of the case studies that form the substance of this book.

Credibility by 'proxy'

Credibility is an important factor with a difficult class. Credibility is earned over time through effective teaching, leadership skill and, most of all, fundamental respect that can keep the punitive side of management balanced with that commitment to dignity, respect welfare and solid encouragement.

In contrast to Tim's and Dianne's stories (pp 1–3) Maria (who had also 'picked up' another teacher's timetable) had come to a new school as a first-year teacher in Term 4. It was her first, significant, teaching load and she was understandably nervous. Fortunately the school had a strong commitment to supporting colleagues, especially in the area of teacher welfare and classroom management.

It was agreed that two classes in particular could well prove difficult for a newcomer to the school – especially a first-year teacher. The staff took a preventative approach working with her to plan the first few lessons, within the unit of work, as a team. They also discussed discipline and referral approaches for after-class follow-up with difficult and challenging students. They particularly discussed how to work with the class in those critical first meetings.

They strongly suspected that if the teacher walked in on day one on her own, as it were, the students would give her a hard time. It was agreed that for the first few lessons the new teacher could establish herself 'by proxy' through team teaching. A senior colleague in the team who knew the students well would introduce Maria and then hand over the class but stay in the class for the first session in a team teaching, mentoring, relationship.

Maria and the senior colleague discussed how the brief introduction would work, what Maria would say to introduce herself and what routines or rules she would refer to in Session One. She was particularly aware to briefly refer to the core rights and responsibilities that linked her leadership of the class with that of the previous teacher. The work for each session for each class was planned with her colleague. They wanted it to look, and sound, relaxed and natural – not as if she was the weak, new teacher who had to have an older, experienced teacher to keep control. They even discussed such issues as how to 'present' themselves to the class, (as two teachers working together); where to stand, and the non-verbal aspects of presentation of oneself to a group.

The senior colleague 'settled' the class in the corridor and directed them into the room. As he stood front and centre, Maria stood to one side, observing him as well as indirectly scanning the class group from time to time. He said, 'Good morning everyone. As you know, your regular teacher is on leave and Ms D will be your new teacher for Term 4.' At no point did he say Maria was a beginning teacher, or that 'I'm here to see you don't cause trouble!' (and so on).

On a pre-arranged cue he stepped aside and Maria went to the front of the room and introduced herself, 'Good morning I'm Ms D. I'll be taking you this term for ...' She never mentioned she was a first-year teacher but added, 'I've taught in many schools [perfectly true] and it's a pleasure to be here working with you all.' She referred briefly to the relevant rules for her subject area and asked a student to put up a poster with several, positive headings on communication, respect, movement and learning. All the time she spoke, her senior colleague stood to one side as if to say 'I'm here to listen to Ms D, not "watch you". I'm here to be part of (not control) your teacher's introduction to this class.' Had he stood watching, facing them, like a duty police officer, or like someone portraying the message that I'm the 'white knight' and 'nothing can go wrong while I'm here', his presence would have conveyed a different meaning.

Maria and her colleague had also discussed how to use confident, assertive correction for behaviours such as calling out, physical restlessness, lateness, talking while the teacher is talking and argumentative student behaviour.

During the on-task phase of the lesson both teachers used correction and encouragement. Maria made a mental note of how relaxed and confident her colleague's teaching and management language and style were. At the close of the lesson they resumed their 'positional places' at the front of the room. Maria reminded the students about homework and smaller reminder slips were handed out. She went through the lesson closure and reminders about leaving the room tidy, and then stood at the door and said goodbye to the students individually as they left.

Maria felt positive about this first session with 'her' class. The students were a lively group but she felt they had conveyed 'status' on her 'by proxy' – they had accepted her as if through her colleague's role present in the room. Also, because she felt better; more secure and relaxed, she also noted her teaching and management had been more effective.

They sat down later to plan the next lessons. They agreed that it might be beneficial if the senior colleague came in after the lesson establishment (during the on-task phase of the lesson) *au naturel*, as if to have a brief chat and then depart several minutes later. The school has an open-door policy, making such classroom visits so much easier.

This approach has a number of benefits:

- The teacher has a positive start with a new class.
- There is two-way professionalism in planning and feedback with a special emphasis on establishment skills in the first meeting(s) with a new class.
- Even apparently small issues such as the actual introduction, how colleagues deal with the introductory phase of the lesson, and cues for teaming have to be thought through.
- The class accepts the *new* teacher more readily within this approach.
- Most of all, the new teacher has a supportive entry into a hard-class setting and this support will extend to problem solving, lesson planning and discipline matters.

■ We also discuss the naturally sensitive issue of whether (and how) a support colleague might intervene in a discipline issue if the class teacher has not addressed significant disruptive behaviour(s).

I have worked with scores of hard and difficult-to-manage classes at both primary and secondary levels. I have worked with teachers in these classes to re-establish a more positive working environment. We have worked together – sometimes with just the one teacher who is struggling with a hard-to-manage class, but often with the whole team at a particular year level. Often it has meant re-establishing the class (p 33*f*); as well as working on behaviour management skills (ch. 5); following up with challenging students; (p 107); improving confidence levels (p 171*f*), and developing personal behaviour plans with students who present with persistent patterns of distracting and disruptive behaviour. We pay special attention to developing common support plans for students with behaviour disorders (p 132*f*).

Whatever we have done, though, we've emphasised an approach involving the support of colleagues. We've worked as a team avoiding the easy blame of:

■ 'Yes, well, what do you expect with a group like 8D. They're all animals.'
■ 'You'll never get anywhere with this class!'
■ 'Anyway, he's a weak teacher. What do you expect – no wonder the class is a riot!'

Avoid easy blame. Blaming the teacher or students is naturally tempting. However, as a long-term solution, it isn't a solution – it's a reaction. Natural maybe, but never helpful.

Reading the riot act may temporarily assuage things (and it's only ever temporary) but it does little for the feelings or professional esteem of the teacher(s) in that class. A class that already has a reputation is not going to change on the strength of a five-minute lecture.

There is no one simple, single strategy that can change a hard class, just as there is no single reason for a class to be (or become) so idiosyncratically difficult to manage, and work with. What my colleagues and I have found is that we have been much more effective when we have addressed the hard-class issue *whole school* (from a year level and team basis). That is the central, underlying theme of this book – we need the support of our peers to 'crack' the hard-class syndrome.

All examples and accounts used in this book come from our collaborative journeys. Where appropriate and necessary, I have modified some accounts and changed the names of students and teachers to protect the self-esteem of all, while keeping to the central integrity of the event or situation.

It is my hope that this book will help in addressing a challenge faced by many teachers today – why is this particular class so difficult? What can we do together to change things? How can we get out of the spiral of jadedness, disillusionment and low expectation to enhance success in learning and social interaction? Most of all, how can we support one another in addressing challenging class groups?

Bad day notwithstanding

There are many strategies, approaches, skills and ideas outlined in this book. Within the safety of print, however honestly issues are faced, it all *sounds* probable, possible and even achievable. And so it is – bad day notwithstanding.

I have had many, many hard to manage classes in my years as a teacher, and I have had to cope with some very challenging and disturbing individuals. When you think of it, every intransigent and disturbed adult, every petty thief, every hardened criminal was once in someone's classroom (unless they had home education). In their embryonic forming that hard reality is the challenge of most teachers. We can't predict, although we're tempted, who such future persons will be (thank goodness). Nor should we predict. John Embling (author of *Fragmented Lives*, 1987) reminds us through his work with disturbed, dysfunctional children that we should not condemn the 'lost' to the 'kingdom of nothingness'. He states that schools can provide 'badly distressed *children* (author's italics) with a safe environment for learning, for interacting with others, for finding some pastoral relief to the nightmare of their lives. This means caring, humane environments, not jungles of violence and mayhem' (the *Age*, 2 June 1987, p 22). Yes, I have seen schools work successfully with difficult students and difficult classes. Such success, though, is hard won. And no matter how caring, how skilful, how well organised, how thoughtful the curriculum, how positive the language and how supportive our colleagues – there is the bad-day syndrome (BDS).

We'll shout on some days. We'll lose (actually *find*) our temper, and we'll say the wrong or inappropriate thing. Tiredness, frustration, irritation and social injustice will strike us. There will be days we'll feel fed up with the unsupportive bureaucracy and the mounting pile of marking. We will be having a bad day – something that should be eminently forgivable (in self and in others). A teacher in one of my seminars once said, 'I don't have bad days! I have bad weeks!' Fair enough.

We can cope with BDS, as can our students, if we're adult enough to acknowledge, apologise (where necessary), learn from it and move on. As Noel Coward once said, 'The secret of success is the ability to survive failure.' The issue of failure, stress and change is explored later in Chapter 9. My point here is that, in a *naturally* stressful job such as teaching, bad-day-notwithstanding should be a normative caveat to anything I've written.

Chapter 1

WHAT MAKES A CLASS 'HARD'?

A loser believes in 'fate'; A winner believes that we make our fate by what we do or fail to do.
Sydney J Harris

What does make a class 'hard'? A bad year? Possibly. A 'reputation class' (5A, 8D, 10L) – no doubt; a class that seems to have an *esprit de corps* expressed in group noise, poor learning habits, resistance to normal classroom management and learning.

- 'It seems like a whole lot of brushfires around your room; you settle one thing down and something else starts!'
- 'It's the noise level – when I walk in it's like being in the playground.'
- 'I come out of 8D exhausted … thank goodness I've only got them for four periods!'
- 'It's like they hijack every lesson; hardly anything gets done!'
- 'It's not one or two students … Lee calls out, Kevin shouts back; Lisa and Cassie are chatting away privately while I'm trying to teach. In wanders Ahmed and Matt late – that's not too bad but all their mates start up: "Whoa, late, eh? Naughty!" It's the seemingly constant hassle of trying to settle them down even before I can begin to teach.'

Even experienced teachers find such classes a struggle. Most teachers have had at least one class like this in their teaching career. If you've taught next door to a hard class, their 'corporate' behaviour can have a through-the-wall effect on your class. And, cruel fate, such classes are sometimes handed out (in the worst timetable slots) to new, even beginning, teachers. So much for teacher welfare.

Cracking a hard class isn't easy once it has a reputation. Of course, early inter-vention is not only desirable but also essential if support is going to be helpful and effective. However, many teachers want to feel that they can deal with such classes by themselves – to admit struggle or defeat early is seen, by some teachers, as a sign of professional weakness. There's the anomaly and yet the earlier the signs of 'hard class' are seen and acknowledged, the easier it is to intervene and effect and enable change.

What is a hard class?

Classes can be considered 'hard' when the *frequency* and *intensity* of the disrup-tive behaviour of a number of its members are significantly affecting the welfare of one or more of their teachers. Such behaviour is also significantly affecting any sense of productive teaching and learning. The other factor is *duration*. If the behaviour of the class (not just one or two members) is well beyond the BDS, it needs to be addressed as a hard-class issue across the whole-year level.

One of the confounding factors here is that sometimes a class is hard 'selec-tively', for just one or two teachers. This may be due to the curriculum offered. It may be due to teacher style, personality, management or discipline approaches. In these cases it is better to work with the individual teachers and the class rather than develop a year-level plan. These teachers, though, will still need the support of colleagues to enable a 'fresh start' with the particular class group.

Common factors in hard-to-manage-classes

All the approaches and skills discussed in this book will be relevant in any hard class.

- Sometimes it's as amazingly basic as the organisation and timetabling of the classes. Having a school policy of deliberately streaming classes (ability streaming) can often create groups of students who believe and act out their label – 'the veggie class' or 'the stupid class'. There is often a correlation between deliberately skewed groups of *learning-problem students* and prob-lems in behaviour. It may well be that the curriculum offered to such students is couched (unintentionally) around a deficiency model. Such classes miss the opportunity of learning from more able peers – indeed they often experience the opposite.[1]
- Sometimes it's the actual physical areas where teacher and students have to work. My first classroom was a bicycle shed (what a gift); and I had to scrounge several old desks to fit it out for my 30 plus students.
- Sometimes it may be associated with the grouping of students. Most schools

work hard at their groupings year by year. If it is known, though, that certain students are catalysts for others' disruptive behaviour, a change of class grouping will have to be made for *everyone's* benefit.

■ Sometimes the hard class is known by all but is given to the teacher new to the school or even to the first-year teacher. Obviously, classes should be allocated with some consideration given to these new teachers (p 5).

■ Sometimes it is the subject area and how it is taught. Some students are more disruptive in subject areas they believe are not beneficial to their perceived needs. I've been in classes where students have effectively said, 'Well, we stuff around because we hate doing ... [the subject area], and this way we don't have to do it, do we?' Teachers in other faculty areas – deemed to be of higher educational value or merit – may be covertly adding to the culture of selective subject resistance. While this does not excuse disruptive student behaviour it should alert us to see where we can realistically address student disaffection.

■ Sometimes it is the beliefs of the teachers that affect their perception of the class and hence their behaviour outcomes with that class. A teacher may label a class as 'All animals – they *never* listen' or 'I can't get anywhere with them'. Such easy labelling may affect how that teacher *perceives*, feels about, and relates to, individuals in the class who may well be behaving positively. There is ample research to show that one's emotional state is not simply the result of external factors. People bring characteristic beliefs to events, and relationships, that can significantly affect emotion and behaviour. That is why teachers A, B and C can all have different outcomes (regarding behaviour and learning) with the same class. The more demanding a person's beliefs about others, and how they *should*, and *must*, behave the more stressed they are when social reality seems to contradict such beliefs (Bernard 1990; Rogers 1992 and 2002). A teacher who characteristically believes, and whose self-talk repeatedly attests, that children *must* behave respectfully and appropriately at all times will find it much harder to work with sulky students easily predisposed to argue with, or challenge teacher authority. Such teachers will interpret the sulky reply to a question or direction as a major assault on their authority. Non-verbal behaviours such as sighs, pouts, raised eyebrows, rolling of the eyes, frowns, slowness and clicking of tongues take on a significant malignant hue instead of being seen as 'normative' student behaviour. Annoying, yes, but 'normative' in some students. This is not to argue that we ignore such behaviour, but it is important to put such behaviours into perspective. A teacher may say, 'Well, I like respect and I want respect, but it takes time to get it with these kids. I'm not going to get stressed out on this. Some students will like me and respect me, some won't – it's self-defeating and anti-reality to *demand* otherwise.' This kind of cognitive reframing is healthier and enables one to feel better. When we feel better we do better. We need to back up any rational self-talk with thoughtful and effective teaching management.

■ Sometimes colleagues are not given the opportunity to explore the hard-class problems and look at whole-school solutions (or at least year-level solutions). In other words, there is a lack of colleague support if the hard class is not addressed on this basis.

■ Sometimes it is the closed-door syndrome –literally. In the past some teachers saw their classrooms as their physical, educational and managerial domain. This is understandable. I fell into that way of thinking early in my teaching career. But other teachers go beyond this to a psychological closed-door mentality. I have seen colleagues plaster the inside of their windows (on both passage and outside windows) with posters so that no one can see in. I have even seen some colleagues totally block off the small glass section on their classroom door and the windows to corridor and playground (!). Is this privacy, or anxiety about what passing colleague observers might see? Many schools now have an open-door policy. It is important that even senior staff perform the normative courtesy of knock, wait and then enter. I have often seen people abuse their 'rank' by just barging in and taking over a class with no regard as to how a teacher might feel, and I'm not talking here about crisis situations either (p 23*f*).

■ Sometimes a class will sabotage a teacher's every attempt to manage the group. Most often this 'sabotage' is exercised by a few key, influential students who garner active (or passive) acquiescence in their peers.

■ Students sometimes pick their teachers as targets; they weigh up very early that this teacher is 'weak' in their eyes. They pick up on tone, manner, body language and the interactive responses and conclude that they can have fun with this teacher. Some students will crow and gloat over how they sent teacher X 'packing', or reduced them to tears, or to a rage. Some students will even bully teachers to satisfy their own pathetic sense of power and control. This issue is addressed at length in ch. 9.

■ Conversely a class sometimes goes wrong because of the way it is treated. There are teachers who believe they can control by fear, intimidation or frequent criticism.

I have seen teachers threaten *whole classes* with detention, (and heard through the next-door – classroom – wall): *'Right, you're all on detention. No – I'm sorry …! (is he?) you're all on detention! You had your chance – you blew it … You're all staying in at lunchtime! I'm sorry–I don't care anymore.'*

One can understand the frustration of the teacher but we can ill afford to lose the essential goodwill of the '60%–70%'.

Effective teachers seek to use detention *judiciously*, fairly, with reasonable necessity. I have spoken with teachers who give whole-class detentions about the 'backfire effect' by the responsible, co-operative students. Some colleagues, in frustration, have said: "I don't care! They're staying back – all of them!"

We can't afford *not* to care. I know some teachers say some unpleasant, foolish, even hostile things when upset or angry. But when calmer, more focused, we need to gain perspective. We will even need to retract … *'Look … I'm sorry. I got really annoyed with you all. I realise it wasn't all of you … I will need to see …'* The teacher can then nominate (at the end of the lesson) those students who will need to be detained to follow-up and follow-through (p 107*f*). Of course that smaller percentage of students will still whinge and moan and complain but at least the '70%' of students will see this as fair.

Some teachers get a reputation – early on – for using unnecessarily punitive measures and mean-spirited discipline because they perceive the whole class to be difficult. They often miscue and mis-target.

Students will find ways to pay back such a teacher. (I've even seen students go 'on strike.') Children today are keenly aware of their rights, especially the right to fair treatment, the right to have a say in how things are, and especially the right of reply when in disagreement with their teacher.

■ Sometimes key powerbrokers in the class have been allowed to become catalysts for disruptive behaviour across the class. There are always several powerbrokers in a hard class; they've learned how to 'work the group' to satisfy their needs for attention and power. It is important not to let these students act as gladiators in a cheering bear pit. Sometimes students from very dysfunctional home environments are given excesses of 'freedom' – they are given too much 'rope' in the belief they can't help their behaviour *because* of their home environment. While we must be sensitive to the needs of such students we will not help them by 're-victimising' them in the school setting. These students need an early message that they will be given plenty of support and understanding of 'where you're coming from', but that cannot be confused with 'allowing you to hijack teaching/learning and safety in our classrooms'. Persistent disruptors need to be given a clear choice to work with class (and personal) behaviour plans or be relocated to other classes. No student has a right to hold a class 'to ransom', as it were. We need to cater for all the students in a class group. We can build up the silent majority, engaging their silent disapproval into active disapproval and refocused behaviour. Thoughtful use of classroom meetings (p 33*f*), classroom behaviour agreements (p 52*f*) and personal behaviour plans (ch. 7) can re-engage the silent majority and enlist their support of the best interests of all students. By making certain rights-infringing behaviour unpopular we can enlist the moral support of the wider group of students (the 60%–70% p 4).

■ As noted earlier, the establishment phase is a crucial time in the development of a class group. We *build* a working relationship from day one as we engage that *natural readiness* in our students:

–What's our teacher going to be like?

–How much 'rope' will he give us? Is he fair?

–Has he got a sense of humour?

–How will he 'control' us? Students normally mean, can the teacher *establish* and *maintain* a sense of order, direction, focus and support in their teaching and discipline.

Every time I have discussed with students what they mean by 'control' they initially struggle, but it fundamentally relates to how they perceive the teacher's confidence in their role, particularly behaviour leadership. They will – normally – respond to fair, *reasonable*, discipline within a teacher's need to clarify rights, rules and responsibilities.

It is important to *teach* a class reasonable entry and exit routines, seat plans, rules for class discussion, simple cues for asking questions or getting teacher support, workable 'noise' levels, basic classroom agreements for learning and fair, and respectful treatment of one another. There are core routines that need to be developed in the first few days and weeks with every class, but especially with the harder class. These are discussed in Chapter 5.

RIGHTS, RESPONSIBILITIES, RULES AND CONSEQUENCES

Doyle (1986, pp 410, 411) notes wide research showing that all teachers introduced some rules and procedures on their first few days. Effective teachers, however, integrated those rules and procedures into a workable system. The rules and procedures were concrete, explicit, functional and clearly explained. Cues, signals and class procedures were rehearsed. In contrast, less effective managers failed to anticipate the need for rules and procedures covering important aspects of class operation or tended to have vague and unenforceable rules. Effective managers were rated higher on clarity of directions and information, stating desired behaviours and more frequently presenting clear expectations for work standards, *responding consistently to appropriate and inappropriate behaviour*, addressing disruptive behaviour sooner, and using rules and procedures more frequently to deal with disruptive behaviour. According to Doyle, the amount of disruptive behaviour did not differ significantly between 'less' and 'more' effective managers during the first week of school. However, in the second and third weeks, there was an increase in the areas of 'call-outs', 'talking in class' and 'movement around the room' for ineffective teachers. Successful managers anticipated problems and ways to deal with them.

Effective teachers will not allow (not establish) poor patterns of behaviour because they know that in doing so they habituate a pattern that is hard to change further down the track. They use management skills and approaches that can balance corrective leadership with conscious respect and encouragement. These skills can be learned, they are transferable and can be developed through supportive peer mentoring. Most of all, such teachers follow up and follow through early with disruptive students, especially the ringleaders and powerbrokers. They do this very early in their leadership relationship with the class group. These teachers are not averse to colleague support in any form because they know that it is only by working with colleagues that problems can be shared, stress can be managed and solutions can be found – not perfect solutions but workable ones.

Put them all in one class?

Why not put all the difficult students in one class – a sort of 'hoon' class – as one brave principal suggested to me (an option he would never have been willing to entertain *personally*).

This novel approach sounds, on the face of it, eminently sensible for everybody (except the teacher who actually has to teach such a class). Putting all the difficult and 'reputation' students into one class can easily result in the following:

- almost no significant role modelling of reasonable social and on-task learning behaviour by students in the 'normal' behaviour range.
- behaviour management is significantly more difficult as key power brokerage and 'hierarchical pegging' take on a more challenging, even dangerous, shape than in a regular class.
- such a class also gets its special reputation beyond any normative hard class that has a distribution of students with challenging behaviours.
- In one sense, too, it is unfair for the teacher and students – there is a perception of an 'isolated' mentality for both.

I'm not saying such a project cannot work, but to set it up within a mainstream school environment sends the message that we can't contain you – the 'troublemakers' – within the relative normality of a classroom setting.

It will be more effective if the school can set up a *partial* withdrawal of students with challenging behaviours (and behaviour disorders) to give educational and behavioural support one-to-one or in small groups (p 132*f*). In such groups key learning and behaviour skills can be taught through dialogue, active teaching, role modelling and rehearsal of academic, and social, survival behaviour skills (Rogers

2004). Furthermore, by regularly being in normative class settings they are subject to the social pressure of their peers. If their behaviour in these normative class settings is so disruptive that learning and safety rights are affected, then school-wide discipline, including loss of privileges through time-out and withdrawal from certain areas, will be a necessary feature of discipline *and* support. The messages for behaviourally disruptive students, and students with behaviour disorders include the following:

- You are always welcome in our classes and our school but not with behaviours that *continually* and *significantly* affect the rights of others.
- Your behaviour is your 'choice', even though your behaviour is affected by conditions, backgrounds and experiences outside the school setting. Our message will be, however, 'that when you come into *our* school this is how *we* do things. We can help you to make better, more effective choices. These choices will help you with your learning, behaviour and relationships at our school.'
- 'You own your own behaviour (YOYOB). I don't own it, your mates don't own it, and your mum doesn't own it. You do.' This is the parallel message to the 'choice' idea. This doesn't deny the need to help, support and encourage students with their behaviour. It does mean students are not merely victims of their poor habituation or life's circumstances.

Labelling the class

Labels are useful in their way – a kind of summary. However, when it comes to global labels used within the context of a whole class, or an individual student, they are perceptually hindering. Labels such as '*all* these kids are animals, idiots, dropkicks ...', 'these kids *never* ...' or 'these kids *always* ...' are global in definition. I have (sadly) heard teachers use such expressions. Such global labelling significantly affects perceptions and beliefs about the *whole class*, let alone key 'powerbrokers', and may make it difficult for teachers to alter their judgment. Actions that are open to a wide range of interpretations tend to support prior labels and hence reinforce negative perceptions and beliefs.

Walking down the corridor to team teach with a colleague she remarked, 'Well, you're going to work with my animals today, are you?' That's how she saw them (no hint of humour in her voice). As soon as we were in the room a student called out some inane comment (I saw it as low-grade attention seeking). My colleague looked at him and said to me (loudly), 'I told you, didn't I, eh?' Actually, in the whole lesson only half a dozen boys and one girl were disruptive, and it was all low level – annoying but low level. My colleague saw, and blamed, the whole class for the behaviours of these students. We had (I believed) a reasonably successful science lesson together but my colleague couldn't see it that way.

Of course my colleague was stressed because of the challenges of leading and managing a difficult class but such labels – frequently used – only reinforced her negative impressions of *all* of the students.

One of the ways to change perceptions is to discuss the same class and key individuals with other colleagues. That may help. I've sat in such meetings where some colleagues, however, cannot find any redeeming features in a student(s):

- 'How dare they …' (they did.)
- 'I can't stand it when they act like idiots!' (not *all*, not *always*)
- 'No way! Those students will not, I repeat not, behave that way.' (They did.)

I am not unsympathetic to these frustrations (I've felt like maiming a student from time to time, I've shouted and I've got angry), but I've put it down to fallibility – mine and theirs. Even when there is intentional fault and blame, harbouring long-term resentment is damaging (very damaging) to oneself and one's professional role. It's not worth it. We can deal more effectively, and positively, with the more challenging individuals in the class with:

- thoughtful after-class chats (p 107*f*).
- constructive conflict resolution with senior colleague support (p 120).
- thoughtful use of classroom meetings (p 33*f*).
- problem solving with the support of colleagues; not 'privatising' our struggle and frustration.
- developing personal, individual, behaviour plans with those students who are frequently distracting, and disruptive, in our classes. We do this on a collegial, team, basis. This is addressed at some length in Chapter 7.

We can often turn around both challenging individuals and the class (as a group); or at the very least we can make things better than they are.

Shouting a class down (or up)

You've heard it, done it or certainly felt like doing it: 'Shut up! Shut up or I'll … !!' (I'll what?). I've heard colleagues from several classrooms away, shouting and even yelling. It's tempting. It sounds strong. It *sounds* like we're 'in control'.

I'm not talking about raising our voice from time to time when it's appropriate. I'm talking about *shouting* a class down. It feels as though we're in control when we shout. It satisfies some teachers – it feels as though they've got back at the class. Worse, some teachers add to the shouting the unsolicited lecture: 'And where do you think you'll be, eh? eh? With that kind of behaviour, where will you end up, eh? Unemployed; that's where! When I was at school ...'

If it works at all – and it might the first time – it has a limited life span. How do we top it? Do we keep shouting to settle them down *each lesson*? And what do they learn from our shouting? By shouting, or using a *frequently* loud voice, we are (in effect) training the students that this is the way it has to be. It demonstrates that *we* don't believe we're serious about them settling down, listening, unless we shout. Furthermore, shouting or frequent and extended use of a loud voice, or snappy tone of voice, unsettles, unnerves, overly excites or even entertains the class.

Settling down a noisy class is never easy but shouting will not work in the long term – and loud teachers correlate with loud classes. It's worth discussing the class-settling options with colleagues in our team; or, better still, watch effective colleagues to see how their verbal and non-verbal behaviour is communicating calmness to the class. (see, later, p 77*f*).

Some effective class-settling options include:
- waiting, standing relaxed and just waiting (silent, casual, look at the watch – not overdone though) and then use the choice of words that indicates what you expect to happen ('settle', 'face this way' and 'listen', 'thanks.' 'By the time I've counted to 20 I want you all sitting on the mat' – this to infants. With infants I like to add (when they are settled on the mat) 'I want everyone facing this way (pause). I want to see everyone *listening with their eyes* and their ears.'
- moving around for brief, 'private' chats and then moving to the positional place at the front of the room (p 21*f*).

- using a small handbell, clapping rhythm, silent teacher hand up cue (as a private signal) or even (at secondary level) light tapping of a glass to indicate you expect a change in residual noise level – then a tactical pause so we can greet the class (always give a 'good-morning'/'afternoon') before beginning the teaching activity.
- writing on the chalkboard while the residual noise drops (I sometimes draw a little cartoon and write 'settling down, thanks everyone') and then wait (tactical pause) and give the first group direction.
- I also find it relationally helpful to add (when the class has settled) a brief 'thanks'.

It is hard to have any effective teaching and learning if there is not a clear, calm, focused start for a class.

Classes that aren't listening

Some years ago in Belfast, (Northern Ireland) I was asked to take a session on teacher stress (a high school staff meeting). Prior to the meeting the principal asked if I would take a couple of Year 7 classes (to 'get an impression'). We walked down a corridor – I could hear the class a mile away. The principal knocked on the door and a harried-looking colleague opened the door. Behind his head I saw several rows of grinning, noisy, unfocused students. The principal said, 'This is Mr Rogers from Australia. He'd like to take your class.' 'Good', was the teacher's reply, and he then walked off with the principal down the corridor. I was left facing a noisy, unfocused group of students whose accents were difficult (initially) to comprehend.

Rather than try to 'get' them quiet by standing at the front of the class and directing them, I walked to the chalkboard, rubbed clean a space and began to draw a map of Australia. I whistled a tune (conveying, I hoped, my confidence and calmness) as I drew sharks, a sun, and a touch of blue here and there. I then wrote on the chalkboard, 'I'm an Australian.' (I knew they'd probably all be watching the TV program 'Neighbours'. It's on twice a day in the UK). Several students called out to me: 'Oi, who are you!?', 'What are you doing here?' and 'You deaf?'. But the overall noise level was dropping with each artistic addition to the chalkboard. I then wrote, 'When you've settled, folks, I'll explain. Ta.'

When the residual noise had significantly dropped (helped by communal shushes and 'shut-ups') I turned and stood, relaxed and 'still', waited and greeted the class group.

When I'd introduced myself (the teacher, you see, hadn't introduced me) several hands shot up; clicking fingers and calling out. I put up a blocking hand, paused, and reminded the class: 'A number of students are calling out. I'm happy to take any questions about Australia. Remember, hands up – without calling out (fair go) – and please give me your first name (pause). Let's go for it.' The first student question was, 'Hey, do you know what's right up to date about the "Neighbours" episodes?' I racked my brains; I'd hardly watched it. We had a useful cultural exchange about sharks, kangaroos, koalas, the weather, and even some history of Oz. By staying calm myself and giving them a focus the students had settled. No guarantees, but it was better than just shouting.

I have also worked with a number of very challenging classes who, *en masse*, demonstrate an indifference to whoever walks in and stands 'up-front' trying vainly to *engage* whole-class attention and – then – to *sustain* necessary attention.

I was asked to work with a difficult Year 9. It was 'home group' time (form-tutor class). My colleague had said that she found this twenty minutes (with her home group) the most challenging part of the day.

As I stood in the front of the room and scanned the group I saw several students chatting to other students outside the window, some boys playfully punching each other and some lads out of their seats wandering to chat …

I could have stood at the front of the classroom (as we normally would) to gain whole-class attention and focus. I sensed that I would be waiting a while. I decided to establish some sense of order, calming and focus by 'going walkabout' to establish a sense of 'calmness' and focus 'Communicating calmness' is a crucial feature of our behaviour leadership. (This is addressed, at some length, later. See p 77*f*)

I wandered and had a private chat with each mini-grouping. I walked over to the group at the back and said, 'Good morning, my name's Bill Rogers; I'll be taking you for English.' I held out my hand and asked for names. Most responded. I had unsettled them by roving into their 'territory' as they perceived it. Ten minutes later I went up to the front – the 'normal' teacher position. Having remembered many names I directed the class to 'face the front of the room …'. I was banking on the fact that this mini-establishment (around the class group) would enable group establishment. 'OK everyone, settle down thanks. [Pause] I need you facing this way and listening. [Pause] Thanks Dean, [pause] Craig, [pause] Darren, [pause] Rebekkah, [pause] and Paul. [Pause] It is Paul isn't it?' He grinned back, 'Yeah, it's Paul!' They were 'settled' now (several leaning back, still a little 'suspicious'; a lot of wry, grinning faces). I introduced myself formally, 'I've already met you, but I'd like to say good morning to you all and explain why I'm here today working in your classroom.'

Now, of course, these approaches imply a sense of personal confidence and self-esteem. I have learned not to be overconfident or believe that any one approach will always work. If the worst comes to the worst (and it does, sometimes) we have to use approaches such as crisis management and time-out (p 114*f*).

What I have learned over the years is that I cannot really control others. I can only control myself (and that's a challenge, especially when tired, frustrated, overworked …). I can lead, guide, engage, challenge, encourage and (at times, when necessary) confront. I cannot, simply, *control* others.

Short-term colleague support (safety valve)

I have walked past classrooms where marginal (even significant) chaos is in progress – much more than healthy working noise or appropriate fun.

In many schools my colleagues, and I, can't simply walk past such a class thinking, 'Well, I'm glad it's not me' or 'I'm glad I haven't get that lot!'. These schools have adopted (among many other supportive measures) a 'safety-valve' option that colleagues can feel free to use if they want to give *immediate* support to a colleague. Such support is as follows:

- Send a student messenger to the class where there is significant disruption to the effect that 'Ms E wants to see these students (named) in Room 22.'
- Ask the teacher if you could 'borrow' a couple (or several) students – name the catalysts – and then direct them to another class (for brief time-out) or have a chat with them out of sight of the room. No doubt the rest of the class will have some suspicions but there's enough 'ambiguity' about the withdrawal to give the class teacher a chance to regroup. Most of all it is carried out without any imputation that our colleague is a 'weak teacher'.
- Knock on the door of the 'riotous' class and inform your colleague there's a message for them at the office. This is code for 'take a break while your passing colleague takes your class'. There needs to be a no-blame climate for this to operate well.

It is important to knock on the colleague's door (it's good modelling); it is basic respect.

When we knock on a colleague's door (where there is 'catalytic conversion' in their classroom) we are aware that our presence can signal support *or* implied censure or even a 'sense of superiority'.

As we enter we say something like, "*Excuse me class (…) excuse me Mr Smith.*" (Always cue the class, and the teacher, respectfully.) Then in a much quieter voice to the teacher, "*There's a message for you at the office.*" The tone is always respectful; allowing our colleague a dignified 'temporary exit' from a very stressful situation.

When the class teacher leaves their class the support colleague settles the class, and works with them until the end of that class period. We *do not* communicate the message 'that the *real* teacher has now arrived and the teacher who has just left could not manage the class'. I have seen senior colleagues glare through the classroom windows at a colleague visibly, audibly, struggling with a hard-to-manage class. As they stand, arms folded, staring through the glass, they communicate to a teacher (already stressed) that, *"You can't cope can you?"* This is how it is seen, and felt, by the colleague struggling with several 'catalytic' students.

Some senior teachers will even storm in and simply take-over the class; ignoring the teacher's professional (and) personal self-esteem. *"Who do you think you are! I can hear this class all the way down the corridor!! Now you get some work to do – you hear me?! Do you?! I'll be speaking to you later!* (this to several students eyeballed as ring leaders). *Do you understand?! Now get back to work!"* The class is seriously quiet, even (temporarily) demure. The senior teacher storms out (with a side glance at the class teacher)… *"Thank you Mr Smith."*

–How long will the class remain unnaturally quiet?
–How does the class teacher feel at this point?
–How (if at all) has the senior teacher assisted the class teacher?
–What will happen long-term with this class with this kind of (so-called) support?

These 'safety-valve options' are merely temporary relief for our colleagues, like the red-card option for the exit of a very disruptive student (p 117). However, if these options are not backed up with significant problem solving, 'restructural' support and personal behaviour plans for students with behaviour disorders, they will be of little value.

Making changes

I had just taken a difficult Year 8 class as a 'demonstration class' for other teachers in the Year 8 team. During the lesson one of the students, Michael, had gone through several attention-seeking episodes (I should have sent him off to time-out, but no, stupidly, I battled on). He jumped up onto a table, and leaped higher still with his hands reaching for the open metal beam. He hung by his hands, emitting baboonish noises. Several of the boys cheered and laughed as I moved across to his hanging feet. I had no bananas and so I said, 'Michael, if you're not down by the time I count to ten, I'm going to climb up and seriously tickle you.' He dropped like a stone and said 'Sh*t! you're not touching me!', and raced off out of the classroom (self-imposed time-out). At least I was able to resume my activity with the class.

I sent a 'responsible-looking' student to admin, to the effect that Michael had 'self-directedly exited our class.'

In the staff workshops I conducted at the end of the day the first question from the staff was, 'How did you manage with Michael and 8D?' When I shared my struggle with the class and his baboon stunt the common response was wearied grins and statements containing the word 'good'. They weren't revelling in an outsider's failure or my 'bad day'. Rather they were, in effect, saying your struggle (as an outsider) legitimates our struggle too. Students such as Michael are difficult to work with in a normal, typical, school setting. By having a healthy whinge about our struggles, our successes and the seemingly impossible tasks, we can always get somewhere with hard classes.

Michael was eventually sent off to a 'special behaviour unit'. In the meantime we'd had him on an individual behaviour management plan, used in-school suspension and had withdrawn him from several classes for safety reasons. 8D dramatically improved.

We won't always be successful with students like Michael – this is reality. We have to have the options of suspension, even expulsion, and alternate 'education' settings to support schools. Weighing up the rights of everyone is never easy, but it has to be just. Safety, fair treatment and fundamental learning can't be compromised because of a *few* students who consistently behave in recidivist ways.

A healthy whinge

After the interesting experience with Michael's class we had a really healthy whinge! I got all the teachers together who taught 8D (and combinations of 8D) and we had a clearing of the air. This is important. While most teachers avoid labelling students and whole classes, it's natural to want to sound off about the episodic stress caused by students like Michael.

I have been in countless faculty and staff meetings (as well as ad hoc meetings) where we've 'let off steam'. We've released the tension that comes from having to teach a group like 8D. The sharing of stressful feelings and 'angst' is cathartic – up to a point. However, *just* whingeing or getting locked into self-defeating dialogue ('We can't get anywhere with them' and 'It'll never change') stifles problem solving. Problem analysis has to follow a whinge with colleagues, and lead us to action planning involving colleague support. There's always something that can be done with a hard class. But if changes are going to occur they need some structure that arises from *reflective and substantial colleague support*.

Action planning

Initially, it may seem all too much: the way that a class pushes and shoves in line, the noise levels, the silly calling out, the physical restlessness, the five-minute settling, the dealing with one incident after another, the off-task behaviour, the lack of work produced – where do we start?

It is essential that the hard-class phenomenon is addressed at the earliest intervention possible. Do not let it degenerate into a Term 2 or Term 3 problem where teachers' energy levels have been significantly sapped by the class and they have almost lost any goodwill necessary for implementing changes.

1 Firstly it needs to be ascertained whether it is a hard class for all the teachers at that year level or grade, or whether only one teacher (or a few) who finds it difficult to lead, and manage, and teach the class. It doesn't take long to ascertain how wide the reputation of a class is at secondary level. If several teachers are struggling it will be necessary to call a special year-level meeting to address the issue, as early in Term 1 as is possible. If it is genuinely only one subject teacher struggling with 9E or 10B then it will be more effective to work just with that teacher and class using the several approaches outlined later in this text:
   - a classroom meeting to enable a *focussed* student voice as well as a sharing of teacher concerns.
   - a classroom behaviour agreement where the class/subject teacher goes through a re-establishment phase to readdress shared (and essential) rights, responsibilities and rules.
   - a group reinforcement activity using thoughtful behaviour-modification approaches.
   - individual behaviour management plans for particular students.

   These approaches all have potential to enable a 'fresh start' with a hard to manage class. A fresh start for both teacher and students.

2 A year-level meeting can acknowledge that several teachers are finding 7E or 8D a challenge. This is, in itself, useful. Teachers will often realise that "It's not just me after all". 'It's not my fault' is an often-heard expression at this meeting. After a normal whinge about the group the co-ordinator of the meeting will raise the *key questions* to ascertain the extent of the problem, how different teachers see the class and individual behaviour(s), and what they are currently doing to address the issue.
   - *How* 'hard' is this class? What do we mean by 'hard' (give specific examples)?
   - Is the class worse at any particular time of the week or day? It is important that in answering this question that the more confident colleagues are not smug about how well they manage 8D or 9C, even if they do not have the

same degree of stress or hassle as others.

- Who are the 'ringleaders', or catalysts, in the class? What behaviours do they typically engage in? With whom? With whom do they normally sit? Does it matter? How?
- Is the behaviour of the 'ringleaders' different across subject areas? Do some students, for example, modify their behaviour from, say, maths to woodwork or is their behaviour consistently disruptive? How? If curriculum, lesson delivery and method are having an effect, what effect do we believe they are having? This is a difficult question because sometimes it is the curriculum material, its delivery and often a lack of commitment in catering for mixed ability that contributes to the hard-class phenomenon.
- Are any of us having *any* success with 6B, 8D or 9C? In what way?

3 Develop an action plan that is based on a year-level approach. Rather than having each teacher simply pursue their own plan, the team will address the following:
- Reassess how they have established their classes, and pursue the benefits of a common re-establishment across the year level through a classroom meeting (p 33*f*) or whole-class behaviour agreements (p 49*f*).
- Decide whether to go for some common rules and routines across the grade, or year-level, groups in question. For example whether to have common working noise procedures, and entry and exit procedures, and whether to publish the rules and expectations in each classroom. (ch. 5)
- Reassess short-term colleague support options if a class is engaged in frequent, and significant, disruptive patterns of behaviour (p 23).
- Clarify the use of a workable time-out plan for key ringleaders (students who act as catalysts for classroom disruption). Make sure the time-out plan is consistent in its application (p 114*f*).
- Develop an agreed procedure for 'tracking' students with behaviour-disorders. If necessary, 'target' ringleaders for individual behaviour plans or if their behaviour is consistently and persistently disruptive, remove them from that year level and relocate the student in another year level with individual work programs. In a larger school it will be possible to relocate students across a year level. It can be helpful, firstly, to discuss with the student how their behaviour is significantly affecting learning (and safety in some cases) in that class and point out that they may have to face being relocated in another group. Make the choice clear, within a rights/responsibility focus. In some cases, the class may need to be split up – this is an exception and would occur only if the whole staff team believed that this would be the best option for the class group. This is not an elegant solution but, on occasion, it may be the most appropriate, and manageable, solution.

■ Consider whether or not any colleagues have been subject to harassment or bullying. If this has been the case, set up due process *immediately* (p 185*f*).

4 Decide on an action plan and the phases of implementation together. For example, the first step might be for all the teachers to run an open classroom meeting with the class in question. We then report back to colleagues and develop their common action from those meetings. If the group is significantly disruptive *en masse*, one meeting will be sufficient to outline the concerns of staff to students and develop a classroom contract for use by all teachers who teach that particular group. When conducting a meeting with a very distracting class it will help to have a supportive colleague jointly 'chairing' and conducting the process (see p 34*f*).

5 Implement and evaluate the plan over a term. There will need to be several meetings with colleagues down the track to fine tune, and plan for, the following term. It can help to include the students in this evaluation.

I don't have any problems with ...

I was standing in the busy staffroom with a colleague. We were on our way to sit down, relax, coffee in hand. We had both been teaching 9C (a class with a 'reputation'). I had found the morning's teaching a challenge. I was already a bit frazzled and I could see why my colleague described this class as her 'worst timetable slot'.

En route to sitting down, a senior colleague stopped to pass the time of day. He asked me which class I was 'working with'. I told him we had been teaching 9C. I briefly recounted the behaviour of some of the 'catalysts' in the class. He could hear (and see) in my voice, and recounting, that we *both* had found the class a challenge. '*Oh 9C ... I don't really have any problem with **them** ...*' Did I recount an easy hint of professional over confidence? I glanced at my colleague. She visibly, psychologically, 'shrunk' back. She didn't say anything ...

When teachers say they 'don't have a problem with ...' (a particular student or class group) they may well be telling the truth; they may be grandstanding; they may even be trying not to appear *as* if they can't really cope with that class. Either way it does not help the colleague who is struggling with that class. They may well feel, and believe, that if this colleague has no problems then I must, in some way, be 'at fault'. 'If others can cope why can't I!'?

Conversely I have seen colleagues emotionally, psychologically, professionally, 'boosted' when a colleague admits they, too, find 8C, 9C, 10E a difficult class (particularly a colleague perceived as a 'successful', effective, teacher.)

When we say 'we don't have any problems ...' (even if true) we may easily alienate a colleague's willingness (and professional confidence) to seek advice, assistance, support.

Tracking students across classes

Students, even from 'reputation' classes, do sometimes modify their behaviour in other classroom settings. It can be helpful, then, at both primary and secondary levels for teachers to 'track' students across classes other than their own. By observing students in other subjects/specialist areas we can get an understanding of how different teachers, settings and programs can affect group and individual behaviour. It is not a spy job – it is showing an interest in our students in other settings.

While I watched Karl in wood design making his CD stacker out of plywood, we chatted:

Student: 'Anyway, what you doing in here?' (in wood design)
Teacher: 'Oh, just wanted to see how 8D got on here, and see what sort of things you were making.'

I also spent time with Karl (and 8D) in textiles and was surprised at the gusto with which they addressed the creation of T-shirts and how adept they were with sewing machines. I noted with interest how the textiles teacher dealt with Karl's whingeing when the sewing machine wasn't free. She said, 'OK, what can you be doing while you wait for a free machine, Karl?' She refocused his responsibility within the task. It was also interesting to see how 'my' students responded with another teacher – the human dynamic in another classroom setting.

As part of the team (the English faculty) I was trying to set up a year-level plan for 8D. I 'tracked' them across several subject areas beyond English. In graphic design Ben asked, 'Hey, you following us or what?' A big grin on his face indicated he'd 'sussed' me. He said, 'Look, you're not a normal teacher are you? I mean you're a shrink or something, eh? I've seen the way you work with us and the sort of stuff we do as a class. I've even seen you making some notes.' So I told him, 'Yes, I'm seeing how 8D "operates" across all subject areas. That's why you've seen me wandering in and out of your classes.' Here I mentioned how they had seen teachers from other classes when I'd been teaching 8D. The students will 'pick up' on what we're doing and it won't hurt to explain our purpose, but keep it low key. It is not helpful to over engage the curiosity questions. At the very least they'll know that all the Year 8 teachers are taking an interest in them.

When visiting another teacher's class it is helpful for the 'host' teacher to briefly introduce the 'visiting' teacher: 'Mr Rogers will be working with us later in the lesson. You know Mr Rogers from English.' At that point the visitor can move either to the far side up the front of the room (leaving the centre of the room for the 'instructing' teacher) or if there's a spare seat at the back the visitor can sit there (as unobtrusive as one can be). At that point the host teacher carries on with their 'normal' lesson or activity. The visiting and host teacher will have discussed the protocols of interclass visits and likely scenarios beforehand.

From such 'tracking' – across several classes – we discuss the following:

- What are the main expressions of disruptive behaviours? How is the calling-out, butting-in and task avoidance in this different setting? Does a change from, say, 'academic' subjects (so-called) to 'non-academic' subjects (for example, maths to woodwork) see any significant behaviour change? If so, what sort of changes? When visiting Karl in woodwork we talked about how he had drawn up the plan for his CD stacker in his workbook, and how he had demonstrated some thought and care in his writing. I commented on his effort and planning. He seemed pleased. This little journey of interest and encouragement seemed to have an effect back in the English classroom. Or at least it changed my perception of Karl (and maybe his perception of me).
- What are the power cliques like here? What seating plans occur in other settings? Does a seating plan help? Do we need to change the seating plan (see below). Do Nathan, Shane and Karl act as ringleaders or powerbrokers? Does 'powerbroker' 'positioning' change depending on subject area and setting? Teachers can use such observation, analysis and feedback to further refine their group plan and also thoughtfully target individuals who may need special assistance or individual behaviour plans.

Changing the seating plan

Sometimes a change of seating may help, especially in a more 'formal' classroom setting (English, history, maths and so on). Some teachers allow students to sit where they want; others use a draw-a-name-from-the-hat approach or alphabetical seating plan. Some teachers use a targetted, student-matched, seating plan. However, if students are simply given free rein: 'Sit where you want', it is then harder to change the seating plans several weeks into the term. In one class I visited, almost the whole back row had formed a power clique. Tables set out in long continuous rows, for example, make it very hard for students to get in and out of their seating, causing several minutes of unnecessary mayhem at the outset of class time, as well as making it difficult for the teacher to move around the classroom.

One helpful approach my colleagues and I have used to correct an unhelpful seating organisation is to encourage the students to work with the teacher to rearrange seating options. We have a brief chat with the class about our concerns regarding seating and behaviour, and its effect on the whole class.

'As you know, we've had some concerns about teaching and learning time in our class. We're particularly concerned about the level of noise during work time;

it's affecting people's concentration and effort. We believe that a change of seating plan helps with overall teaching and learning in our class. Read this carefully (the sheet) and choose wisely.'

OUR CLASS ...

As your teachers we are concerned about the level of noise during whole-class teaching time and seat-work (eg: talking while the teacher is talking, and calling out ...)

We will be changing the seating plan and we need your assistance. We believe a re-arrangement of the class seating will help with overall teaching and learning.

Write down the names of two fellow students who you know won't hassle you, or make it difficult for you to get your class work done (see over).

We will use your suggestions in the new seating plan starting ---------------

We can't guarantee every selection but we'll do our best (choose thoughtfully).

Thanks.

Year level co-ordinator:

Subject Teacher:

Bill Rogers and colleagues (2005, Term 1)

I have seen teachers begin a new year by saying to the class, *'OK guys, sit where you want.'* Students then move swiftly to organise their seating arrangement into 'the cools' and 'non-cools'. This can be extremely distracting – even disruptive – in more challenging classes. I have seen teachers allow absurd table groupings where a single table group is over-dominated (in numbers and personality) and other table groups have one or two students and empty seats.

As with all seating arrangements it is not just the physical organisation of the seating that is important it is also thinking about who sits with whom.

Students need to learn that we do not always have to be sitting with the best friend (or the half best friend!). *'We've got plenty of time to be sitting with our best friends. You've got plenty of time to be with your friends outside the class-room. We've got four periods of English a week so we need to learn to work alongside, and with, a range of people in our class ...'.*

It is important, too, that students know there will be time (on occasion) when we will be working in friendship groups. (We will let them know *when* those occasions are appropriate.)

It will always help to develop our seat plans with our faculty or grade colleagues in the establishment phase of the year.

The students know that we will use their suggestions but that the teacher is the final umpire. When the class comes into the room the following week the new seating plan reflects their involvement. By engaging their support we almost always have a better outcome for the teacher and students in the subsequent weeks. That, coupled with a reconsideration of rules/routines/management practices and teaching methods resulted in a more relaxed and productive class (and teacher).

The repairer and rebuilder

There are teachers whose relational, managerial and collaborative skills single them out as key bridge builders. These are teachers who can go into hard-class settings, not as 'white knights', but as staff working with regular classes to repair and rebuild. Before the spiral of negative feelings, low expectations and burnout occurs, these colleagues can often set up classroom experiences that rekindle group spirit, re-establish a framework for educational and social harmony, and rework the delivery of curriculum to enable relative enjoyment and success. It can be helpful, especially at secondary level, for senior staff to be aware of where these talents are in their teams and utilise these skills as early as possible when a class, and its teacher, is struggling on a day to day basis.

Footnote
1. Jones, P. and Tucker, E. (eds) 1990, *Mixed Ability Teaching – Classroom Experience in English, ESL, Mathematics and Science*, St. Claire Press, Rozelle, NSW.

Chapter 2

CLASSROOM MEETINGS

Sitting in the staffroom with a music teacher (the tea getting cold) she started to share how a Year 8 class had become her 'worst time-table slot' each week.

These students had given their teacher 'hell', as she had described it. The music lessons had degenerated into teacher-student slanging matches, little on-task work and a feeling of constant frustration by the teacher whenever she faced the class. Several of the girls, in particular, were sullen, sulky and unco-operative. There was calling out, task avoidance, talking while the teacher was trying to teach and so on. Lessons were basically the 'horizontal tyranny' of the strongest class members.

Conducting a classroom meeting

I encouraged my colleague to conduct a classroom meeting with the Year 8 students. I suggested we could plan, and conduct, the meeting together. My belief was that if we could invite the views, perceptions and feelings of the students we could perhaps find some starting points for change. She had never run a classroom meeting and so we agreed to run it together, based on my initial observations of the class. It is my belief that when people believe that their common concerns and viewpoints are heard, and taken seriously, there is a basis for common understanding and potential change.

I joined my colleague for a lesson, just to observe what I've already noted above. In the last ten minutes of the lesson I walked to the front and directed the attention of the students. They settled and I introduced myself and shared – briefly but specifically – what I'd observed in the past forty minutes. I said in a calm voice, conveying seriousness of tone as I scanned their now quiet faces, 'As a teacher in our school, I'm concerned, very concerned, about this class and how learning and behaviour are not going well. I'm *not* going to give you a lecture because you know better than anyone what it's like in music – here. I just want to invite you to have an open meeting with me and Mrs P next Tuesday to discuss what's really happening in music, why you think it's happening and how you believe *we* can change things here. We're going to have a classroom meeting. When you come in on Tuesday you'll see the chairs in a circle. I'll ask a student to keep a record of what we discuss and suggest together. I'll also ask a volunteer to write up our suggestions on the whiteboard.' Several hands went up, but the bell was about to go. I put up my hand to block questions and said, 'Look, I know you've got a lot of questions already, but think about it and be ready for next Tuesday.' I directed them to leave, considerately (row by row); there was a residual whinge from a small cohort of students (p 96*f*).

Already I felt that the teacher's current teaching style, discipline and curriculum delivery were key factors. Although she was an accomplished musician and a 'fine piano teacher' (in the words of other colleagues), she had clearly lost the 'working good-will' of a significant number of students in this Year 8 class. And she agreed. As an older teacher she was very demanding on herself and at times intolerant of typical adolescent behaviours that could have been refocused with skill and a little enthusiasm. Some changes in teaching methods and some collaboration with the class would help. I thought about how I could assist her in these areas without discouraging her. That was difficult enough, but my real concern was what the students might say about her *as a teacher* at the classroom meeting. I discussed with my colleague how the students might react and what they might say when given a 'voice'. I didn't want her to be hurt by ill-considered, thoughtless or mean-spirited comments. I wanted to work towards a co-operative model with teacher(s) and students.

The following Tuesday the students came in and name tags were given out (mainly to help me). They took their seats with some visible unease and natural, nervous, laughter.

Once settled I explained what we would be doing for that class period.

Step 1

I said, 'I want firstly to hear what you have to say about how you feel things are in the class – both positive and negative views.' It is important as teachers that we show we do care for their input. When students are allowed to express their views freely it helps to clarify the problems, and why such problems exist in the perception of teacher and students alike. It also stimulates a more co-operative atmosphere that is united to problem solving. Most of all, it conveys genuine concern.

Some teachers are worried that the students will make ridiculous suggestions and some do. Some will make ambit claims. This too is normal. If the teacher manages this well within the rules, students soon bounce back to the more serious agenda. The main thing at this stage is to elicit their responses and not to put them down for their ideas or use the classroom meeting as a pulpit for our frustrations alone. It is important to use this first stage to reflect their point of view in order to clarify it, for example 'Are you saying . . . ?' or 'You seem to be saying . . . Is that correct?' (eg: 'are you saying this [be specific] happens every lesson?'). Reframing or paraphrasing their point of view without judging it is the hard part. Save any judgment until later in the meeting; *the class can make its judgment within the fair test of how suggestions fit basic rights and responsibilities*. When sharing our impressions and feelings (as the class teacher) it's important to remember some basic rules. (See below)

Step 2

'I'd like to share my concerns and feelings with you about how we see things here in music,' I said. Here we went through (briefly – no big added lecture) the behaviours, how we felt about them, and how we believed they had affected teaching and learning.

CLASS MEETING RULES

It is important to have some published rules for running classroom meetings. Ideally, such rules would arise out of group discussion. Basically these rules focus on the right to a fair hearing and respect for others. These rules are shared with the group prior to the meeting. Students are also asked if they have any questions, or concerns, about the 'meeting rules'.

Treat others with respect:

- When we share ideas and opinions, we do so without attacking them or putting them down.
- Keep your hands and feet to yourself.
- Speak one at a time and listen when others speak.
- Primary level teachers sometimes use 'talk tokens'. Each student has three coloured discs. Students put one disc quietly on the floor in front of them after each verbal contribution. This slows down the more garrulous. I have even used this with a Year 8 class successfully. At lower and middle primary level students often use a 'focus' – an object or toy that is held by whoever is speaking in the meeting. When the speaker has this 'focus' no one else is allowed to talk. Once the novelty is settled it 'norms' itself as 'a routine'.
- It helps to look at others when you speak and listen to others when they speak.
- We make decisions together based on the rights and responsibilities of our school. We will review our decisions in a week's time.

It will be important for the teacher to enforce these rules in a relaxed but firm way where necessary. Even a bit of humour, defusing or light turn of phrase can help keep a relaxed flow to the meeting.

Students noted that a lot of lessons were boring because they do a lot of filling-in of sheets, theory and copying. The teacher later admitted it was her way of coping with their behaviour, but some students saw it as a punishment. A few students also particularly complained about the teacher's management style. That was hard to hear and I paid particular attention to how we addressed their concerns so that it did not become an 'attack' on the teacher. It is crucial that at all times we 'address the concerns, we are not here to "attack" each other.'

Step 3

We then 'brain*waved*' suggestions for change (I don't like the term 'brain-*storm*'). With some of my classes I have used the term 'surfing the brain space' (STBS).

At this stage it's normally helpful to just list (or have a student recorder list) the suggestions on the whiteboard. If they are outrageous ('Get rid of the teacher') then a clear, brief, firm reminder of the no-put-down rule is enough. Avoid over-servicing silly comments or gratifying their attention seeking (we can always follow up with such students later).

On some occasions we will need to direct a student to leave the classroom for time-out (p 114*f*).

I emphasised, and my colleague joined in, that we were looking for ideas that would help us all to treat one another with respect, to learn well and most of all to enjoy our time together in music. 'We're not saying it can always be fun, but we are saying we'll work hard to improve things to make it as enjoyable as possible – we need your help and your support.'

The need to have some fun and freedom are (according to Glasser 1991) basic human needs. This is an interesting and important understanding, because if teachers ignore this fundamental aspect of 'social belonging' children will easily find their own versions of fun!

Step 4

We then went over the fairly long list of suggestions and referred from time to time to their original concerns and ours. The solutions that best fitted everyone's needs were written on the whiteboard. One of the suggestions was to do group work and we discussed how best we could form the groups and how we could blend whole-class teaching time with group work time. It was a valuable meeting and the students certainly saw *our* perspective as teachers; we too acknowledged and took seriously the perspective of the students.

The outcomes we all agreed on were:

- less whiteboard, copying, work and filling in sheets
- a reappraisal of class rules and consequences
- no group detentions (an early recommendation)
- no shouting or 'slanging' matches (we'd remind them of the fair rules, which would now be published)
- more group work
- respect cues for getting teacher attention and support
- respect routines and expectations for noise level in class and (fairly) getting teacher assistance
- another meeting in a week to review how we're going, then a meeting in three weeks and then once a term
- more positive feedback and encouragement ('Be more positive...' was frequently mentioned). We noted (as their teachers) that 'being positive has to work both ways.'

My colleague and I added a few extras ourselves such as possible afternoon teas together and some short break times in longer sessions.

Step 5

We thanked them for their participation, showed appreciation for their effort and assured them that the issues they raised would be followed up. We noted, too, that the decisions made would be evaluated and their involvement in the process would continue.

Things did improve. There were a few setbacks and we did need an extra meeting to fine tune a few things. What really helped was colleague support – classroom meetings of any kind are not easy if teachers haven't had previous positive experience to draw from or if they lack initial confidence.

We also did some work on peer mentoring and reskilling. I could see the relational tone improve between the class teacher and the students as my colleague took extra time on such things as personal greetings, remembering and using students' first names, changing negative correction to positive correction, inviting suggestions on units of work and respecting student opinions about music and music tastes and, above all, a conscious effort to encourage students in their efforts. The effort and outcomes were worth it.

This approach – the classroom meeting approach – is used widely in schools to address issues of common concern. These can be anything from playground issues, teasing and bullying, to issues such as lying, stealing, cheating, put-downs in the classroom, homework concerns and noise levels. Many teachers at the primary level run regular classroom meetings (once a week) to enable issues to be raised, addressed and worked through.

The purpose of classroom meetings is basically to widen the students' view of who is affected and how they are affected by the kind of behaviours we are discussing:

- How do other students feel if and when …? How might the teacher feel if and when …?
- How does such behaviour (always be specific) affect learning and any of our basic rights at school? Such as our right to respect? Who else does our behaviour affect? Our parents?
- What might happen if we choose this approach? How do you think it will change things if we do it this way? (Be specific.) Note that all class decisions need to be fine tuned by the teacher at the close of discussion.
- Do the decisions made as a class, about the class's behaviour, fit in with the school's code of rights and responsibilities?

One simple test my colleagues and I use for student suggestions in a class meeting is the 3Rs test (I have adapted this from Nelson, 1987).

- Is it *related*? Are our proposals related to how we can realistically address disruptive, inconsiderate behaviour; even bullying?
- Is it *reasonable*? If it can't be implemented, or if it's too impractical, costly (for example, build a new classroom or have a refrigerated air-conditioning unit in class) or unfair, we won't do it. But we can have an afternoon tea during our double-class period if we plan it well.
- Is *respect* kept intact? Does the suggested solution(s) keep the basic respect intact between one another? Outcomes, decisions and consequences should not set out to hurt or humiliate anyone in our class.

Open meetings

The two basic kinds of classroom meetings we've used are 'open' and 'closed' meetings. These meetings are the formative, foundational, basis for a 'fresh-start' with the class.

Open meetings give students the direct opportunity to share their ideas, feelings and needs. The preferred seating plan for such a meeting is the three-quarter circle. An open meeting can combine class dialogue or a written exercise. One of the standard written exercises I've used for many years is the 3W Sheet (see Appendix 4, p 204).

Each student is given a pro-forma sheet containing three key questions. These questions are explained prior to handing out the exercise. Students are encouraged to fill in the pro forma exercise privately (the use of personal name is optional). Students answer the following questions on a separate sheet:

Students in a Year 6 class listed the following in response to a classroom meeting using the questions noted:

1 What's working well in our class?
- I like school because of my friends.
- We do some good things here, such as that project and what we did for science.
- Sometimes the teacher does interesting stuff like …

2 What's not working well and why?
- I don't like the seating here.
- I think my teacher has favourites.
- I don't think the teacher likes me.
- I reckon the teacher shouts too much – so do most of the class.
- We don't have enough free time.
- There's too much boring work – like all the writing (referring to the writing of notes on the chalkboard).

3 What are some things we can change – and how?
- It would be better if we could do different things, not just writing (this student's perception was unfortunately narrowed but she had a point).
- Don't have favourites.
- Examine both sides of the story when someone is in trouble (this from a very articulate and earnest student).
- Some more free time would be great.
- Get some better library books such as …
- It would be great to have some outdoor games and equipment.

---

1 **What's working well in our class?** For example, are there any activities you particularly enjoy? Are there any lessons you can recall that went well? What made those lessons go well for you? Do you have an opinion as to *why* some things go well here in our class? It is important to start with the positive questions first, otherwise some students will use the written feedback activity to 'have a gripe session' on paper. Basically we're asking what they like, enjoy and feel works well at the moment and why? This can include comments about the teacher, class, activities or environment. Students are reminded that if a comment about the teacher or other students is particularly personal they should focus on the behaviour and not 'attack' the person. This is crucial when addressing question 2.

2 **What's not working well and why?**

3 **What are some things we can change – and how?** What can *you* do to make this classroom a better place? What could we *all* do to make this classroom a place where learning, personal safety and fair treatment work better for all?

Some teachers will use the format of the 3W Sheet as part of an open-forum problem-solving meeting. The students sit in a circle. The teacher goes through each question and the feedback is noted on the chalkboard as well as on a written copy. If this format is used it is essential that normal 'classroom meeting rules' are re-emphasised.

It is essential to always keep written notes on any classroom meeting so that effective reflection and monitoring can be made. We often nominate a boy *and* a girl to (each) take running notes

Closed meetings

Unlike open meetings, where students are encouraged to freely share their point of view, a closed meeting is conducted almost exclusively by the teacher.

The procedure for a 'closed' meeting may be as follows:

- The seriousness of the issues (raised by classroom behaviours) is stressed by having a respected senior teacher conduct the meeting with the regular class teacher. It is not, though, an exercise in reading the riot act. The teacher(s) will convey (in their shared communication) the seriousness of what is happening in terms of the behaviour of *this* class. The tone should be firm but calm, 'formal' and serious – not attacking the students. The focus, and emphasis, are on their behaviours and how those behaviours are affecting basic rights and responsibilities. Students, in this kind of meeting, would normally be sitting in their desks (at their tables).

- The teacher(s) outlines, specifically, what behaviours are causing concern. Wherever possible, brevity of explanation is the aim – not a long lecture or moral invective.

- It can help to have the behaviours and issues of concern written up on a large clear poster attached to the whiteboard.
- The teacher will also have to re-visit the essential rules for fair, respectful, helpful, co-operative behaviour 'in our class.'

It can help to publish such rules on a large poster (able to be seen from the back of the classroom) focusing on the three critical areas:

- *To learn well here we …*
- *To feel safe here we …*
- *To show respect we …*

Under each key heading (see later p 52*f*), on each poster, are the key elements of those rights eg. the *right* to respect …; the *right* to learn without undue distraction or disruption; the *right* to a safe place (this includes *both* psychological and physical safety). (See Appendix 6a, 6b for an example of *role posters* for secondary-age students.)

The aim of this kind of meeting is to address the following:

- Explain what the class is doing, what the class is like (at the moment) with respect to behaviour and learning. We then clarify how such behaviours affect fundamental rights and responsibilities.
- Re-establish the 3Rs – rights, responsibilities and basic rules. Make copies of this available later in the session.
- Re-establish some key expected routines (as they fit in with school rules) and classroom practices. In subsequent classes these work practices can be outlined and monitored. These 'routines' will address 'noise levels'; how to have a fair class discussion (hands-up rules); appropriate movement etc.
- Rearrange the class seating plan (p 30) if it is thought this would help.
- Outline key consequences for disruptive behaviours *beyond* fair reminders of 'our classroom rules.' This will include time-out if necessary. Point out that there will be no group detentions.

The key emphases of this kind of meeting are:

- 'We cannot allow the levels of noise and disruptions (noted earlier) to continue, especially the frequent talking while the teacher is talking. If there are any genuine complaints or concerns about the class, or how your regular teacher "runs" this class (or any of your regular classes), Mrs D and I are prepared to listen to your concerns and to personally speak with you. We will take your concerns seriously and seek to do something about them. There will be time later in this session to raise questions.' (An alternative is to conclude this formal, 'closed', meeting with the 3W Sheet, in Appendix 4, as a class-written exercise.)

- 'If you need help with your work or behaviour we can always give you some individual assistance. I know it's difficult to ask for help but that is what we are here for. We'll be having another meeting in a week's time to see how our "fresh-start plan" is going.'

- 'We have not contacted your parents – yet. This isn't just a threat, folks. We believe *you* can help change the way this class works and that your behaviour, individually and as a group, is something you can sort out without our having to hassle your parents.'

- 'I'll be speaking to several students – I'll let them know privately later – about the option of moving classes if some of you can't handle the options we've just shared. At this stage we don't want to split up our class.' (This option of moving students must be available at any year level where some students evidence *repeatedly* distracting, and challenging, behaviours and are resistant to change.)

'Thanks for your time everyone – I look forward to hearing how the fresh start goes in our class.'

In the closed meeting it is important to combine an air of serious concern with formality, tempered with an acknowledgment of care and hope.

Mini-class meetings

Mini-class meetings are sometimes used where it is suspected that a larger meeting might prove a bit taxing for the class teacher.

Having observed a very noisy and unfocussed grade six class, my colleague and I decided to conduct mini-classroom meetings.

I chose to withdraw three students at a time (while my colleague was teaching) and we sat in the corridor and quietly went through the key questions (noted earlier). 'What's working well *and why*...? What isn't working well *and why*? And what are your fair (and realistic) suggestions for change?' I assured them we (the teacher and I) would follow up the concerns even if it took several weeks. Some of their concerns addressed playground issues, being blamed for 'stuff' they didn't do because they were in Year 6, and unfair treatment ('Luke gets blamed a lot but he doesn't always do what the teacher says he does; she doesn't always see other kids do stuff too!'). They were clearly aware of the noise level in the class and the general 'task avoidance.' I asked what we could do about this. 'We could try to be quiet,' was the sheepish reply. 'How?' – I asked. It was the start of a re-appraisal of necessary routines for class learning. We discussed the difference between 'playground voices' and 'partner voices' (in a small space like a classroom.) Most of the students clearly wanted a classroom where we could learn without loud, distracting, voices and 'hassling behaviours.'

After this exercise we took the findings back to the whole class for a more formal meeting to address the need to re-establish our class rules and routines especially noise levels (p 86*f*).

Like any meeting format the mini-class meeting needs to be well planned. Conducting the meeting with a colleague gives some emotional security and a chance for mutual reflection and feedback later.

I've also found it helpful, on occasions, to conduct class meetings in another classroom to emphasise that this meeting is 'special.' We take the rules and our notebooks with us and return with our shared outcomes.

Another variation is to use the 3W Sheet (p 39*f*) within the 1, 3, 6 method. This combines individual and group focus. Students fill in the exercise on their own, then join a group of three other students (after ten minutes) and share their responses. After five minutes each group of three combines to form a group of six (or thereabouts) and five minutes later receives the feedback. Or the teacher can conduct the exercise individually and give the feedback at the next lesson (or the next day at primary level). The main point to stress is that we want the students' feedback.

Meetings to deal with put-downs

Put-downs and teasing in class

Put-downs and hurtful teasing are an annoyingly common feature of a hard class. If ignored or tolerated ('Oh, they're always speaking like that'), if not consciously and firmly addressed, it can become 'the norm.' I've been in classes where teachers have seemingly given up on frequent student use of 'idiot', 'stupid', 'dropkick', 'gees you're a dummy!', 'poofter', 'gay-boy' and so on. While much of this is *sotto voce*, in my opinion it is still unacceptable. I have heard *some* teachers (and some social commentators) suggest that this kind of language is almost always 'banter' or 'street language.' A classroom might be representative of the street but it is not, itself, 'the street.'

Teachers have both a right, and a responsibility, to address the nature and use of language in our classrooms.

This issue can be addressed in the first instance by having a clear classroom *understanding* about what we mean by 'respect', 'fair treatment' and the use of 'positive language' – 'In our class we use language that helps people to feel good about themselves and good about others. This means no put-downs or slanging off at another class member.' It always helps to express *the right* to respect and fair treatment within an equally fair rule (see Appendix pp 205/208). This rule is developed during the establishment phase of the year.

It may also be helpful to run a classroom meeting to address the issue if a pattern of hostile and put-down language starts to emerge in the group (see later).

Wherever we hear put-downs; 'shafting'; nasty teasing and name calling; homophobic or sexist slurs (verbal or non-verbal) we need to immediately remind the student(s) of the class rule.

It will also be important to follow-up with students – on occasion – to reinforce the rights and responsibilities of 'respectful communication in our class.'

During one of my lessons a male student referred to a female student's head covering as a 'tea towel'. This student (a Muslim girl) was understandably, and visibly, annoyed.

Jeff had called across the classroom to her and said, 'You've got a tea towel round your head.' He grinned and enjoyed the little chorus of laughter from several boys. I looked at Jeff and said firmly (without shouting) and with a strong assertive tone, 'Jeff! [here I dropped my voice to a serious tone] that's a put-down. Our class is a no-put-down zone. That language is totally unacceptable.'

With behaviour such as put-downs and abusive language it is important to register to the student (and the class) the seriousness of the issue at stake (there is *always* an 'audience'). This will come across in the assertive (non-aggressive) stance of the teacher. Jeff responded quickly, 'Gees! I was just joking!' The sad thing is this is probably true. Jeff didn't see any religious, cultural or emotional significance in the girl's head covering – just an opportunity to have some 'fun.'

'Maybe you think it was a joke, Jeff, but what you said was a put-down and that can hurt.' I blocked with my hand to both students and said 'I'll speak to you after the class.' Later in the lesson I (quietly) asked Halina if she would be willing to stay back after class and explain to Jeff why his comment was upsetting.

At the close of the lesson I asked Jeff and Halina to stay back for a few minutes. I briefly explained why I'd asked them to remain after class. Halina very quickly started to complain about what Jeff had said.

'Halina, if you're comfortable could you look at Jeff? He's right here. Explain to him what he did, and said, and how you feel about it.' She looked him in the eye and explained she was quite upset because the head covering was from her religion and she had to wear it. Jeff looked at the floor, sheepishly. I asked Halina what she wanted to do about it. 'I just don't want him – Jeff, I mean – to say things like that.' I asked her if she could explain that to Jeff as he was standing right next to her.

She repeated it again to Jeff. He replied that he didn't mean to hurt her and that he was just joking.

I asked Jeff what he could do to fix things up and assure Halina that she could feel safe – and respected – in our class. I reminded him of our school code about rights and responsibilities. He apologised to Halina and said he wouldn't say 'stuff' like that again.

I find it helpful in after-class chats – or more extended mediation meetings – to have the 'victim' and 'perpetrator' (it's not always easy to sort out who is who sometimes) face each other and proceed through a basic process:

- This is what you *said* (or *wrote* about me, or *took* from me in class) ...
- This is how I feel about it ...
- I want it to stop because ...

It is then important for the teacher to invite the perpetrator to respond, but emphasise the right or rule affected and ask the perpetrator what they will do to fix things up or ensure that this will not happen again. On the occasion where the put-down(s) have had a nasty, 'invective', tone it will be helpful to finish the meeting by telling the perpetrator to meet the teacher in a week's time to 'see how things are getting on'. This lets the perpetrator know we take the issue seriously. This lets the offending student know he is 'on notice' (as it were.) This approach, at least, empowers the victim and directs the perpetrator to account for their behaviour (it will not be excused). It also enlists a commitment to stop this teasing, put-down or verbal abuse. More serious incidents will need to be addressed through the school's due process for harassment/bullying. If a teacher (secondary level) hasn't got time for such an after-class meeting, it would be important to set aside a formal time to meet with the student.

A class meeting to deal with negative language and put-downs

A classroom meeting can clarify the issues for all; give a chance to air feelings, needs and concerns about hurtful language and teasing. Such a meeting also 'educates' as fellow class members feel their concerns, grievances, are heard and values about respect and perspective-taking are aired and discussed.

- Have clear guidelines for the meetings. (p 35)
- Plan ahead – advertise that next week there will be a special class meeting to look at negative language, put-downs and 'slanging off' at others in our class (not a nice term but unfortunately common with some students).
- Use the conventions for classroom meetings. (pp 34–38*f*)
- Print some key common put-downs used by class members on a large chart, for example, 'That's a *dumb* idea!', 'Gees you're a dickhead, poofter, slag, bitch,

mole, dog-face' and so on. Some students may not see these pathetic epithets as put-downs and may trivialise, or excuse, such language in the guise of having 'fun'; especially when they merely use them conversationally. Even 'stupid', 'drop-kick' and 'idiot' are hurtful to students, apart from the fact that it is inappropriate social language, and hardly contributes to a socially constructive environment.

- Discuss the use of put-downs:
  - –How do people feel when such words are used?
  - –Why is such language inappropriate?
  - –Why do people speak this way – what are they trying to achieve?
  - –How does the use of such language affect our basic rights and responsibilities?
- Discuss other more productive ways of speaking that can convey displeasure, disagreement or annoyance without putting someone else down. A student may make a comment in response to a teacher's question in a class discussion and another student may call out, 'No, stupid. That's not it!' Discuss how the recipients (teacher and students) feel in exchanges like these and invite other ways of communicating disagreement or questioning another's ideas, opinions or perceptions. Such language is thoughtless – it doesn't think about other people's feelings.
- It is also worth discussing the sensitive issue of swearing. Prior to discussing this with the class, it is worth clarifying with our colleagues how we can raise the issue and pursue a purposeful discussion. We want to avoid *merely* a negative approach such as 'don't swear in school.'
- List suggestions of things to say or do, and choose those that fit in with our:
  - –right to learn
  - –right to feel emotionally (as well as physically) safe
  - –right to be treated with basic dignity and respect (regardless of race, gender, religion, ability or disability.)

It can help to publish these communication reminders in a positive form as a class reminder about considering others when we communicate. (See Appendix pp 205/208.)

Class meetings and group establishment

Another form of classroom meeting commonly used by teachers is that of 'establishing roles of student and teacher.' We begin the discussion by asking a series of questions about 'roles', 'behaviour' and working relationships in a learning community like a classroom.

- Ask the class what makes an effective teacher. The answers come thick and fast ('knows how to keep order', 'has a sense of humour', 'is interesting', 'kind', 'fair').
- We then ask 'What makes an effective student?' I like this question because the answers always indicate that students *know* what they need to do regarding 'listening', 'having relevant materials', 'taking turns', sitting 'still' and 'raising their hands'. They also talk about the 'role' and responsibility (or expectations) regarding attitudes such as working hard, being on time, co-operating with others …
- 'What kind of teacher would I need to be to enable those rights to be enjoyed?'
- 'What kind of students would you need to be?'
- 'Well, it seems you know what an ideal class could be like. I'll do my best to be that kind of teacher. Let's discuss some of the routines and agreements about working together that can help you do your part and help me do mine, so we can work effectively as a class.'
- The teacher then works on some basic classroom agreements (rules) and routines for smooth running of the class. These can be published and displayed when working with that class.

Last year we had a very difficult Year 7 and I was asked by the principal and guidance officer (school psychologist) to become involved. The main difficulty at the time was a large group of girls (nearly the whole class) splitting into 'gangs' and the beginnings of some physical hostility and aggression. The decision was made to involve these girls in regular class meetings, which I ran very 'tightly', especially to begin with. Four of the very difficult ringleaders actually met with me once a week where I discussed their week and we talked about ways to deal with problems.

I also had them on individual contracts monitored by their teachers. I think the sense of being listened to, even though I often encouraged them to understand the consequences of their behaviour and didn't agree with some of their methods, helped enormously.

To start with, at meetings I tried some of the issues they all agreed on to begin the problem-solving process, for example a special area just for Year 7. There was a tennis shed to which, as members of Year 7, they felt they had special rights. This issue was non-threatening and non-divisive. As they gained confidence in the process and the guidelines we moved on to more 'touchy' areas. The classroom meetings had a significant impact in changing a volatile situation. It gave the girls, in particular, a 'shared voice' helping them to gain some perspective and reclaim behaviour ownership.

Colleen

Chapter 3

DEVELOPING A CLASSROOM BEHAVIOUR AGREEMENT

> *George Eliot (Mary Ann Evans (1819–1880) was once asked*
> *'Are you an optimist or a pessimist?'*
> *'Neither,' came the reply, 'I am a meliorist.'*
> In Potter (1950) p 81.
>
> [A 'meliorist' is someone who believes that the world may be made better by our human effort – considered, practical, supported, persistent, effort (even that grade 3, grade 6, 8D, 9C or 10E) Bill Rogers.]

The purpose of any classroom meeting (as noted in Chapter 2) is to give students an appropriate voice about the issues that affect *everyone* in that class.

Any such meeting will aim at:

–*raising our conscious awareness* about issues and behaviours that cause concern to members of the classroom community.
–*giving a focused and guided voice* to address those concerns.
–*making assessments* about these concerns (how common, frequent, serious, the effect of such concerns are on one another ...).
–*mapping out areas for change.*
–*having a workable process to enable that change.*

A **classroom behaviour agreement** is a way of refocusing and re-establishing a classroom group. It is a collaborative process (based on the classroom meeting format). The areas of focus for change are:

- Our shared rights;
- Our responsibilities that support our shared rights;
- Necessary rules for our class community (these rules give formal protection to our rights and highlight our responsibilities);

- The consequences that follow from our behaviour choices;
- How we support one another in our class. This area of focus particularly addresses those occasions where students need help with personal behaviour plans (see p 132*f*).

The *framework* offered below can be utilized with any age group (Fig. 3:1). Obviously such a behaviour agreement will vary in the language used, as well as the degree and the *amount* of written language. For example at infant level (age 4–7) we often use digital photographs – with a page for each of the key areas noted in Fig. 3:1. The language used in the behaviour agreement is always inclusive: 'we', 'us', 'our', 'all', 'everyone here …', 'together …'.

Eg. '*In our class we line up* (without pushing or shoving).' This would be appended to a photograph children lining up in a relaxed, considered way.

'In our classroom we use our partner-voices.
We use our partner-voices so we can concentrate.'

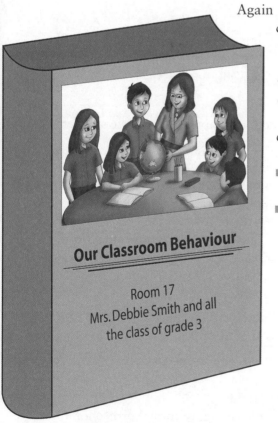

Again these statements would be appended to a photo of children sitting (say) at a table group working away 'happily' and co-operatively.

Fig: 3:1 outlines the key focus areas teachers use to develop behaviour agreements with a grade-class (or a form group at secondary level).

The teachers working collaboratively with the class demonstrate the following:

- The teacher takes the students' views and perceptions seriously.
- The teacher values the students' input by publishing a class agreement that can be used as the basis for teacher–student dialogue, management, conflict resolution, and repairing and rebuilding. For example, whenever students are behaving disruptively those students are affecting the due rights of the other students (and of the teacher). The students will be reminded of the right they have affected and of the relevant rule as developed within the classroom agreement. They may have to face an appropriate consequence (within the class plan) but the teacher will always offer behavioural support wherever appropriate.

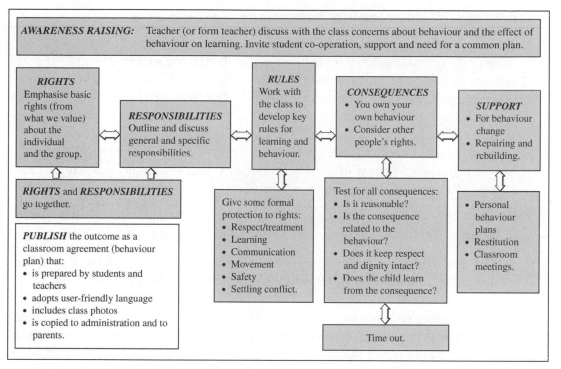

Figure 3.1   Class Agreement: Behaviour Plan

One of my colleagues has the following covering statement on her class behaviour plan. I've adapted it slightly for publication here.

Note the inclusive language and positive tone. This first page of the plan sets the basis for the subsequent sections on rights, responsibilities and rules, (see Figure 3.1). The key to a such a classroom 'plan', or agreement, lies not in the published document itself; it is the process of collaboration between teacher and students.

WELCOME TO OUR CLASS (ROOM 21).

- This behaviour plan has been discussed and developed by the students in Class XX. It is a record of how we behave towards others and wish others to behave towards us.
- The plan applies to all people who come into our class and will be used until the end of term four.
- Any new students (or adults) entering our classroom will be taken through the plan by a classmate, who will answer questions and explain our rules in more depth.
- Our written rules are displayed on the classroom noticeboard.

Rachel

Basic steps in developing behaviour agreements

I was developing a class behaviour agreement with a difficult Year 10 some years ago, and several students argued that it was the teacher's job to 'control' the students in class. I pointed out that as Year 10s they could, if they chose, walk out, scream, yell, work, sleep as the case may be. They choose to behave based on what they believe about their needs at school. We had an interesting discussion on the expectations of teachers and students. The students finally agreed the teacher's job was to teach, lead and guide but that – in reality – we are all responsible for our own behaviour in terms of its effect on others. This discussion led naturally to a spirited discussion on fundamental rights and responsibilities.

Rights

With any age group (five–18 years) it is important to focus on the basic, non-negotiable, fundamental rights we should expect to enjoy at school:

- *The right to respect and fair treatment* – it will be important to discuss basics such as personal space, treatment of school property and one's personal property, and even basic manners (such as ask before you borrow – don't just take). In this way a right is explored as the fair and reasonable 'thing' to do and also the behavioural expectation that goes with such a right.
- *The right to learn, without being distracted by others* – a discussion often follows on hands up, waiting turns and fair share of teacher time.
- *The right to feel safe and be safe* – this right addresses issues such as emotional and physical safety. All issues of bullying and harassment have to be dealt with from this essential and non-negotiable right.

'A right' is an expression of what we value. It is also an expectation of how things ought to be – it is (of course) no guarantee things will be that way. This is why we need the corrective side of behaviour management – the rules and consequences.

The rights and responsibilities section of the class behaviour plan gives the class a structural framework against which responsibility and accountability are measured. Some class contracts outline the essential rights of all members of the school community: students, teachers and parents (Rogers 1998).

With infant and middle primary age children we would not normally use the word *rights* as such. We would develop the concept of 'right behaviours' as those behaviours that are fair, considerate of others, helpful to others. In short how we, too, would like to be treated in a place that aims: to be *safe*; to be *fair*; to *convey respect* to each other and respecting the place we 'live' and work (for a third of our day!)

My colleagues and I find it helpful to begin a discussion on rights and responsibilities by having three, key, **focus questions**:

- How can we learn well here (in a way that helps others?)
- How can we show respect to each other here?
- How can we feel safe here? (we always distinguish between physical and psychological safety). 'Being safe' involves recognising that we '… all share the same place, and space here. We are all here for the same reason. We all have similar feelings … how can we respect others' feelings here?'

A discussion about these understandings enables a sense of shared place, space, and belonging. It also highlights the *responsibilities* that go with those rights.

Basic responsibilities

From upper primary level onwards students are keenly aware of their rights (perceived and real). It is essential to point out that rights and responsibilities go together. Some responsibilities will be expressed as expected, responsible, behaviours (co-operate, share, act safely, do your best, and so on) and other responsibilities will be more specific (be on time, have relevant materials, and so forth). By brainwaving with students and listing outcomes on a whiteboard, the teacher illustrates common, and more focussed, understandings about responsibilities.

RESPONSIBILITIES

Responsibility is when you take control of your own thoughts and actions.
We all have responsibility:

- to care for each other and ourselves
- to respect other people's work
- to set a good example for the school
- to treat belongings and resources with respect
- to control our noise level
- to keep clean the area where we work.

From a student behaviour plan [*Jackie, Grade 4 teacher*]

Class rules

It is always important to clarify the purpose of rules with students. Basically good and fair rules give some formal protection to one's rights. Rules are not mere impositions. If students have not had a decent discussion on rules at primary level, it can help to focus on the rules in our society – in football clubs, on the road, in swimming clubs, in board games (try playing chess without rules!). I've often had interesting discussions with students about rules 'at home.'

We might discuss the following questions:

- Why do we need rules?
- What would happen if there were no rules to guide us, remind us and set standards?
- What makes a rule fair or useful?
- What sort of things happen when rules are broken? – and why? What sorts of things *should* happen – and why?

When my colleagues and I develop rules we seek to:

- Keep the rules as simple as possible.
- Make sure classroom rules tie in with school-wide rules.
- Phrase rules in a positive way, or at least have a balance of positive and negative aspects of the rules. For example, 'Hands up in class discussion – no calling out and no finger clicking' and 'Keep hands and feet to yourself – no hitting, no hurting and no play fighting'.
- Keep rules few in number. The basic test of a rule is whether the rule focuses on the basic rights and responsibilities of the issue it addresses. Is the rule essential to social harmony and learning? ie: *is it safe?*; *is it fair?*; *is it showing respect to others and the environment?* With older students at secondary level, the term classroom agreement can be substituted for classroom rules if such a change is perceived as helpful.
- Avoid nitpicking rules (for example, 'No one leaves the room unless every piece of litter is picked up' and 'If you are caught chewing gum, all gum will be confiscated and thrown away').
- When publishing the rules, we utilise inclusive language. For example:

    Our classroom rules are:
    –When we communicate we … (followed by key examples …)
    –To show respect *we* … (followed by key examples …)
    –Moving safely in *our* room means … (followed by key examples …)

    See Appendix, pp 206–208.

SAFETY IN OUR CLASSROOM

We take responsibilities for our actions while at school:

- We use equipment appropriately and safely.
- We look after our property and the property of others.
- We wear only sensible clothes and safe jewellery, and tie back our hair if appropriate.
- We think about the possessions we bring into school and check that they are appropriate.

In some settings the rules for safety would need to be more specific (for example, 'Leave all toys and playthings – footy cards and so on – in your locker before you come to the mat' in lower primary) older students need reminders about mobile phones; I-pods; expensive electronic games etc. In one high school where uniforms were not worn, we put up a montage of photographs in each home classroom to indicate acceptable and unacceptable dress code.

In some classes there could be a lower degree of specificity concerning the rules because of the natural levels of consideration, thoughtfulness and social awareness. Many rules and routines have their highest focus and utility in the establishment phase of the year (p 74*f*).

PROBLEM SOLVING IN OUR CLASS

- We settle disputes peacefully whenever possible.
- We talk about problems rather than keeping the problems to ourselves.
- We ask the teacher for help in solving a problem or we can ask for a student mediator* to help.
- We discuss problems during circle time.
- If we fight as a way of fixing problems there will be immediate time-out.

* Some schools have peer (student) mediation programs to support problem-solving processes, where senior students (from Year 5 or 6) are trained to mediate in class and playground settings to enable students to work through problems to reasonable resolution. Where issues are serious, of course, they refer the problem to a teacher. The training program involves conflict-resolution skills, communication skills and problem-solving skills. Mediators can be called on by students or teachers to assist other children in solving a problem. For example, two students come in from play uptight and crying. In the short term the teacher calmly directs them to sit separately. When they have cooled down emotionally, the teacher asks if they would like a mediator to work with them. A note is sent to a Year 5/6 classroom requesting an available mediator to come to work with the two students. The teacher directs the three students to work quietly in the corridor, and report back later (if appropriate).

Dianne [Grade 6 teacher]

It can help to have key headings for rule areas so that the teacher can refer briefly to the rule, whenever reminding or correcting students – 'Remember our rule for communication'. The teacher might also need to add briefly 'Hands up, thanks'. Having discussed and published the rules, the class now has a framework within which to encourage responsibility, and give a basis for corrective (and supportive) action by the teacher.

Consequences

A consequence is the stated (or negotiated) outcome that relates back to behaviour that affects others rights in distracting, disruptive or hurtful ways.

With all consequences there needs to be 'degrees of seriousness.' The consequence for repeated lateness is different in nature from the consequences for bullying or hostile and aggressive behaviours.

When discussing consequences with the class, students will often be tougher, in their views of punishment than some teachers. Based on their backgrounds at home and school, they may see only the punitive side of consequences; some may even see consequences as a teacher or adult payback. Students do not easily see a consequence as an expression of just, and fair, accountability.

It is important, therefore, to discuss with the class the purpose of consequences.

- Is the consequence *related* to the behaviour? For example, should picking up litter be a consequence for bad language? Would a written or verbal apology or a 4W Form (Appendix 2) be more appropriate? If students damage any school property perhaps they should do several jobs around the school as a 'civic-duty' consequence.
- Is the consequence *reasonable*? If students use art equipment inappropriately (for example, flicking paint on the window with a brush) does that mean they lose all rights to all art equipment or just brushes for the lesson? There would also need to be a follow-up consequence as well (for example, cleaning brushes and the window).
- Does the consequence *teach* students anything about their behaviour? What does a student learn from writing lines? Or merely copying out the school's code of conduct? At least with a 4W approach (whether written by the student or as a basis for teacher-student dialogue) students are challenged to reflect on their behaviour and work with the teacher towards an appropriate consequence.
- Have a *severity clause* built into classroom consequences, such as time-out, within or away from the room. Students need to know that when their behaviour is *continually* disruptive they lose their rights – in the short term – (especially their right to stay in that room with persistently disruptive be-

haviour). It is essential to clarify this severity clause at any age level.

- Distinguish between *short-term* consequences, such as students being directed to work somewhere else in the room or having time-out if their behaviour is persistently disruptive or unsafe, and *longer term* consequences that will need to follow after students have cooled down and the class audience has gone.

- Most importantly a consequence needs to be applied with *certainty* and not intentional severity. Keeping the fundamental dignity and respect intact is a way of both respecting the basic treatment right of our students while still holding students accountable for their behaviour. The message that we emphasise to the class, and the individual, is that it's the *behaviour* that needs to be addressed and worked through. The emphasis is not on teacher payback or revenge, for example, 'You could be out playing now, couldn't you, eh! No, you decided to leave a mess, didn't you? Now you're missing recess and it serves you right!'. This teacher rightly has the student stay back to clean up the personal mess, but instead of focusing on the behaviour so that the student remembers the certainty of consequential outcome the teacher is more interested in the severity message.

- *Link* consequences to repairing and rebuilding (support for behaviour change). The purpose of all discipline is to enable students to be reflective of, and responsible for, their behaviour and its effect on others. This is a challenging goal. If we want to help students in the future to be more self-aware and more responsible, we need to help them beyond the consequence so that they will repair and rebuild those behaviour and relationships patterns that are causing them problems. Some students will need support from their teachers to *specifically* focus on ways to enable behaviour change. The use of personal, or individual, behaviour plans helps students by identifying behaviour goals. Teachers assist students to target, practice and reinforce new patterns of behaviour. (See Chapter 7.)

Some consequences (such as those affecting safety, harassment, fighting, bullying and drugs) will be school-wide and non-negotiable. Many classroom consequences, though, will be negotiated by the grade teacher, based on the principles noted earlier.

Support for behaviour change

Regular use of class meetings at primary level is an important feature of supporting positive behaviour and keeping the class plan on track.

Once the class plan has been discussed through its key stages (Figure 3.1) the class can work with their teacher to write the class plan (or behaviour agreement)

CONSEQUENCES

A consequence happens when you choose behaviours that are hurtful to others' rights.

A consequence must have something to do with the behaviour and must be fair. A consequence will also be related to the problem and respects the individual.

- You will be asked to explain your behaviour to the person affected. You will be expected to explain to the appropriate person your feelings and reasons for your behaviour (the 4W Sheet – Appendix 2).
- We have a class response book where you can write an answer or response to your behaviour.
- If your class work is not up to standard you will discuss it with your teacher and you may be asked to redo it.
- If you disrupt the learning of others or affect their safety you may be asked to work away from others or take 'cool-off-time' and 'thinking time' (time-out, in or out of our class).
- Consequences can also be worked out during class meeting time. We will try to help with problems as a class. We will support the individual while trying to deal effectively with the problem. Class meetings are open to everyone. Consequences are recorded in the class response book, which we will use to follow through with the solution.
- If you forget your homework you get an extra day in which to do it. If you forget again you will do your homework in 'catch-up time', or do a set piece of work. Your parents may have to be contacted to support your homework plan.
- We can develop organised action plans to arrange individual consequences. We can also develop individual behaviour plans to help you change things for the better.

Year 7 (adapted) Secondary behaviour agreement.

–Don.

based on the basis of the following principles:

- Adopt user-friendly, simple language relevant to the age group (see boxed material on consequences).
- Keep the overall emphasis positive where possible.
- Include class drawings, or photo montage on the cover, and throughout the text, to personalise the plan.
- The last page of the agreement notes the following: 'Our class has discussed, drafted and edited our behaviour plan and we agree to use it.'

At primary age level it can also help if a copy of the class agreement goes home to each parent from that class. Of course, the teacher would need to have a covering letter, supported and countersigned by the principal, explaining the purpose of the plan(or 'agreement') and how it fits in with school-wide policy (Rogers 2006).

It is important that any relieving teachers also receive a copy of this class agreement (it normally runs to about 6–8 pages with pictures and photos included). Key aspects of the class plan can be recorded on classroom posters to set the class tone for the establishment phase of the program. Some schools conduct a parent information night where the common (school-wide) philosophy and practice regarding the use of classroom behaviour agreements are outlined for parent discussion and feedback.

It is also important that students and parents see the positive benefits of the process and practice of classroom behaviour agreements: this includes the welfare and well-being of all the participants, the challenges to responsibility, and the positive outcomes in learning and behaviour.

The consequential chain

Students need to learn the consequential chain and how it operates, in the school community. In *serious* cases all behaviour is directed to the principal and parents are notified, but the grade subject teacher is always involved in some way in the consequential process, even where the student is suspended.

As a part of the classroom discussion on rights, responsibilities and rules the teacher(s) will explain that consequences have *degrees of seriousness*. 'If you have been reminded of the relevant rule, or given a simple (fair choice) or a fair direction, remember that what we're seeking to do is to help you take ownership of your behaviour and consider others' rights. If you make it difficult for students (or the teacher) to feel safe here, to learn (or teach) or be treated with respect, one of several things will happen:

- You will always, *always*, be asked to stay back and meet with me (or sometimes another teacher) to explain your behaviour and sort out ways to change things for the better.
- In class you may be asked to work away from others in the room (or even just outside the room).
- You may be asked to take "cool-off-time" and "thinking time" in the class, away from others, or even just outside the class.
- You may be directed (not asked) to leave our classroom for time-out in another room.

'You see, as your teacher, I cannot allow any of you to behave in ways that make it very difficult for others to learn or for me to teach. I cannot allow any of you to hurt others here.'

DEVELOPING A CLASSROOM BEHAVIOUR MANAGEMENT PLAN: ONE TEACHER'S STORY

My teacher-centred approach was not going to work with this class! Their social skills were not strong. It was pretty obvious that I had to change the group dynamics as well as address the issue of poor social skills. I believe that the success that I had with this class was largely due to establishing more positive relationships with, and between, the students so that they valued what we were doing – not an easy task with a difficult group that I saw only once a day for forty minutes.

I started by looking closely at what I was doing. I was also a part of this group – a group I had to work with for the year. It was vital that I made a difference. Until the class could accept each other and develop a more positive, supportive classroom environment we would achieve nothing.

I put myself into their shoes. I tried to anticipate what discipline problems I would encounter the next day. I planned how I would handle each problem and even rehearsed what I would say. I also had an exit/time-out plan in place that I had developed with the assistant principal.

I spent as much time planning my discipline plan as I did the content of the lesson. When problems occurred I wanted to be able to deal with them in a manner that reduced stress.

It was essential that the class own its behaviour. I was totally honest with the students. I told them that I was really unhappy with how we were functioning as a class and that on several occasions I had shed a few tears after the lesson. I explained that I was under a lot of stress and we needed to address what we were doing – a brave thing to admit to a Year 9 class! The discussion that followed focused on how we liked to be treated and the rules we wanted to put into place to ensure that each one of us felt valued.

With this difficult class it was obvious that I needed not only to concentrate on social skills but also to ensure that the material we covered was interesting, relevant to them and enabled them to realise some success. I strongly feel that the development of relationships is an important part of a behaviour management plan, as is catering for the needs and learning styles of students. It is not just a case of having a good discipline plan. Co-operative learning experiences were also invaluable in helping me establish positive relationships.

In coping with a difficult class I needed support from my colleagues, and at first it was not easy to discuss my problems. I received a lot of help from an assistant principal as well as a teacher who had 'rescued' me on several occasions when it all became a bit too much. I now tell my story as much as possible to encourage others who have difficult classes not to be afraid to admit it. As an experienced teacher it can be hard, but I found that many others were then prepared to discuss their problems with me and help me as well.

We were able to turn things around using a 'recipe' of a carefully thought-out discipline plan, the establishment of rules, routines, responsibilities based on valuing each other, relevant and interesting programs and, above all, a sense of humour and senior staff support.

Once the students could see that I was a part of the class and was interested in them and the youth culture, we were off first base. It was hard work developing social skills and positive relationships in the room, a well thought-out discipline plan, and interesting lessons catering for individual needs. However, my teaching became far less stressful and, by the end of the year, I was actually enjoying the class. The end-of-the-year class barbecue and the flowers from the students said it all.

Step 1: Personal review
- How should I start?
- Where should I start?
- Am I prepared to change from a teacher-dominated approach? Will this threaten and weaken my authority and control?

Step 2: Clarifying the issues
- Identify the problems.
- What behaviour do I consider to be disruptive?
- How often do disruptions occur?
- How do I normally, characteristically, react to disruptions?

A tape-recorder became my best friend for a week. I recorded several of my classes and identified the following problems:

- overreaction to minor disturbances, often leading to a win-lose argument
- some students treated differently from others for the same misbehaviour
- teacher-imposed discipline – student ownership of behaviour not apparent
- too many instructions at once
- lack of social skills in a number of students
- same misbehaviour occurring every lesson
- no clear class expectations – goals/aims often not discussed
- teacher indecision
- many teacher commands; few teacher requests
- no group cohesiveness; poor working atmosphere
- lack of assertiveness by teacher
- students often removed from room – no follow-up.

Step 3: Action planning
- I read as much literature as possible relating to the issue of behaviour management, for example: *You Know the Fair Rule* (Rogers 1998) and *Behaviour Management – A Whole-School Approach* (Rogers 1995).
- I talked to my colleagues about concerns and looked for ideas, strategies, approaches and support.

Step 4: Action
- I noted misbehaviour in each lesson and how I responded to each instance.
- I planned my approach to similar problems I expected next lesson.
- I discussed *exit-from-the-room procedure* for serious disruptive behaviours. The discipline problem was not to be handled by the assistant principal or year level co-ordinator, with the exception of fighting, but was to be dealt with by me at more appropriate stages. The 4W Form was to be completed by the student (see appendix in this book).

Step 5: Class discussion
- Classroom expectations, rules and consequences were discussed with the class. The rules were clear and expressed positively wherever possible.
- How our rules matched school policy was also discussed.

Step 6: Discipline
- I started by choosing behaviours I would tactically ignore, and used non-verbal messages and simple directions.
- Over time, I gradually used other behaviour management approaches that focused on positive correction and encouragement.

- I ensured that all problems were followed up.
- I found it essential to reinforce positive behaviour once a disruptive student was back on-task.
- I was continually working on co-operative learning approaches to develop more group cohesiveness.

- Initially it was time-consuming but now considerably less time is spent dealing with disruptive behaviour.
- Teacher stress and frustration have reduced considerably, and a more positive, respectful classroom behaviour has been created.

Roxanne (High school teacher)

Chapter 4

DEVELOPING A CLASS BEHAVIOUR PLAN USING GROUP REINFORCEMENT

A major purpose of behaviour modification is to change the child's world into one where appropriate behaviours are naturally reinforced.
The teacher needs to intervene at first, but once the world has been changed, the situation should ideally be self-reinforcing.
Biggs & Telfer (1981)

Introduction

With very disruptive classes where a significant number of students seem to be constantly off-task, unfocused, loud, fractious and so on, it may be helpful to restructure the whole class using *group reinforcement*. Rather than simply setting up individual reinforcement programs with individual students, the teacher restructures the class into mixed-ability groupings. These groups are then encouraged in positive academic and social behaviours by the use of systematic reinforcement. An individual's behaviour can benefit the group, and vice versa, and is selectively reinforced by the allocation of tokens, which are traded for *rewards* (as the students see it). It is not an elegant educational philosophy but as a short-term refocusing plan it can enable the kind of success that can regenerate positive teacher and student relationships.

I am aware, of course, that to include any form of behaviour modification suggestions one risks the simplistic objection that one is merely interested in ends. Not so. Any educational and management approach is replete with values and ideals. It is my view that any method that diminishes a person's fundamental freedom and dignity should be called into question or not used at all. This view comes from what we value about people. I do not believe one can (or should) reduce complex human behaviour to stimulus and response, or some facile reductionism that says by simply applying conditions at A we can produce outcomes at B. Utility is no proof of value.

My purpose in including group reinforcement is to demonstrate that, with the students' full knowledge of what is happening with a 'reinforcement activity', a class can refocus on positives and begin to celebrate group and individual effort in learning and behaviour. The 'rewards' that form a key part of this selective reinforcement are a way of motivating a disruptive class. They are a means of acknowledging and affirming those behaviours that benefit the group and that are considerate of mutual rights. In time that affirmation and acknowledgment should be a normative feature of our leadership and relationship with our students. With group reinforcement a *process* is structured to enable that normative outcome. Whenever I've used this approach it has been in open discussion with students and never pursued as an end in itself. Behaviour reinforcement can act as a kind of 'social circuit breaker' – a *means* of changing the power brokerage in the room and utilising it for the benefit of all. With many groups I finish the program after several weeks and run a classroom meeting to discuss the lesson learned, the changes observed and future direction of the class.

There are countless studies showing that task performance, positive reinforcement, group motivation and positive behaviours can be enhanced by group modification (see particularly Brown, Reschly & Sabers 1974; Rogers 1998). One study with a 'head-start' classroom (in USA) showed that group reinforcement at infant-age level significantly reduced the incidence of aggressive behaviours (hitting, biting, pushing, shoving and kicking). This study combined group reinforcement with time-out procedures. Any act of aggression was immediately associated with time away from the group using in-class time-out (physical separation for cool-off time) where students cooled off for three minutes, with an audible timer to signal for teacher and students their readiness to rejoin the group.

The 'reward' cycle operated on an hourly basis, with all groups (of four) having the opportunity afresh each hour to see their efforts affirmed and rewarded. The key to this program was that if one group member was aggressive or significantly off-task, the whole group lost the extrinsic reinforcement for that hour (Brown, Reschly & Sabers 1974, p 415). This program was directly related to the positive class explanation of rules and the process. The reminder was given each day to the whole class that the 'reinforcement process' was in operation. Ideally class groups ought to work co-operatively without the inducement of rewards. We have found, however, that some groups of students significantly benefit from this reinforcement stage. The reinforcement program can also act as an 'experiential precursor' to co-operative group work. The overall aim of any reinforcement program is to fade out the extrinsic modification by the teacher to allow the classroom to operate under naturally occurring co-operation and subsequent feedback and encouragement by the class teacher.

The process

This program relies on the use of basic behaviour modification principles and pure novelty to refocus the group. I have adapted this approach from McCarthy et al (1983); Brown, Reschly & Sabers (1974); Barrish et al (1969); Wilkes et al (1981) and Rogers (1998).

My colleagues and I have used the following approaches to refocus classes of five-year-olds and 15-year-olds back to calmer, quieter, more task-focused groups (Rogers 1998). As one science teacher said of the very difficult Year 8 group we had been working with, 'Up until now I haven't been game to bring out any equipment and do experiments! I couldn't have trusted them. Now we're actually starting to work together.' In this case the group reinforcement programs not only saw significant changes in student behaviour, the class teacher became more positive in his perception, focus, and relationship with the class group.

Preparation

In preparation for the programme the teacher lets the class know that the class will be working on a new group programme. We explain that this will involve small groups working together as 'learning groups'. 'To help our groups support and encourage one another in our learning there will be points "granted" for positive behaviour; (considerate, helpful, thoughtful and co-operative behaviours). These "points", when added up over the week, indicate our effort. We will celebrate that effort with a range of options: board games; group games and activities; certain kinds of free time …; (even food!).'

N.B. We prefer to use the term 'points granted' than 'points given for rewards'. In fact we prefer to use the word 'celebrate' rather than 'reward'. We want to avoid notions of bribery or coercion.

We normally set a 'group reinforcement programme' to run for two to three weeks to heighten the novelty that is a key feature of the programme.

Presenting the programme

We find it helpful to outline the programme to the class using several prepared charts. These charts enable the teaching phase of the programme, and remain (posted) as a visible *aide memoire* for the class during the programme.

Chart 1

This chart contains the class rules expressed as behaviours. These rules may have come out of a 'brainwave session' (p 53). It is important at primary level that the chart outlines the rules simply, clearly and behaviourally. The following examples are rules from a Year 1 class:

- Line up without pushing and shoving.
- Enter the room quietly.
- Place all toys quickly in the locker and sit on the mat.
- Put up your hands to ask questions (no calling out).
- Stay in your seats at your tables (monitor gets materials).

Chart 2

This chart is for leadership selection (used at middle and upper primary and secondary). The teacher highlights that when students select a group leader 'these are the qualities to focus on':

- someone you look up to as a leader
- someone who can help the group co-operate and get the class work done (without yelling or threats – this point is made verbally to the class)
- someone who can help the group work by the fair rules.

Chart 3

This is a chart with four or five columns in which to list each group leader, the members of the groups and the 'points' granted.

Chart 4

This chart contains the 'rewards' available for points earned. These 'rewards' can range (depending on age or group) from stickers, stamps, free-time activities (board games, computer games, extra reading time, a class game and so on) to a special class video. The points allocation ranges from 10 to 100. At 10 points, for example, each student in the group gets an 'energy enhancer' (a dangerous jelly bean!) and at 100 points there is a class video, or an afternoon tea, or board-games …

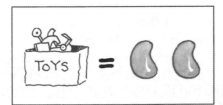

The points are always allocated to the *group* even if only one member of the group is doing the right thing at the time. In this way the group reinforces the individual and vice versa. The number of points corresponds to the effort applied by the group over time.

Note: Before embarking on any behaviour modification activity using 'rewards' (especially edible 'rewards') check with your team leader or with administration. Some schools have strong philosophical/educational reservations about 'reward programs'. Some schools will allow 'rewards' such as free-time activities but no edibles, so it is worth checking in advance. Some teachers discuss with the class what special activities they would like to do and these are listed as 'behaviour enhancement outcomes' or 'celebrations'. This is preferred rather than use of the term 'reward'.

Formation of groups

We normally introduce the program to the group in the following way:

- Share with the class your concerns about class behaviour and learning but keep it brief. It may help, with older students, to have the issues/behaviours listed on a poster. Outline the changes you would like to make with the class: 'We're going to be working in groups over the next four weeks. We will need five teams of five (or six) students and we will need five (or six) leaders for these teams.' The poster has a clear, large, bright heading: 'Our classroom teams'. Underneath have Chart 2 (points for leadership selection) and Chart 3 (team groupings). This stimulates initial interest.
- For the selection of the leaders, the class teacher should outline the qualities of a leader (refer to Chart 2). Hand out slips of paper on which students are to write the names of two students they think would make 'good leaders' (someone they would take notice of, listen to, work co-operatively with; someone we all respect). Students are asked to write down one name if they can't think of two. I have had students ask if they can put their own name down! I explain that it is a choice about *others* in the group and say, 'If others believe you're a good leader your name will soon show up.'
- Nominate a student to collect the 'leadership selection' slips and note the recurring names. These will usually synchronise with your own views of responsible leaders. At infant primary level the team leaders are chosen by the teacher and the team members allocated by the teacher. While organising leaders from this 'secret ballot' the teacher will give the class some busy work to go on with. It can even be a sheet or two of suggestions on how to improve our class (Appendix 4).
- Write the names of the five or six leaders on the group chart. Invite these leaders to come to the front of the classroom to privately select their team members (one at a time) from the class list until *every* name is selected. It is important to conduct this process 'privately' at the front of the room, to avoid

public selection and any sense of shame at being chosen last. At lower/middle primary level, team members can be allocated by random selection of names out of a container or the teacher can allocate group members to guarantee mixed ability. I have found it helpful at upper primary and secondary levels to brainwave with the class how they could form themselves into five or six groups smoothly, without hassle. We then select the most helpful idea and set them to it. From the outset it is important to invite the co-operation of the group (our ongoing goal).

■ Read out the teams (there will be a few cheers – let that go). Call for group attention and ask the groups to organise themselves to sit in teams. I've found it helps to have a large poster attached to the chalkboard showing where each group will form itself with tables/desks. Allow five minutes for each team to do this quietly, considerately and co-operatively. They can receive points for their effort. The restructuring of the class group into small groupings/teams changes the power dynamics of the group. With the behaviour modification process, the groups (and 'relocated' powerbrokers) begin to refocus their attention on benefiting the group contingent with the 'rewards' process. Our overall aim – obviously – is to move from a 'rewards' focus to naturally occurring reinforcement by the teacher *and* the students.

The 'reward' system

Explaining the 'reward-system' is a crucial step in the process:

■ Once the class is settled into its new groupings (five minutes at most) we explain that points can be gained by the groups and as these points add up they can be traded for a range of 'Behaviour enhancement outcomes' or ('rewards'). Go through the list of rewards briefly. If *all* groups get to a common target, for example 500 points, the *whole class* can have a class treat. This could be a video as a class (from teacher selection, not an open choice) or special afternoon or BBQ (I've had those.)

■ Point out that groups can *gain* (avoid easy use of the word 'earn') points as a group, or individuals can help their groups gain points by:
  –lining up without hooning, pushing and shoving
  –settling in their group quickly and quietly
  –working by our fair rules
  –co-operating in their group
  –reducing working noise levels
  –leaving their area clean and tidy.

■ In effect we, initially, allocate a point for all efforts and then, as the lesson progresses, points are granted for extra effort. We become more discriminating. If any student complains we point out, calmly, that the teacher is the referee, and that 'hands up', or 'lining up quietly' is the fair thing anyway. If a student is really objectionable either take a point off the team's score (the group will apply reflective group pressure) or point out (calmly, briefly) that this behaviour is not helping the group to gain points. Be careful not to take too many points from a team's daily score as it slows down motivation. It is better to say, 'You could have gained points if …' and leave it at that.

■ Make sure each group gets to at least 10 points in the first session. Acknowledge all their efforts (even if not granting a point *every* time!)

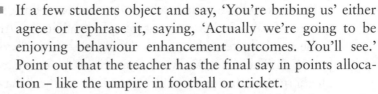

■ If a few students object and say, 'You're bribing us' either agree or rephrase it, saying, 'Actually we're going to be enjoying behaviour enhancement outcomes. You'll see.' Point out that the teacher has the final say in points allocation – like the umpire in football or cricket.

■ The giving of points on the class chart is the primary reinforcement. The secondary reinforcement is the group's acknowledging the efforts of their peers and later the BEO itself. When putting up the points, do it casually, without a big fanfare, for example 'Craig, you've got your hand up – point for your team.' Leave it at that. We don't need to thank him – just briefly acknowledge and visually allocate the point on 'the points board'.

The process in operation

The lesson material doesn't need to change *per se*. When using this approach, though, some teachers will set up special group activities to enhance group co-operation.

Many teachers have commented on how it has changed their perspective as teachers. They start looking for the positives in their students, not just the negatives. As the teacher becomes more positive, the class tone changes as the students perceive themselves differently. I've had classes say they actually start to enjoy their work.

The normal classroom discipline (including use of time-out) still operates within such a programme. It is important that any student's attempt to sabotage the program be dealt with swiftly – either immediate time-out (with positive follow-up) or allowing the student to work separately. In one very boisterous and unfocussed Year 6 class, where I had developed this programme, one of the boys loudly, and attentionally, refused to join a group. I invited him to do his work separately, away at a desk of his own. I gave him the choice of joining a group, at any stage, saying, 'Just let me know.' He joined a group in the second week.

It is also important that the teacher reserves the right (as umpire) to change any leader who is not keeping to their 'job profile'. This would normally follow a private discussion, after class.

Some teachers enhance the points allocation by having an audible timer go off at random times during the session. The group most on-task at that point (umpire's decision) can gain points too. Other colleagues have a tape-recorder going that gives out a random signal every three to five minutes. The class soon gets used to it.

Do not let students themselves allocate points on the points chart as it can easily get out of hand with a feisty group. Only the umpire (the teacher) allocates points. Some teachers keep the points tally hidden from the students. I like to keep the points chart visible. We work consistently to see that no one group gets too far ahead of the other groups.

Behaviour modification at lower primary level

Most of the guidelines noted earlier are relevant not only at primary and secondary age, but also at lower primary – kindergarten to Year 3. At the lower age level:

- The grouping of the students is directed by the teacher, as is the allocation of the leader.
- Students in each group have a badge with their group motif (colour, animal name, plant name, but not a football team name).
- The allocation of points can be tied in with other activities such as the noise meter (p 86*f*).
- It can help to have the points allocated on a five-minute (or ten minutes) allocation so *every group* gets some chance of scoring. Special effort rewards can be allocated for high scores. To enhance a *whole-class* ethos, as well as a *group-by-group* ethos, the group points can be tallied into a whole-class allocation so the whole class gets a reward when the whole-class tally reaches a target of, say, 100 or 200 points. Any points target has to correspond to the 'working currency' we establish at the outset.

One such novel approach involves each group having a poster with a drawing of its group car (different coloured car for each group corresponding to the colour of the group badge). The object of the game is for each group to fuel its car for the journey. The fuel is the points gained by the group's effort. As the cars get to 5 (fuelled by the 5 points gained) each group member gets a jelly bean. When the group gets to 25 points, each group member gets a sticker (it may take a couple of hours for some groups to get to this stage in the journey). The motivation is primarily in the fuelling reward (allocation of points) and the members' interpersonal encouragement. At 50 points the group can finish five minutes before the end of the period and do an activity (quietly) of their choice. At 100 they can try the balloon game (see below).

Another novel approach is that each group has a poster depicting a basketball's journey to the ring. Each part of the ball's journey is coloured in (5 points for each part of the ball's journey) and there is a small reward for each five points achieved. When the ball finally reaches the ring the individual group has a group game or activity.

One popular activity is for a member of the group to come up to the balloons fixed to the wall and pop a balloon. Each balloon has either a group game possibility inside (on a piece of paper) or a reward for each group member (a canteen voucher, a photocopy voucher entitling the students to make ten photocopies, a pencil for each group member, or a special game or activity).

Whenever considering the use of such 'rewards' it is important to be aware of:

- a 'currency profile' where students see the overall value of individual rewards, or group rewards or even whole-class rewards.
- emphasizing the effort exercised by students – not just the reward itself.
- acknowledgment for the student's effort when giving points verbally. Eg: 'Michael and Sean; you remembered to pack up quickly and quietly (without reminder) – point for your team.'

Maintaining the programme (primary and secondary)

- Keep any corrective discipline positive. Use rule reminders (refer to the rule chart) or direct a question: 'What are you doing, Craig?' When he replies, 'Nothing!' we quietly, clearly, remind him: 'Actually, you're working very noisily. What are you supposed to be doing?' If Craig says that he doesn't know, calmly remind him, refer to the class rule, or ask his team to quietly remind him.
- Tactically ignore any residual sulkiness; sighing; muttered whinges; eye-rolling … when any student is unhappy with a points allocation or teacher correction. Follow up one-to-one.
- Utilize the skills of the group leader where appropriate (upper primary) and the leader can then refocus her/his group members.
- Use time-out for any persistent disruption.
- Rotate group members during the course of the programme if you think this would help.

- Increase the time needed to gain points and increase the points required for 'rewards', but discriminate in the allocation of points.
- Change the group leader once a week if possible at primary level and every second period at secondary level. However, if the groups are working really well, it may be appropriate to leave the leader in place or ask the group what it thinks.
- Fade out the program within four to six weeks maximum.
    - Keep the tenor of the whole programme positive. At the end of each day briefly remind the students what they have accomplished and the difference it has made.
    - Conduct a classroom meeting at the end of the programme to share with the students what they have learned through this 'activity', this 'process'; what they see as the benefits (or otherwise) and where we might move on to from here. Discuss the benefits of the programme beyond the 'rewards' themselves. Ask the students *what*, and *who*, really made the difference to their behaviour together; they did.

Many teachers move on from group reinforcement programmes to co-operative group activities with *naturally occurring* 'class rewards' that need no points allocation.

One of my favourite, naturally occurring, rewards with a difficult Year 6 was to have a morning tea once a week with monitors for tea, coffee and hot chocolate and a plate of biscuits taken around by a monitor. Students were rostered to take orders, make the drinks and clean up/store away. They loved it – and we more than amply completed the set work for that term.

Support from colleagues

Teachers with a very difficult class may want to consider the group reinforcement programme but may not be confident in planning and delivering the process. Colleague support will always help – there may be a colleague on staff who has used such a programme. At the very least, having a colleague plan the programme with you and help you set up the first session (day one is the hardest) will make you feel better. Invite a colleague to visit and observe a session, or part of session, and ask for descriptive feedback – this can help fine tune the programme.

Group reinforcement is not a cure-all. There are no guarantees that it will work with a hard class. However, I have had many, many, teachers tell me that this program has been a great 'circuit breaker' with a class that was seemingly 'off the rails'. It has rekindled teacher and class success, and with some teachers has saved their sanity.

One of my American colleagues, who directs a behaviour clinic in Okalahoma, has used a reinforcement game with attention deficit hyperactive disorder (ADHD) students. The reward schedule is based on a simple board game where students spin a spinner and a piece is moved along a board. As they don't know what the rewards might be, this increases motivation and decreases dissatisfaction. The number on the reward card corresponds to a number on the board. Over 50% of the game cards provide activity-based rewards involving movement. Examples are: wiggle your whole body while counting to 50; act like a tightrope-walker in a circus; and have a game of Pictionary. The cards also give the opportunity to pick up a sticker or 'animal cracker'. Up to 10% of the cards give students an opportunity to pop a balloon (p 70). The chance to spin comes from points gained from their groups.

The game is available along with a video program (McNeil 1994).

Students in co-operative working teams

One of my colleagues in a Melbourne secondary college has his machine shop (Automotive class) run on the basis of teams or groups of three or four. The teams are of mixed ability and are rotated from time to time. They have rostered job descriptions involving monitoring and clearing away of equipment, and special afternoon teas from time to time. There is a tape playing music during the on-task phase of the lesson (tapes selected by students but no heavy metal). The tape is turned off for lesson transitions.

Each activity in the units of work is noted on a work card with easy visuals, all in a plastic folder.

The basic behaviour rules are discussed within the whole-school code on Day One, and the safety rules are published and placed near each machine. The class virtually runs itself. The students respond very well to the goodwill and trust communicated by the teacher. Goal-based learning and assessment and student co-operation are emphasised in all the units of work. This teaching method, when coupled with a positive and interesting classroom (workshop) environment, enhances both learning and social behaviours.

In a Year 7 textiles class we had each group of five students working on three key projects (with their visual/written learning cards) over time. In each group there was a noise monitor to keep working noise to partner voice level ('work talk' with no 'playground talk'); a materials monitor, which meant that only a few people were moving around the room instead of 20; and group leaders who kept the group on-task, focused, and reminded their team of the rules (where necessary). Most of all the group leaders encouraged the group members to support one another. To introduce the scheme the teacher (with a colleague for moral support) had a class meeting. In the meeting we discussed the present concerns about the class and then invited their concerns and shared her team proposal. She used the selection method for student grouping (noted on p 38*f*). The class rules and group responsibilities were published on bright attractive posters. The class had a celebration at the end of that term and regrouped for Term 3 as a more settled and a more co-operative group.

I have seen teachers at every level of education enhance student co-operation in the following ways:

- The classroom environment is attractive and functional (especially important at secondary level) with everything from seating plans to use of pot plants, curtaining, posters, work displays (even if it's taken down each lesson it's worth putting it up for that class at secondary level).
- An emphasis on 'visual-learning' (and some appropriate kinaesthetic learning activities) – as well as obvious 'auditory learning'.
- A teaching style that invites student opinion and co-operation, and conveys that trust is adopted.
- There is a move from a positive establishment structure (Chapter 5) to opportunities for co-operative learning lessons. While it is not always possible to have a co-operative grouping approach in each lesson, it is important to blend teacher-directed learning with co-operative learning options to enhance socialisation skills as well as group learning skills.
- Periodic classroom meetings are held to obtain classroom feedback. While this approach is used more often at primary level, secondary teachers are increasingly using classroom meetings to invite student participation, dialogue, problem solving, action planning. At the very least we can invite student feedback on aspects of our teaching and their learning, and the delivery of curriculum and the support we offer as their teacher(s) (Chapter 2).

Chapter 5

ESTABLISHING A CLASS AT THE OUTSET

In the morning when you rise unwillingly
let this thought be present –
I am rising to the work of a human being.
Marcus Aurelius
(The Meditations of Marcus Aurelius V
120–180AD)
Trans. G. Long, Grolier: The Harvard Classics

Introduction

When a group of students sits down for the first time in a classroom with a teacher standing 'up-front' there is a *group readiness*. This readiness is sometimes a testing time for teacher and students – especially with a class that seems to present as challenging from that first meeting! The students are ready to see how, what, and in what way leadership, teaching and learning will take place in *this* class; what the limits (if any) are; and how the teacher will communicate and enforce any limits. However challenging the class we need to utilise their 'natural readiness' and establish – with them – a place of shared rights and responsibilities.

There are a number of routines, aspects of room organisation, procedure and expectations that are basic to day one and week one – the *establishment phase*. What we establish tends to have a significant *initiating effect* from day one. If, for example, the teacher appears to 'allow' the students to run into class, wrestle for the tables, repeatedly call out, throw things and so on, it tends to convey a powerful initial expectation. Of course, if we have a *disastrous* day one, it doesn't mean we can't turn things around, but it does mean that such turning around is harder. It will mean that we will need to enlist senior colleague support a.s.a.p. This support option is discussed later (Chapter 9).

I was discussing the establishment phase with a large high school staff recently and we decided it would be helpful if we reappraised our establishment procedures within, and across subject, faculties. It surprised some teachers that they were not sure what they actually did, or said, when establishing their classes at the outset of the term:

- Did we line students up outside a classroom or just let them go straight into a classroom?
- How did we settle the class in the first few minutes?
- How did we gain and maintain the attention of the group? What did we say and do to that end? Does it matter what we say and how we say it? If so, why? Why not? Were some ways of gaining group attention more effective than others? If so, why?
- Did we have seating plans or did students sit in friendship groups? Why? If we had a seating plan, what difference did it make to class focus, attention and learning?
- How did we deal with typical early disruptions, such as students arriving late, students calling out, students with notices to hand in, students arriving with hats on and students chewing gum etc.? Some teachers, for example, felt it was important to remind students about hats and chewing gum, while others said it didn't matter to learning.
- How did we deal with disruptions to the lesson such as calling out, butting in, requests to go to the toilet, and so on?

We asked ourselves what we were trying to achieve in the establishment phase. We agreed that basically we wanted to convey:

- a sense of order, focus and purpose in our classes.
- a positive tone in teaching, learning and social exchange.
- some clarity and consistency on rules, and – as important – the *rights* basic to those rules. We also wanted to clarify the core routines for the smooth running of life in our classroom.
- the expectation that students are responsible for their behaviour, especially in how it affects others' basic rights, such as the right to learn without undue pressure, interference or interruption (by other students); the right to be treated with respect and dignity (whatever one's race, background or gender) including respect for property; and most of all the right to feel (and be) safe in this place (all harassment and bullying is an attack on one's right to feel safe and be treated with basic respect.
- our teaching and management style – a style that conveys respect with appropriate assertive leadership.

A number of basic aspects of classroom establishment followed on from these aims.

'Lining up' and entry to class

Think for a moment; how do we actually settle 25 students with multiple energies outside a classroom (especially an outside demountable classroom on a cold day)? It sounds incredibly basic but how do we lead 25 or more students into a classroom with some sense of co-operative calmness and order?

I walked down the corridor to the 25 Year 9 students outside Room 27. I could see at the front of the group, by the door, a tall boy holding another boy in a headlock. I asked him his name. He replied, 'Queen Boadicea!' and grinned. I looked him in the eye, in the hope this distraction and diversion would refocus him. I said, in a quiet, firm, 'aside': 'OK Queenie, let go of your mate, keep the hands and feet to yourself thanks.' He grinned back; turning attention back to the group I asked them to settle, said 'Good morning' and directed them into the room. The lad (Queen 'B') told me later he had been learning about this ancient British Queen – a 'war Queen – and had 'taken a fancy to the name'(!).

What sort of things do we say to settle and initiate group focus in the corridor? It's worth thinking about some key phrases to use based on verbs, for example 'look', 'settle', 'walk quietly', 'sit at your seats', and 'sit on the mat a metre from my chair' (this to infants creeping up to examine my socks!). It sounds a little 'mechanical' when put clinically on paper like this, but with a smile and hand gestures, thoughtful directions, and reminders, can convey positive expectation and tone to the group.

Consider the following:

- Do we go in first and have the students follow? Do we send half the students in and then go in, or do we let them all go in first? It's worth discussing this in relation to our age and subject needs. For example how do we set up appropriate entry to subject areas such as textiles, physical education and art?
- Do we remember to greet our students on the way in or just wait for them to settle? At secondary level, especially upper secondary, there is often no 'lining-up', as such, and a greeting *as* students enter telegraphs a positive, respectful, teacher-student relationship. I like to stand by the door with a brief greeting to students as they come in. Of course, at primary level the teacher is already in the room before the first assembly bell. Lining up normally occurs at recess break.

Before the students actually go in to class it can help (at primary and lower secondary levels) to briefly remind the students of *expected* behaviours. 'Before we go into our classroom, what do we need to remember about hats; coats; drinking bottles and where we sit ...?'

Positional placing (in whole-class teaching time)

Where do we sit, or stand, while we seek to gain the attention of the group? How do we *wait* for the residual noise to settle? How do we signal that we want whole class focus and attention, and what cues do we use?

It is helpful to convey the impression and expectation that when we stand (or sit) at front-centre of the classroom that we require the group's attention. If we wander and pace the front of the room we may cause unnecessary (even involuntary) restlessness and visual tracking in our students. By *anchoring* ourselves and our words in that positional place (front/centre) we can build the association that when the teacher is here *group* attention and focus is expected.

Of course, it is important to look calm and relaxed with open body language (not tensed up with arms folded or slouching), feet a little apart. If we look *as if* we expect the students not to listen and not to co-operate, we may see the students behaving correspondingly. Standing upright – but relaxed – scanning the room and giving some tactical waiting time conveys teacher expectation.

If we talk above their residual noise (and in difficult classes there will be residual, settling noise) we establish a possible norm that it is acceptable for students to talk while we talk. The waiting time may seem like five minutes, but it normally isn't. I know I've timed it on many occasions.

As we scan the room, we demonstrate that we expect the residual noise to drop. A *non-verbal signal* can help as a preface to the brief waiting. The signal can be tinkling tapping on a small glass jar, rhythmic clapping, a raised hand or something else. One of my colleagues often begins whole-class attention and focus by drawing an oval on the chalkboard. He then scans the room and draws bright eyes on the oval shape (and turns again, quietly, to look at the students). He then draws the ears on the now, emerging, head (and turns again) and finally draws a smile. The attentive face on the chalkboard is now complete. It is another way of saying, to the class, 'Eyes and ears this way thanks.' He makes sure the face (in those first weeks) is gender inclusive and idiosyncratic each day!

Whenever we stand at the front of a classroom to signal for *whole-class attention and focus* it is important not to *simply* stand and wait. With restless classes we need to cue them as well.

Non-verbal cues are obviously age-related. I find it helpful to wait *initially* (standing still, relaxed, front centre) for the residual noise to settle, *then* cue with a tinging of a small glass ... Then as we scan the class, '... *Settling down ...* (pause). *Looking this way thanks* (pause). *Looking this way and listening.*'

This is a variation of the 'old' group direction of: '*Stop ...*', '*Look ...*', and '*Listen ...*'. We may need to repeat this a couple of times. '*Settling ...*', '*Facing ...*', '*Listening ...*' are all positive, behaviourally-focused, directions. They are given in preference to:

'***Would you*** *please face the front and listen ...?*'
'***Can you*** *please be quiet ...?*'
'***Would you*** *stop talking now and listen up ...?*'

We avoid asking questions where we need to give *directions*.

The tactical pause (in the direction eg '*Settling (...) Facing (...) Listening (...)*' allows take-up-time; allows some cognitive registration by the students.

Communicating calmness

One of the most challenging aspects of behaviour leadership – with *groups* of students – is that of communicating calmness. When standing, facing a really restless, and fractious, group of young people. What we say, and do, in these first few minutes is crucial. Our calmness – in tone, manner, language – can communicate positive expectancy that students can, and will, co-operate with us.

By 'calmness' I do not mean that we are – necessarily – unemotional. It is possible to be calm *and* assertive. 'Calmness' is about being confident in ourselves, in our role, as teacher leaders.

When teachers are characteristically loud, or overly anxious; when they pace and sigh; when they stand and simply 'wait and hope' for the students to settle *their behaviour is communicating something at that point.*

When we stand at the front of the classroom and scan our class of students do we 'look' and 'feel' calm? I do not mean that we do not experience some natural anxiety with restless and challenging classes, I mean are we able to convey a sense of calmness and purposefulness at this point in the lesson?

The behaviours inherent in *characteristic* calmness can be learned. It is not easy; it is possible.

■ The first person to calm, in restless, and tense, situations is the adult, not the child (or the group). Our own sense of control, and calm voice, and focused language will telegraph calmness and 'invite' calmness in return. ('A soft answer turns away wrath but a harsh word stirs up anger.' Proverbs 15 verse 1. The Bible). When a teacher's voice, tone and manner is *characteristically* loud (even kinaesthetically loud) it *adds* to the residual tension. If a teacher's directional language is couched in negative terms, '***Don't*** *be so noisy*', '***Why*** *are you so noisy?!*', '***Why*** *can't you settle down?*', '*Do you have to do **that**?! Do you?!*' The students will perceive the teacher as being threatened by their behaviour. Some students will even interpret overly negative behaviour in teaching as an 'invitation' to 'fight-back' (to argue, to challenge, or defy).

- Our calmness is measured by children in how we communicate *characteristically* – not how we communicate on our bad days.

- How 'secure' do we sound, and look, in our voice and manner as we 'scan' the class group and wait/direct the group to settle? Even if we need to raise our voice a little to *initiate* attention ('*Settling down ...*'), once all the students' noise level starts to drop we – correspondingly – lower our voice *level*, '... *eyes and ears this way (...) Thank you.*'

- Are we aware of what we say – the actual words we use – to remind and direct the class to 'settle', 'to relax', 'to face the front' and 'listen'...? It is worth discussing with our colleagues, the 'kinds of verbal cues' we use to initiate and sustain whole-class attention.

    When I am teaching infants I find it helpful to direct them to listen with 'their *eyes* and their *ears*'. '*I want everyone* (scan the faces) *looking this way and listening. I want you to listen with your eyes and your ears.*' I have had many children call out as I remind them: '*You can't listen with your eyes!*' I will *tactically* ignore the students who call out and *briefly* acknowledge and affirm those who *are* listening with eyes *and* ears. I will also briefly explain how we *can* listen with our eyes as well as our ears.

- I also find it helpful (with any age of student) to thank them *when* they are settled. As we scan their faces, as we see them settle into their seats and relax and start to attend to what the teacher is saying, a brief (non-patronising) 'thanks' is well meant. '*Thanks. You're much more relaxed now* (keep scanning the class). *You're much calmer. Well; good morning everyone ... today ...*'. I would rather 'wait' for corresponding calmness in the class group before 'formally' saying good morning and starting the lesson activity. If I talk above their residual noise in effect I habituate that it is OK to chat, move around, fiddle (with toys, objects on their tables) *while* I am beginning a 'formal' class activity.

    Our voice, now (at this point of the lesson), is quieter, relaxed, pausing where necessary for take-up by students.

- By scanning the faces of our class group (during whole-class teaching time) we can make brief eye-contact with each of our students, we can briefly (and importantly) engage and tune-in to their responsiveness; we can also briefly engage those who are still distracting ...

    '*Craig* [pause] *Michael* [pause]. *You're still chatting* [pause] (*describe* their behaviour – briefly – rather than asking them 'why' they are chatting ...). *Looking this way and listening* [pause]. *Thanks.*'

- Tactical pausing is a 'small', but important, feature of communicating calmness, in our communication to the group or the individual. Some teachers *rush* their language; long sentences with no pausing. Tactical pausing (a few seconds) allows cognitive take-up of what we have said to the group or the individual.

■ Communicating calmness is enhanced by basic preparation of the actual lesson activity (catering for visual as well as auditory learners). Our assurance we have prepared a reasonable lesson enhances our confidence. Enhanced confidence enables our calmness (p 171*f*).

■ Communication calmness – lastly – is about being prepared for the annoying, but common, distracting behaviours in restless classes: talking while the teacher is talking; calling out; students 'fiddling' (secreted mobile phones, toys, pencil cases ...); students who walk in late ...

   We need to have planned for the sorts of things we want (and need) to say *when* these distractions occur. This level of planning is as crucial as the planning of any lesson activity (see later in this chapter).

It is always important to have a positive start to the session or day, especially a greeting and a get-to-know-you session on Day One. At the beginning of most lessons I also like to have a brief morning 'chat'; or a *brief* relaxing game or activity to 'calm' and focus the group.

One of my colleagues uses a game to teach, and maintain, class settling; he calls it 'target time' (Pearce 1995). A nominated student times the class as they respond to a prediscussed agreement to be settled, and ready, in sixty seconds from entry into class. This necessity is taught and discussed as a class routine in Session One, Day One. The amount of time that can be lost by students wasting 5 to 10 minutes a lesson over a week and a year is also discussed.

Our target:
o Take a seat.
o Sit and 'relax'.
o Focus on the front of the classroom.
o Have relevant materials.
o Be ready to join in and contribute.

THANKS Mr. Rogers.

After we have signalled for whole-class attention, and focus, we may have to briefly address any disruptions to group attention, for example a student who walks in late or students calling out or talking while the teacher is talking, or fiddling with pens, rulers, toys etc. It is important to address these disruptions quickly and unobtrusively as possible with a refocus to the whole-class teaching and learning; keeping the flow as relaxed as possible. If we over dwell on these disruptions we send mixed signals to both the class and the disruptive student (Kounin 1970; Robertson 1995; and Rogers 1998).

It is important to learn students' names quickly and keep using them in all teacher–student dialogue (even when disciplining students). I've seen teachers talk to students without making any effort to use their names. For supply (or temporary relief) teachers it can help if they ask a 'responsible-looking student' to draw a seat plan for them. I normally ask a student to do this on the way into the class. I have a prepared A4 sheet on which is written: 'To help me to learn the names of everyone in the class, please draw a plan of the room. Tables with first names will do. Thanks, Mr Rogers.' It hasn't failed me yet. The student passes it back to me and I can do a check, as well as use it during on-task learning time as I'm moving around the classroom. It is worth doing this each class period at secondary level as students may change seating positions each week if there is no set seat plan.

Clarifying cues for questions, discussion, attention and help

We know that we will experience a range of distracting and disruptive behaviours with our more 'challenging classes.'

It is, therefore, important to plan ahead how we will address such behaviours as calling out; several students talking at once; overly intrusive lateness; students distracting by 'fiddling' with objects during whole-class teaching time.

As noted earlier it is essential to have clarified the class rules and routines with the students in our first meetings. These basic rules, *and routines*, are the reference point for our leadership and discipline where necessary. Most importantly, though, they are the focus for group expectations about behaviour and learning.

Calling out in class

If several students are calling out, the teacher can give a whole-class reminder, 'Remember our rule for asking questions.' It is helpful to use plural pronouns (where possible) eg: 'our class', 'our rules …'. The active verb 'remember' is more positive than 'don't forget'. As the teacher says this, they hold up a blocking hand, eyes scanning the room. A variation on this would be a (group) conditional direction, 'When you've got your hands up, without calling out, I'll answer your questions.' Similar language (and non-verbal signals) can be used

when addressing an individual who is calling out. A pleasant, invitational tone will carry the meaning and it won't sound as though we're 'in contest' or putting a student down. The teacher then acknowledges a student with his hand up, 'Tim, you've got your hand up, what's your question?' If a student persists in calling out we will need to clarify the consequences (the immediate, or *deferred*, consequences).

By teaching and reinforcing these cues from Day One we set the tone for whole-class teaching and learning time. In contrast, if we ignore, or negatively correct ('Don't call out!' or 'Don't talk while I'm talking'), we set an unnecessarily negative tone. We may also end up with habituated factional noise and annoying distractive behaviours.

Tactical pausing

Much of a teacher's intent and tone is communicated non-verbally. When correcting students we aid the registration of intent by adding brief tactical pausing between using their name and the direction or reminder about appropriate behaviour.

Two students are chatting while the teacher is teaching. She looks at them and says, 'Sarjam [pause], Sarjam [pause]' – she has to repeat because he is not attending – 'and Milan [pause], You're talking.' This *describes* what she sees. That is sometimes enough. She may need to add a behavioural direction, 'I need you to face this way and listen [pause]. Thanks.'

The brief tactical pausing also allows 'take-up time' (Rogers 1998) as the teacher 'brings their eyes' back to the whole class, resuming the flow of the lesson.

Cues for on-task teacher assistance

It is wearying for teachers to have several hands up, some clicking their fingers, to ask for teacher assistance during on-task learning time; or the 'crocodile' line of Grade 3s, work in their hands, waiting and waiting for teacher feedback, and having a hair pull here or a little bored punch there.

There are a number of routines we can establish with our students:

- 'Checking first with three students at your work area before you check with me.' Explain on Day One how they might do that. Discuss *why* and *how*.
- Number the hands, 'I see one, two, three. Michael, Jude, Chris, I'll see you in turn. Remember to go on with your spelling list [or whatever] until I come.' It

can help to have a class understanding on alternative work to do in 'wait time' (eg: work sheets/class novel/on-going project).

■ Set up class mentors who can confer with students either at their own table or a spare area in the room. This approach can work at any year level.

■ Infants go to a 'wait table' and quietly read and the class teacher calls them up in turn.

■ Have a 'ticket-system' (small numbered-laminated-cards). Students take a ticket and are called up (in turn) for teacher conferencing. Students go on with other work options while waiting.

■ Some teachers use a teacher-help board (THB) at upper primary and secondary level where students can write their name and be assisted in turn.

The teacher-help board

The THB is a simple technique (a visual prop) that can be used in any class/subject. It is ideal in such subject areas as art, textiles, information technology, manual arts and home economics. In these situations teachers often have their backs to students and there is frequent mobility by students during on-task learning time. Because of the nature of the subject area the teacher can hardly expect a simple hands-up rule.

REMEMBER

1 Check the set work yourself: What am I actually being asked to do now?
2 Check with a classmate (remember 'partner voices').
3 Write your name (quietly) on the THB. Go on with your set work.

Thanks: Mr. Rogers.

Figure 5.1

The THB is made up of two charts. One chart has space for several names to be written consecutively from one to five. This 'chart' can also be a small whiteboard. The other chart contains reminders on how to use the THB (Figure 5.1), for example **Remember** (before you write your name up here):

■ Check the work requirement yourself. Read it carefully and ask yourself, 'What am I asked to do here? Have I understood it? Where do I start? What do I need to do first?'

■ Check the work quietly with your partner, or check with three other students before me. (It needs to be explained that this means 'the student *next* to you, not the student behind or in front of you, or the other side of the room.')

- Write your name on the THB, and I'll come round in turn.
- While you are waiting for me, carry on with the other work options (general, or specific, worksheets; class novel; spelling list, and so on).

The purpose of the THB chart has to be explained on Day One: 'It's your responsibility to consider my share of time and help for all students here. This is one way we can do that. Let's give it our best shot.' If any students are abusing this 'system' a thoughtful after-class chat with those students will help (p 107*f*).

Planning for transitions

I have been in classrooms where the transition *between* the whole class teaching/instructional phase of the lesson and the on-task phase is significantly unclear. In some instances students do not know when the teacher has finished teaching and when they are supposed to start the next phase, or (worse) whether there is an on-task phase at all(!).

Transitions need to be clear, with visual (on the whiteboard) explanations – steps, page numbers and noted examples – so that students don't start the attention-seeking whine, 'What do we have to do again?' Poor transitions can contribute to a significant rise in noise level, boredom or confusion. I've seen teachers hand material out *while* still talking, instead of completing the task explanation and getting a few key students to act as materials monitors.

It is also crucial, in the first few lessons, to emphasise and maintain expectations about on-task behaviours *before* transition to on-task learning time.

For example:

- how to get teacher assistance;
- appropriate movement around the classroom;
- noise – *levels* (during on-task);
- toilet (and leaving the classroom) procedures;
- early finishers.

Students without equipment

Teachers sometimes get into long, pointless arguments with students over not having pens, pencils, rulers or workbooks/paper and may even send students to a co-ordinator over such a small issue. Asking a student to get equipment from another student can cause needless delays and hassles.

My colleagues and I find it helpful (in secondary and upper primary classes) to take a box containing pens, rulers, pencils, paperclips, name tags and A4 paper. The box is coloured and each writing implement (for students) has a tip of coloured tape to track it back to the box. My students know it as the 'yellow box'. I also take a pile of lined A4 paper. Being prepared helps to minimise unnecessary disruption. My rule of thumb for students is that if they forget (or do not choose) to bring required materials on three separate occasions (in close succession) we'll have to sit down and make a plan together.

Helpful hints

Here are a few helpful hints:

- Have a few extra sheets that have been photocopied from the set text for those students without a textbook or who have 'forgotten'.
- Have key tasks or task requirements (such as 'Page set out' and 'Five steps in writing a draft') published in a user-friendly form around the room. It saves repeating the familiar over and over. Have a class noticeboard with daily items/reminders. This caters for visual as well as auditory learners. I've been in classrooms where teachers have given all the instructions for a learning task/requirement in one teaching style alone – spoken (not even the reference to page numbers written up for visual learners).
- Have a tray for completed (to be marked) work with ongoing learning activities for early finishers.

Gaining attention

If students are not actually *attending* to the teacher and the learning experience, it is clear that little effective teaching can take place. Gaining and *sustaining* attention is not merely some 'starting technique'; they are essential to effective teaching *and* learning. It includes the ability to build a rapport through having teaching and learning experiences appropriate to the age situation. I've seen, for example, classes at lower primary where all the expository teaching was oral/aural and went on for too long. There were no visuals, no engagement with the students by question and no involvement by a brief role-play up-front, not even a regular scan of faces and 25 pairs of eyes. If teachers are going to engage and motivate learners and learning they need to consider how to gain, sustain and focus group attention both in the whole class and on-task phases of the lesson.

Management skill has to be applied in combination with solid lesson planning and thoughtful use of the curriculum. Here, again, planning with colleagues will assist in motivating, and meeting the needs of, our students.

Teacher A teaches grammar to a Year 6 class. The unit of work is 'punctuation'. The students are restless and bored, and there is little relevant application during the on-task time. The teacher has talked a lot and has used the text, but in a way that stimulates little interest or understanding. The rest of the lesson consists of examples of punctuation read out by the teacher and a resultant worksheet.

Teacher B teaches fundamentally the same unit, but begins by talking about a bicycle having a puncture, 'Who's ever had a puncture on their bike?' The teacher then uses the concept of puncture as 'a hole in something' (to puncture). This is enhanced by the teacher drawing a rough picture of a bike with a puncture and a sad-faced lad looking at his bike.

From the concept of 'puncture' she talks about a puncture kit (to fix the hole). She then extends this to an analogy about *punctuation*, and the need for a 'punctuation-kit'.

Reading a set piece of unpunctuated writing she asks how can we fix this unpunctuated writing. The class makes a *punctuation kit*, containing small cards, denoting the tools to fix the text: 'Capital letter'; 'full stop'; 'comma'; etc. "*So, how can we use our punctuation tool-kit to fix this piece of writing?*"

She has engaged the class, drawing in many students who would not normally be so focused on the learning process.

Of course, this kind of teaching is harder with poorly motivated students and subject areas deemed a waste of time by some students (and even some teachers). I've been in schools where languages other than English (LOTE) seem to be rated as 'nonessential' or 'unimportant' and beyond the core curriculum. Some teachers will even subtly convey that view to students and not actively support subject areas such as LOTE. This is especially difficult for teachers who, for example, are already at a disadvantage if there is a negative attitude in student's homes about foreign languages.

All subject areas need to be given due credibility and support at faculty and staff meetings and particularly 'in front' of students. Year heads especially should convey the appropriate status of subjects so their students can't simply hijack subject areas they think are not 'relevant' to them.

Monitoring 'working noise'

My colleagues and I have found that it is important to *teach* and monitor 'working noise', particularly in classes with a reputation and in schools where classes are streamed. In 'bottom set' classes (a disturbing 'label') behaviour and learning problems are often associated. In such classes we've found noise monitoring and feedback a useful way to teach healthy 'working noise' or 'partner-voices', or '*inside*-talk', or 'work talk' (as one of my primary colleagues describes it to her Year 3 class).

The noise meter is a visual display of cartoons and a coloured 'signal' wheel to indicate different noise levels (Figure 5.2). The pictures need to be clear, blackline drawings, able to be seen from the back of the classroom. The four drawings indicate:

1 hands up (and listen when others speak, one at a time, without calling out) when we are on the mat – at upper primary level the picture indicates students sitting at their desks/tables with hands raised (see Figure 5.2)
2 partner communication/working noise/using 'partner voices'
3 reminder that class noise level is getting too loud
4 too loud – we need to stop and re-focus back to our 'partner-voice' level.

The central colour wheel signifies noise-level zone by colour (white = **1**, green = **2**, yellow = **3** and red = **4**). It is an ideal teaching activity for primary level for the establishment phase. White is for up-front instructional time, green is for on-task time, yellow indicates that the noise level is too high and red signifies 'Stop'.

It is important to initially discuss with the whole class what the colours and pictures signal (about noise level) by discussion or even role-play. Students are taught and encouraged that if they forget their partner voices (green zone) during table learning the teacher will point the arrow to yellow as a reminder/warning. Elected noise monitors on each table group will remind their peers to use partner voices when the teacher signals yellow. Only when the teacher puts the arrow on red will she verbally signal the class to 'stop, look and listen'. She will then briefly remind them to stay in the green zone (and remember their partner voices). The whole activity is designed to encourage co-operation, keep verbal directions to the minimum (for example, yellow zone is a non-verbal reminder) and enhance visual non-verbal teacher reinforcement. It minimises 'Shush' and 'You're getting too loud'.

Some teachers link the 'noise-meter game' to a points tally and free-time activities. However it can easily stand alone as a means of establishing and teaching healthy working 'communication' and '*levels* of voices' during a lesson.

I've used the noise meter, in modified forms, right up to Year 9. For upper primary and secondary levels I often utilise a simple whiteboard graph that gives feedback on class noise level during on-task learning time. The vertical axis nominates whisper zone at 2, and the upper limit of partner communication at number 5 (on a scale of 0 = total silence and 10 = major migraine level!).

The horizontal scale is marked from 0–30 signifying the time-divisions of the on-task phase of the class period. The horizontal line is divided into three-minute or five-minute time slots. Every five minutes the teacher can quietly walk to the whiteboard to give feedback (non-verbally with a coloured marker on the bar graph). Peer pressure will do the rest. Like the noise meter the graph needs to be explained and encouraged (in a fun way) as a way of helping us to manage class noise to enable positive learning. Points can be allocated relative to the effort by the class to manage their noise level and targeted to a score (say 20) that allocates free time (of, say, five minutes) towards the end of the class period, or the points tally (of 20) can be built up over two class periods.

Figure 5.2

Dealing with disruptive behaviour

It is important to consider how disruptions can be dealt with in the key phases of the lesson: entry and settling; whole-class teaching time; transitions; on-task learning time and at a lesson's closure. Here we will deal with the *whole-class* teaching phase (when the teacher requires group attention and students are facing directionally the same way) and the on-task phase (when students are engaged in on-task learning in groups, pairs or even individually).

In the whole-class/instructional phase of the lesson

In the 'establishment phase' of the year (as noted earlier) there is a group readiness – students are expecting us to clarify the rules, and routines, and to exercise some leadership or control of the class *as a group*. As children progress through their schooling journey they experience a variety of management styles from authoritarian to *laissez faire*. They also learn to 'read' (early) their teachers' characteristic leadership style. We need to communicate our discipline style in a decisive but confident way if we are going to set a positive classroom tone.

It is very important to avoid talking over residual noise level when settling. Teachers talking over or through students' chatter conveys (at the very least) an ambiguous expectation of how things will be. It may be enough to use the tactical pause (p 77*f*) or to give a general reminder: 'Several people are talking. Face this way and listen. Thanks.' It is also important we communicate a *confident* voice; scanning the eyes in the room, with relaxed but upright body language; blocking with a hand briefly and beckoning (to the talkers) with the right hand once or twice as if to say, 'I expect you to do it, folks.' The scanning of the class group enables eye-contact with each class member; it also shows our focused interest. Brief, scanning, eye-contact also enables us to gain feedback on how we are 'coming across': Are we sustaining their attention? Do they seem to understand? Do I need to reframe, clarify, extend? It is difficult to convey in print the powerful effect of non-verbal behaviour. John Robertson (1995) notes the following in the introduction to his book *Effective Classroom Control*.

> Gestures, vocal variations, facial expressions can reveal a teacher's insecurity or boredom. Unlike words, their meaning is often ambiguous and can only be interpreted reliably if we have other information, such as the status of the speaker and what he is saying. Nevertheless, when there is any discrepancy between the meaning of the words being spoken and the non-verbal behaviour accompanying them, it is the latter which we take to reveal the real feeling of the speaker.

Giving thought to language skill and our non-verbal communication will help consolidate our communication as teachers. The 'presentation of self' (Goffman 1972) is an important factor in behaviour management. If we look sloppy, indifferent, overly tense or anxious, and if our voice tone manner is *characteristically* off-hand, sharp or unnecessarily negative, those aspects of self will override what we say.

Non-verbal skills such as tactical pausing, positive scanning and eye contact, upright bearing, pleasant tone of voice (assertive when necessary), expectancy in one's voice and the positive use of gesture add up to a 'global' presentation that students very quickly pick up on.

Corrective language in behaviour management

Our conscious approach to corrective language is also very important:

- Try using positive verbs or participles wherever possible: 'Do' rather than 'Don't' and 'Look this way, thanks' rather than 'Don't talk while I'm talking'. For example, 'Leave the windows for now, and face this way.'
- 'Damien and Ibrahim, this way and listening. Thanks.' (In a whole-class teaching context) 'Thanks' contains a little more expectation than 'Please' when it's said positively.
- 'Hands up without calling out' rather than the simple negative 'Don't call out'.
- Use simple *descriptors*: 'There's paper on the floor' rather than 'You've made a mess down there' or 'It's noisy at this table' rather than 'Shut up here' (we should avoid ever using such a negative – if tempting – phase).
  - Use the language of 'choice' when appropriate (Rogers 1998). 'Yes, you can go to the toilet *when* I've finished this story.' Compare 'No, you can't go because I've just started this story.' The following are more invitational: 'When/then', 'Yes/when' and 'After/then'.
    - Use inclusive language when giving group directions: 'In *our* class *we* have hands up without calling out. Thanks.' Then look for a hand that is quietly up and reinforce it quickly. 'Yes, Tim, what's your question?'

Class clowning and silly comments can sometimes be met with *tactical* ignoring (where appropriate) or with a repartee or a defusing comment where comfortable. Humour is a very powerful way to defuse and refocus attention away from tension, but it depends on one's personality and ability. It should not be confused with sarcasm or teacher put-downs.

On other occasions we need to address 'clowning' comments, or behaviour, with a clear direction or rule-reminder.

The teacher needs to avoid unnecessary attention with 'clowning' behaviour, but, if given, we give it briefly:

'That's not a helpful comment right now' and move on with the flow of the lesson.

If a student puts another student down, loudly, in front of his peers, it will be important to directly 'eyeball' the student and using a firm assertive voice name the student: 'Jason!' We drop our voice to a serious tone and add the clear statement, 'In our class we have a rule for respectful language' or *'That's* a put-down and that hurts. Our class is a no put-down zone.' It will also be important to follow up students who put others down (p 107*f*). (See also p 205)

If put-downs are frequently heard in class (even 'quiet' put downs), it is worth following up with the perpetrator(s) and the victim later. It will also help to conduct a classroom meeting to address the issue (p 43*f*).

When using corrective language in behaviour management there are several principles worth considering:

- *Avoid unnecessary confrontation* (or embarrassment, or sarcasm, or 'cheap shots' … just to score!).

  For example, if a student is late (even five minutes late) we do not ask him 'why' he is late (in front of his peers). We welcome him, direct him to a seat and resume the lesson flow. We ask for reasons (re: his lateness) later in the lesson.

  I have seen teachers get into long-winded (and heated) discussions about a student's lateness often generating conflict with the student and entertainment for the watching peers.

  If a student (or students) are fiddling with pens, ruler, pencil-case (whatever) while we are engaged in whole-class teaching – we do not talk over the residual noise *or* simply walk over to the students and take the distracting objects off them. I have seen teachers snatch Walkmans; I-pods; mobile phones … and seen students yell back and even swear; it is their property. It is enough to briefly *describe* what they are doing, and direct them to put it away in their pencil case/bag or on the teacher's desk until recess. Eg: *'Michael (…) Sean (…). You're fiddling with your pens and pencil cases. It's really distracting.'* This 'describes the reality' – it raises their behaviour awareness. If several students (in different parts of the room) are fiddling with *objects d'art* it is enough to say, *'a number of students are fiddling with pens, rulers, pencil cases (…) it's really distracting.'* Sometimes I find it helpful to add, *'Maybe you're not aware that it's distracting, however it is.'* As they start to put the objects to one side, it is worth adding a brief thanks and resuming the flow of the lesson. Brief, respectful, least-intrusive. Sometimes we will need to add a *directed choice* to the *behaviour description.* *'Michael (…) Sean (…) I want you to put those little cars in your pencil cases; or I can put them on my table until recess.'* Most students put them away. *'Thanks'.*

By giving a 'directed choice' we avoid unnecessary confrontation. If the students refuse to put the distracting object away it will be necessary to clarify the consequence. *'If you choose not to put it away, I'll have to follow it up with you after class.'* *Simply* snatching an object from a challenging student is a recipe for conflict.

N.B. If we ever give such a *deferred* consequence, the effectiveness lies in the respectful communication – in front of the student's peers – and the certainty of the follow-up later (see p 107*f*).

■ *Keep the focus of correction on the 'main' or 'primary' issue or behaviour.*

It is very easy when we get frustrated by annoying, distracting or disruptive behaviours to focus on a student's 'secondary behaviours': the way they sigh, pout, raise their eyes to the ceiling, screw up their mouth … When we address a student's behaviour (say calling out) it is not uncommon for a student to lean back in their seat, roll their eyes and sigh as if it is such a big deal that we asked them to remember the rule(!). Some teachers get easily drawn into such 'secondary' behaviours and the focus of correction shifts from the calling out to the student's body language.

Teacher: 'Why can't you do what I ask instead of making it a big deal!?'
Student: 'Yeah well other people call out don't they!?'
Teacher: 'Don't you speak to me like that …!'

The teacher, now, only hears the student's sulky, pouting, tone of voice. The calling out is now overshadowed by the student's 'attitude' – his 'secondary' behaviour as it were.

My colleagues and I find it helpful to *tactically* ignore much of this kind of non-verbal 'secondary behaviour' and keep the corrective focus on the main, or 'primary' behaviour *at that point*. We can always follow-up with the student's 'attitude' away from his audience of peers later (p 107*f*).

■ *Use positive corrective language where possible.*

Non-verbal cues can be effective forms of reminder/correction. When a student is calling out a teacher will often raise their own hand (as a least-intrusive corrective reminder); or the hand on head to indicate hats off; or the hand portraying a volume switch being turned down to overly loud students …

A good deal of our corrective discipline is expressed in reminders, directions, questions about a student's behaviour. Sometimes we need to assert and, even, command.

Mostly, though, verbal reminders and directions are appropriate, and adequate, for the typical distracting behaviours we face in the classroom.

Where possible we seek to keep any correction brief and 'positive': *'Jason and Kyle (…) facing this way and listening'* is more 'positive' than, *'Don't talk while I'm teaching ...'.* 'Yes – *when*' is more 'positive' than '*No you can't because ...*' A directed question: '*What is our rule for ...?*' is more focused than an open interrogative: '*Why are you out of your seat hassling other students?*' When we use questions, we avoid questions prefaced by (or including) interrogatives eg: '*Why are you calling out ...?*'; '*You shouldn't be calling out **should you**?*'; '***Are you** late?*'; '***Are you** two talking ...?*' Questions need to direct a student to *behaviour awareness*: '*What ...?*' '*When ...?*' '*How ...?*' '*Where ...?*'

Eg: '*How are you supposed to come into class when you're late?*' This *quiet* aside to two lads who barge into the classroom in the middle of the teacher's lesson without knocking or acknowledging her.

'*Where are you supposed to be sitting when you do your class work?*' This to a student sitting on the table instead of in his seat (at his table group). '*What's our rule for ...?*' This quiet reminder question to a girl playing her I-pod while doing class work. The 'direct' questions *raise behaviour awareness. Positive* corrective language is not always possible and we need to be assertive at times. The ability to convey assertion is not inconsistent with the ability to be firm *and* respectful. Assertion is a crucial feature of our behaviour leadership and is addressed at some length later (p 171*f*).

- ■ *Keep the fundamental respect intact.*
  At the end of the day the students will hear our intent, our respect, our confidence, our like or dislike *within* what we say. We cannot force ourselves to 'like' every student; we can convey civility and respect.

These fundamental principles of behaviour leadership involve us thinking about what we *characteristically* say, and do, and why.

Some teachers write the name of the student on the chalkboard as a public signal, indicating a clear warning that if the talking continues the teacher will put a tick against the name. The addition of a second tick means an after-class meeting or detention. With more challenging classes this method may well invite an unnecessary power struggle and should be developed only within a clear team approach and the backing up with consistent follow-up and follow-through of difficult students.

Following up students after class is an important factor in establishing the certainty of consequential outcome. (This is explored in Chapters 6 and 7.)

It is crucial to distinguish between short-term correction (what one can say in the immediate emotional moment) and longer term follow-up when the audience of peers is not around. The teacher *and* student can then work through the behaviour concern more calmly (one hopes) in this one-to-one setting (see later p 107*f*).

Discipline in the on-task phase of the lesson

Behaviour management and discipline during the on-task phase of the lesson can be more directly personal (because we are now able to move around and alongside students).

If a student is chewing gum, the teacher can use a non-verbal signal to indicate the bin or an incidental question: 'Dave, are you looking for the bin?' I've taken the rubbish bin many times to the student(s) to invite co-operation on gum disposal.

If two students are talking loudly, the teacher can say, 'Dave, Karl' and signal non-verbally across the room, by making a volume turning-down signal with thumb and forefinger. The teacher could walk across and quietly say, 'Talk inside your heads *while* you're working.' Context and the student's age will modify our language but we need to consider the points noted earlier about brevity, focus on behaviour, keeping the language positive where possible and avoiding arguing or unnecessary confrontation.

Corrective discipline will vary depending on the situation and can be expressed in a variety of ways:

- Correction can be expressed as a 'conditional direction'. Maria asks if she can do the next activity but she has left a mess on her table. We could reply, 'Yes, Maria, you can, when you've cleaned your work area.' (Note that 'area' is preferable to 'mess'.)

- Simple directed choices: 'Darren, I want you to put your basketball cards in your bag or you can leave them on my desk.' This is more invitational that snatching the cards or just holding out your hand. If the student protests that he wasn't looking at them the teacher can gently block or refocus by saying: 'Maybe you weren't. They are distracting. I want you to put them away in your bag and carry on with your work.'

- It also helps to leave the student with a task-related direction, reminder or question after such a 'choice', for example: 'What should you be doing now?' or 'Carry on with your work, thanks Darren. I'll be back later to see how you're going.'

- Direct questions focus on the student's present behaviour (or issue) and invite 'behaviour awareness' responsibility. For example 'What are you doing?' rather than 'Why are you calling out' or 'Why haven't you started work?'.
  A student is 'off-task' talking to a friend. The teacher has tactically ignored the apparent time wasting for a while, but she now walks across to the students casually and directs a question at them both.
  Teacher: 'What are you doing?' (The teacher is not hostile in tone, or manner, – just relaxed, and decisive.)

Student: 'Nothing' (said a little defensively).

Teacher: 'Actually you're talking quite loudly to each other.' (She gives some brief, factual feedback.)

Teacher: 'What are you supposed to be doing at the moment?' (Her tone is pleasant and her body language is relaxed.)

Student: 'We're not the only ones talking.'

Teacher: 'If other people are talking I can remind them' (brief *partial* agreement). 'What are you supposed to be doing? (She refocuses.)

Student (sighing): 'Our project.'

Teacher: 'OK, carry on with your project. Do you know what you have to do …? I'll come across later and see how it's going.' She smiles as she leaves them with a general task reminder.

- Also, during the on-task phase teachers can sometimes call the student aside for a brief private word or even go into the corridor for a 60-second reminder. For example, Frank had walked to the bin with a piece of screwed-up paper. En route he tapped it on three students' heads. It created the effect he wanted. He walked back to his seat grinning. Should the teacher ignore this? There is a time for *tactical* ignoring, such as ignoring the sulky pouting face or whining while focusing on the behaviour that precipitated it. In the case of Frank, however, such 'ignoring' would be seen by the other students as de facto acceptance of his behaviour.

The teacher called Frank aside, away from the other students, just outside the door. She still had line-of-sight back into the room. Frank sauntered over, face screwed up, and said, 'Yes – what do you want?' In a low voice the teacher said, 'Do you know what you just did in class?' (The class realises she is 'disciplining' him even if they can't hear what is being said.) 'I was just putting some litter in the bin,' moaned Frank. 'I didn't want to embarrass you in there, Frank,' she said, 'but you actually tapped three students on the head with the litter on the way.' Frank replied, 'Gees, I was just mucking around – they are my mates.' The teacher terminated the correction by saying, 'Even if they are your mates, Frank, in our class we keep our hands and feet to ourselves, thanks. Come on, back to class.'

I've had students say, 'You can't make me' or 'I don't care' or the insouciant 'So?' when I've corrected them. In this case *partial* agreement can help refocus the student's responsibility. Rather than walk across and push the boy's feet off, or confront him with detention, we can clarify the consequences and heighten his 'choice': 'If you choose to sit like that, you're choosing to have me follow it up with you later,' or 'I can't make you, but if you continue with your feet up, I'll have to follow it up at recess.' If he replies, 'Don't care,' the teacher can say, 'But I do. We observe basic manners here – I'll see you at recess.' He then retorts, 'No you won't!' If he continues with what he perceives as counter challenge, we will need to utilise the back-up time-out plan (p 114*f*). It will be essential, though, to follow up with this student (with a third party if necessary) at a later time.

I've been in classes where teachers ignore these small events (feet up, playful punching, gum chewing, loudness, throwing pens to each other and so on) so that in time there is a general noisy, distracted, unfocused *habituated* 'culture' in the room that contributes to the hard-class definition of the group. If a boy has his feet up we signal him ('four on the floor, thanks') with a non-verbal simulation of chairs legs – four fingers pointing down. 'But I can still hear you,' the student replies. 'I know you can, (partial agreement) but considerate manners in our room are feet and chair on the floor. Thanks.' I resumed the lesson; he slowly put his feet down with a loud sigh. If he hadn't I'd have cut my losses at that point (with a reminder of a deferred consequence) and carried on with the lesson. Effectively this avoids an unnecessary power struggle (in the emotional moment), puts the responsibility back where it belongs – to the student – minimises attention to the student, and keeps the focus on the main issue (with the assurance this will be followed up later).

Some teachers ignore what they should address and address (sometimes overdo) what they should *tactically* ignore. Getting a reasonable balance isn't easy. Discussion with colleagues on these issues will help, as will observing effective teachers in their own classrooms and focusing on how such colleagues utilise their corrective language and manner, and how they deal with behaviour issues. It can also help to sit in on their follow-up with students if they are comfortable about this. Peer mentoring (*elective* peer mentoring) is probably the most effective way of learning 'on the job'. This is further addressed in Chapter 9.

If we choose to ignore events that significantly affect our rights as teachers, we effectively indicate acceptance. I was team teaching in a Year 8 class and saw a student walk right in front of the teacher while she was teaching the class. Apparently she'd had it happen many times before! It made her whole-class group attention difficult, and stressful. If such behaviour has been frequent, over time, it may even be a form of harassment and needs to be addressed at that level. No teacher should accept continual abuse of fundamental respect and fair treatment. The issue of teacher bullying is addressed at length in Chapter 9.

Closing the lesson

It is important to have a clear ending to the lesson that isn't rushed with work not collected, chairs still 'out', litter on the floor, students 'beating the bell' and so on:

- There needs to be a clear cue to the class for the end-of-lesson transition. We return to the positional place (at the front/centre or some familiar place where eyes and ears of our students can be seen en masse). This is sometimes called *anchoring*. The teacher gives a non-verbal signal (the class bell, clapping, the tinkling of a glass or even the simple waiting for 10 seconds) and the direction 'stop (what you're doing), look (this way) and listen' *before* the directions about packing-up. If we speak over students' on-task noise, half the students may have already packed up but the other half may still be engaged in chatting, finishing work and so on. Some teachers give pack-up directions *while* still moving around the room, this also adds to restlessness in some students while the directions have registered, or connected, with others.

- Summarise the key aspects of the lesson where appropriate and where necessary. Review the key aspects of learning with the class if there is time.

- On Day One, pack up early enough to go through the actual routines for pack-up and exit from the classroom.

- Regarding homework reminders: a reminder sheet can help, or at least write the information on the whiteboard rather than a hurried verbal reminder. Many teachers use a homework book for all homework, even if the homework is on a sheet. Some teachers give homework certificates for five days' completed homework and a 'reward' after five certificates. With all routines, a check with colleagues will give insight into a range of options for creative homework. Some schools run homework clubs for students who would have little hope of completing homework at home because of family dysfunction or space problems. These clubs are run with the support of parents, and afternoon tea is provided to charge up the batteries and enhance the relaxed tone of homework club.

- Clean-up routines need to be especially focused, and practised, in areas such as art, textiles and manual arts. Posters on the wall or a few cartoons can help with the key steps in cleaning up the clay area, or around the lathe or sewing machine … (I taught art for two years at primary level). These posters should be located in the key areas: wet area, paint brushes area, clean-up/storage, tool areas, use of machines and so on. Again, it is catering for visual learners (words and pictures). At lower primary level a laminated card on each group's table can carry several clean-up reminders with little cartoons of what students need to do before the bell (and at the end of the day).

- It may be helpful to allocate room cleaning on a monitor system with monitors for key requirements/roles. The monitor system is rotated so all get the chance to do all the jobs required.

- Little games like 'beat the clock' can help at lower primary level. 'Listening everyone. By the time I've counted backwards from 60 (or sung two verses of this song) let's have a clean floor, chairs under tables, felt-tip pens with lids on in your containers ...' Have the list on the wall or on their tables (with a little picture against each task).

- Have a final, calm settling time prior to the school-wide recess bell.

- Have a positive close to the lesson even if it's been a bad day or a bad class. Avoid saying, 'You're the worst class I've ever had! Do you hear? Yes you – you, Damian Scraggs – you're the worst!' If we've had a bad day, of course we need to acknowledge it – briefly: 'OK, it hasn't been the best day lesson-time today. I'm especially concerned about ... [here be specific and brief]. Tomorrow will be a new day. I'll expect better from you (and me) such as ... Enjoy the rest of this day, everyone. I'll see you tomorrow.' Of course, we'll keep back the one or two individuals for a brief after-class chat or make an appointment to discuss behaviour or learning concerns (p 107*f*).

- It will help to direct the students from the class 'row-by-row', or table group by table group (even up to Year 10!)

- If several students 'race off' when the bell goes, we'll call them back. When they are settled, remind the class that this is not a group detention but a brief, group, reminder. Class detentions are hated by students because they are unjust and do not achieve the so-called 'peer-pressure' objective. After calming the class the teacher will direct the students to leave again – considerately this time. The teacher stands by the door giving a goodbye to the now more-subdued members of the class as they leave. The teacher has established a small but important routine. We'll need to do this over several lessons with some classes until we have a positive class exit.

- Remind students to put chairs under the table (even at secondary level): 'Do the next class a favour, folks' or – at period 6 –' Do the cleaner a favour and pick up any litter near your table – everyone. I'll give you a hand. Drop it in the bin on the way out. Thanks.'

- Lastly, remind students to leave the room in a way that considers others who are outside in the corridor: 'We walk (we don't run). Thank you, see you tomorrow.' Some teachers will just let the students race off – literally – when the bell goes, to barge into yet another horde of 25 plus students across the corridor.

Encouraging the individual and the class

In a hard class there is sometimes a tone of jadedness, even of defeat – teachers are discouraged by what they face day after day. This can sometimes show up in their characteristic language. Teachers may actually be unaware that they are frequently using discouraging language: 'When will you ever learn?', 'What's wrong with you, eh?' 'Can't you understand this work by now!?' 'I'm sick and tired of your stupid behaviour'.

I recall working with a team of colleagues 'cracking' a couple of hard Year 8 classes. After a team-teaching session one colleague said, 'How is it possible to stay positive with that lot, especially that cretin Steven?' I understood his feelings – it isn't easy. We feel that these students have let us down, or that they do it on purpose, and that they don't deserve anything positive from us. One of the more common remarks I've heard from some teachers is, 'why should we even praise such and such; they hardly ever behave well. Why should I praise them when they do – that's what they're supposed to be doing anyway!'

Encouragement is the necessary, even essential, balance to correction. It is the *conscious* effort to acknowledge and build up what is positive in individual students or in the group.

I've seen teachers transform a class by consciously, and frequently, making the effort to acknowledge and affirm students' effort; publicly (where appropriate) and often in the quiet word aside from the main group.

Some of my colleagues jot down, in a notebook, students' extra little efforts or a contribution in their work or social interaction so they can quietly pass it on later, for example 'You started quickly …' 'You were courteous and thoughtful when …' 'I like the way you handled that, Paul', 'That's a tidy desk there, Halid – looks well organised' or 'Look at the progress you've made in this … Lisa'. [Be briefly specific]

When a student hands in minimal written work, for example, it's tempting to comment only on poor work, just give a mark out of 10 or just fill the page with red (negative) marks. We need to acknowledge the effort the student has made: 'Well, Michelle, that's a positive line about Van Gogh's loneliness being the start of his madness. It helps the reader to understand. It will help if you go back and check the second point in the essay topic about how it affected his artwork. Check the underlined words for spelling and check for the date. I look forward to seeing your revised paper. Thanks. Mr Rogers.'

Encouragement gives a bit of 'courage' – through positive feedback – along the way to improving, or consolidating, something in one's work or behaviour. Sure, this approach takes a little longer until it becomes habit, but it develops a more positive and constructive tone in the learning environment generally and with each student in particular.

Thoughtful encouragement acknowledges, and affirms, students' efforts and leaves the primary evaluation to them. What we convey is our confidence in their ability to progress. This can be done in the following ways:

■ Describe the effort (or thought) we see in their behaviour, their work and their attitude: 'David, that's a tidy desk', 'That's a clean work area – brushes all washed' (art), 'You've got your hand up' (whole-class discussion time).

- Recognise the improvement made by the student (even 'small' improvements).
- Reframe comments from the easily negative to the positive. For example, 'This is a noisy line' (said to a class lining up) and 'Don't you know what *quiet* means, eh?' becomes 'Settle down everyone, we've all lined up then?' The teacher comments on the students who have settled and gives them a 'good morning' (a smile) and makes a non-verbal hand gesture to the several noisy and physically restless students. 'Right, let's go in quietly and sit on the mat ready for story-time ...' Those few words preface expectation and are preventative management.

Encouragement creates the atmosphere conducive to positive learning: 'Look at the progress you've made' (specify), 'You've got a real talent for ...' and 'I've got confidence in you because ...' This challenges the student to look forward and to be specific about things that can change the present for the better: 'That helped a lot, Hung. It looks a lot tidier in the reading corner now. It'll be easier to find the books, eh?'

Encouragement works in the following ways:

- Acknowledge even the little that the students accomplish, and help them to focus on areas that they may need to work on or what still needs to be done: 'It's very tidy over there. The lids are on the felt-tip pens. What's left to do?' The teacher points to the pencil shavings.
- Avoid disclaiming *after* encouraging. For example 'You've got your hand up, Michael. If you had you're hand up all the time it would be so much better, wouldn't it, eh?' Also, avoid using encouragement in a way that seeks to manipulate the child.
- Some students will benefit from a personal plan for their class work or behaviour as a way to motivate and encourage (p 132*f*).
- A positive note (or phone call) home can be very rewarding for a student, especially when previous phone calls (or letters) have been of the 'We are disappointed with ...' variety. Some primary schools use a good-news book

between parent(s) and school to acknowledge the students' assets, special talents, contributions and so on.

■ Observe and note social skills (primary). When a teacher observes a student displaying thoughtful social skills – in the playground for example – the duty teacher makes a note and passes it back to the grade teacher.

■ Classroom meetings (primary) are often used as an opportunity/occasion to give positive feedback to class members (peer feedback). When students give feedback in a classroom meeting setting, it is important that they acknowledge what it is they like or appreciate about their peer(s). For example, 'I appreciate Michael's help in maths because ...' or 'Lisa is kind when she ...'

■ It is also important for the whole class, and especially for the hard class, for the teacher to make a conscious effort (BDN) to begin and end the day or session positively (p 96*f*). Particularly if the lesson (or class behaviour) hasn't been 'the best'!

■ If students don't always respond to our encouragement, we still need to keep it going anyway. We don't need to add qualifiers, such as 'I really mean it!' or 'Well, if that's the way you feel, I won't say anything nice.' Their unenthusiastic or even negative response ('I don't think my work's any good!') may be a form of attention seeking, or just habit. Maybe they haven't had much encouragement at home.

■ Basically, it's treating people with respect – even if they don't 'deserve' it.

Motivation

Motivating a hard class is a challenge, especially in subject areas they don't always enjoy. Motivation requires a reasonable balance between intrinsic and extrinsic motivation at work in individual students and in the group.

Intrinsic (personal) motivation involves:

■ the need for 'challenges' in learning situations
■ meeting fundamental personal needs such as the need to belong, the need for fun and the acknowledgment of worth
■ the natural drives for interest and curiosity – this is where teachers utilise novelty, prior knowledge, selecting topics likely to interest, engage and connect with the particular age/group
■ likelihood of success – if students believe they're not going to be successful academically or their reputation is already 'shot', they've got nothing to lose. That is why it is important to cater for mixed abilities within the group and, where appropriate, peer mentoring, and developing a balance between co-operative group learning with individual learning.

Extrinsic motivation involves:

- creating a context that enhances the naturally occurring intrinsic motivation students bring to schooling contexts. For example the classroom meetings approach (p 33*f*); the group establishment approach (p 74*f*) and the group reinforcement activities motivate students' needs to have a say, and to feel they are significant and can appropriately influence how things are in their class.
- the status of the subject, marking, or parent expectations (even sibling expectations) – these may be powerful extrinsic reinforcers for students for good or ill (for example, 'Why can't you be more like your brother?').

Children respond to a range of motivators and reinforcers:

- Many students appreciate a certificate when they know they've put in the hard work, the effort, in both academic and 'non-academic' areas. Cultural activities, community service or school service, as well as in academic and sport areas all deserve acknowledgement and affirmation.
- I've worked in a number of secondary schools that have instigated what they call a 'gold card' (the size of a Bankcard). This laminated card carries the student's passport-sized photo with name, date of birth and signature. A gold-card holder is a student who is consistently cited as someone who is making the effort across a wide range of areas to be a contributing member of the school community. Gold-card holders are entitled to discounts on a range of local services (shops; restaurants; sports clubs) and additional library borrowing. It is a way of acknowledging the larger group of students who 'consistently do the right thing' (as one school notes). It is an affirmation of a student's social effort, maturity and responsibility.
- As with all extrinsic motivation, it is important to be careful not to set up a situation where students behave well only *because* there's a pay-off. Staff will need to discuss how they can best motivate individuals and indeed whole classes without over-dependence on 'rewards' alone. By planning curriculum, lesson units and teaching methods in teams, we can share experiences and approaches we have found to be beneficial in motivating positive learning experiences with students.
- Teacher motivation can energise a class and pull it out of the spiral of negative feelings and lack of success. I've seen very challenging classes turn around within a term when teachers have:
  –planned together and worked as a team
  –moved away from easy blame and labelling

–involved students in the re-establishment process (p 49)
–provided challenging material that seeks to 'connect' with students' understanding and (where possible) their needs
–acknowledged and affirmed the effort of individuals and the group
–not given up.

'Pupils are typically reported as liking teachers who can keep order (without being too strict), are fair (that is, are consistent and have no favourites), can explain clearly and give help, give interesting lessons, and are friendly and patient' (Kyriacou 1986, p 139). Studies of classroom discipline indicate that much pupil misbehaviour actually stems from a sense that a teacher who is unable to fulfil such demands (that is, the demands of the teaching and management role) is felt to be offensive by pupils and thereby provokes them into misbehaviour (ibid, pp 139–140).

I've had many classroom meetings with students where we've analysed, as a class, where they believe things are going wrong and why (p 33*f*). The common refrain to much of their feedback is:

- 'You can do what you want in here and he won't check up.'
- 'I hate this subject and I hate how it's taught – I mean it's the same each time we come and there's no different things.' (I think the student meant 'no vari-ability'.)
- 'Sometimes she'll yell at us and then she doesn't care what happens on other days!'
- 'He's got his favourites.' (Very common.)

I've had students say, in effect, that in some classes they will even engage in group 'payback' – that is, if this is how it's going to be we might as well get some satis-faction here. I've seen classes 'lay down tools' and refuse to do *this* subject with *this* teacher, because he's given group detentions and refused to listen to class concerns.

These students are not just simply being difficult (there's always one or two ringleaders who will capitalise on any unfocused group energy). They are often reacting to what they perceive is unfair or poor treatment of them as a class.

If the teacher can fairly acknowledge student discontent *early* and seek their co-operation, changes can occur. Of course, if the spiral of discontent and failure is allowed to become embedded into Term 2 or 3, it will be very much harder to really turn things around. In a supportive school environment colleagues will be alert to the 'hard-class signals' and *invite*, and offer, colleague support. This sup-port can range from moral support and sharing of ideas and strategies, through to reinforcement activities (p 62*f*) and colleague mentoring (p 165*f*).

Core routines

When developing core routines we best develop them with our grade-team (or faculty) colleagues.

This does not mean each class has 'total sameness'; it means we develop the necessary core routines that will *enable the relatively smooth running of 20–25 or more students* (in a confined, physical space often with uncomfortable furniture; lack of air conditioning on those hot, hot days; for 50–60 minutes or more six times a day, five days a week, four terms a year…!).

- Develop the core routines across year levels (grades – fine-tuned (obviously) across subject areas where 'classroom movement' and group noise level will necessarily vary).
- Clarify the *core* routines within each grade team/faculty team before communicating them at classroom/subject-class level.
- It will help to publish the core routines for each class group/grade.
- Discuss with the class group *why* these routines are necessary; invite discussion and clarification.
- The key to the development, consolidation and reasonable 'habituation' of fair routines is reasonable teacher consistency; relaxed vigilance.

If we have established (eg.) a routine such as: considerate entry to our classroom; hats and sunglasses off in class; find seats, relax and settle for whole-class teaching time. There is little point in such a routine being communicated and published when the teacher routinely allows pushing/shoving/wearing of hats, loud, persistently talkative settling …, calling out, talking over other students while the teacher is trying to say 'good morning' and begin a teaching period. *Any* routine has to be explained (even modelled with young children) and *maintained* and *consolidated* by on-going teacher encouragement and necessary correction.

Being 'overly friendly' with a new class

I have sat down with many teachers (over the years) who have shared how they feel about 'losing a class'; of having 'the class slip away' from them. They often recount how hard they tried to 'be their friend'; to be 'their buddy' … Why has the class turned out so difficult?

Some teachers recount the brief 'honeymoon period' when students seem to respond positively to these warm overtures of friendship. They all recount how their classes quickly became places where peer socialisation was uppermost; teaching and learning became a difficult second best.

In the establishment phase of our relationship with a new class we need to

Note on wearing of hats etc.,

When 'settling a class' in the corridor, (or just outside the classroom) a teacher will briefly remind students of the 'routine' or 'rule' for hats. Not by asking 'why' students have got hats or sunglasses on ... but a brief, *descriptive*, reminder, 'Jason ... Sean ... you've got hats on ...' Often this kind of reminder is enough; it raises the 'recognition factor'; it raises behaviour awareness *for* the student. Even a non-verbal cue to hats off is often enough. If a student protests, or refuses, a *brief*, second, reminder (without arguing or threats) is adequate. If the student refuses to 'take the hat off' the issue for the young lad is not (now) the rule/routine – it is often an issue of 'contestable behaviour': win/lose. It is pointless to try to force the lad to take his hat off. It will be important to follow-up – later – (away from his peer audience) to clarify expected behaviour re: hats.

The issue about hats/sunglasses 'coming off' (*en route* to the classroom) is to draw that distinction (for students) between 'social time' and class time. Hats/sunglasses are outside apparel. Taking them off 'signifies' that change of place, space, and reason for being together in the classroom.

communicate that we are a respectful, confident, teacher-leader. (Not the overly, got-it-all-sorted-kind-of-confidence!) Our confidence rests in our ability, our skills, and our willingness to lead, and engage, young people in the teaching and learning journey. Confidence is also not about 'bossiness'; it is about planning for teaching and learning and establishing appropriate adult-minor relationships based on mutual respect. We are not – primarily – their 'friend'. Of course we need to be 'friendly' but most students have plenty of friends of their own – they hardly need us as 'their buddy'.

I have seen teachers self-disclose very personal details of relationships, preferences and personal history that are *not* appropriate in teacher–student 'relationships'.

One can be friendly, courteous, show 'warmth' and care without being 'a buddy' or (in some cases) trying to be 'one of them' (as if we are a student!).

This is a sensitive, and difficult, area to discuss with some teachers. It is a matter of responsible balance; particularly in the establishment phase of our relationship with a new class. Students can only make inferences (and judgements) about us from our behaviour. If we telegraph we are simply 'a buddy' ('... *let's all work together as friends ... come on guys ...*') many students will miscue or start 'having some fun' with this 'teacher-buddy'. I have seen many teachers try to be 'one of the lads'; joking and swearing 'at the students' level'. I have seen those same teachers get very disappointed, even angry, when students then treat the teacher correspondingly – 'as one of the lads'!

Students can *sense* when a teacher is confident (in themselves) – as an adult leading young people and as an adult in a particular role. They can sense the teacher's confidence from the teacher's posture; tone of voice; their ability to convey calmness and a sense of purpose and order (p 78*f*).

This is no mean feat but the skills of confidence can be learned; it is not a matter of mere personality alone. We chose a profession where confidence, and the ability to lead, guide, engage and motivate others is crucial to our role and crucial to our usefulness to those we teach (p 171*f*).

We develop confidence when we develop the skills essential to our profession; we confirm that confidence under the natural pressure of day-to-day teaching. We *enhance* the development of our confidence when we are realistic about the challenges we face; when we forgive ourselves normative failure and set-backs and when we *learn* from our failures and set-backs (pp 178–185).

Chapter 6

FOLLOWING UP WITH DISRUPTIVE STUDENTS

Winning or losing points becomes a conflict in itself and not just a discussion about conflict. It is something of an absurdity to try to solve one conflict with another one.
Edward De Bono, Conflicts:
A Better Way to Resolve Them (1985)

I had finished the lesson. I had reminded the students about leaving the room tidy ('I'll give you a hand', 'tidy tables', 'chairs under ...' and 'litter off the floor'). Just before the bell went I took my notebook from my top pocket and read out the names, 'I need to see Leigh and Darren for a few moments after class.' Darren groaned and Leigh pushed back his chair and swore loudly under his breath, grunted, and then scowled and sulked. 'What'd I do anyway!?' he asked. I wasn't about to start any discussion. Leigh and Darren had been play punching earlier in the lesson – the final straw being the pen jabbing in the last five minutes of English.

I said, 'I can see you're uptight, Leigh, I won't keep you long.' I farewelled the class, and Leigh and Darren stayed back. Leigh stood against the wall near the door, sulking. I spoke briefly with the boys, separately, and covered the following:

- I acknowledged how they might be feeling (they'd be missing some recess). 'I know it's annoying to have to stay back after class.'
- I focused on the behaviour and how it had affected basic rights (especially learning and basic safety).
- I invited some feedback from each student ('we were just mucking around ...!')
- I even 'mirrored' (p 111) their behaviour and they laughed when I briefly mirrored their so-called 'play fighting'.
- I invited their feedback, again, and we finally made a brief verbal plan about where they would sit next lesson.
- I wrote down their suggestions, determined to hold them to it next lesson.
- We separated amicably. It hadn't taken long.

In the establishment phase of the year it is important to follow up classroom incidents that, in the heat of the moment, indicate a need to follow up and follow through beyond the classroom correction. Students are often more amenable, later, when they are calmer and away from their 'peer-audience.'

Sometimes the follow-up will merely be an after-class chat to clarify an issue of concern. At other times it will be a consequence such as: cleaning up a mess; completing a piece of class work (not completed in class time); filling in a 4W Form (p 202). When pushed for time an appointment will need to be made with the student to follow up beyond the classroom. If the situation is particularly disturbing it may be helpful for the initiating teacher to invite a colleague to facilitate and support the follow-up process.

NOTEBOOK TRACKING AND FOLLOW-UP

A second-year teacher reported to me that he'd taken my advice on the notebook idea and was following up significant behaviour issues and learning issues after class. He pointed out that he'd also used the 4W Form as a link in the consequential chain. He said, 'The students didn't like that – they moaned: "Why don't you give us lines like the other teachers?".'

I asked how the notebook tracking and follow-up had gone. He said, 'By the end of the first term I was buggered [his word] but second term was a breeze.' He wasn't being smug or overconfident; he pointed out that the students realised he was serious (and supportive) about his follow-up and about students needing to reflect on, and own, their behaviour.

Another colleague of mine commented that the notebook (especially in Term I) takes 'pride of place in my shirt pocket; it somehow makes me feel a little more in control of my own behaviour – just knowing it's there. It's a way of reminding myself of the importance of consistency in following up with students.'

Guidelines for follow-up

To help with consistency of practice concerning follow-up of students it is important to give consideration to fundamental practices such as the following:

1   Consider, as a staff, why such follow-up is important in the first place, and what we are seeking to convey to students and (by proxy) to their peers. Fundamentally, we need to convey *certainty* of consequential outcome, not intentional severity of outcome. With harder classes our follow-up can 'weed out' the merely destructive students from the very difficult and challenging or those students with behaviour disorders. It can reduce an early domino effect of behaviour (students believing that if we just 'let their behaviour go' that we

don't care, or that 'it doesn't matter'.) By following up with
students early (even on Day One) we show that:

■ we care and we are concerned about their behaviour, their
  learning and their welfare.

■ we want to give them some assistance (not a long, or
  nasty, lecture though).

■ we genuinely appreciate their side of the story and
  where appropriate we do take their feedback seriously and will give students a right of reply.

■ we expect them to work with us not against us.

It is important that we convey concern and offer support. Follow-up is not an opportunity to 'win' at the
expense of a student 'losing'. Some teachers use follow-up
time to hammer home emotional payback ('How dare you
think you can speak to me the way you did! Who the hell
do you think you are. You wait till I tell your parents!').

2 Follow up on important, not trivial, issues. It is worth
discussing with colleagues the sorts of issues that would
normally merit an after-class chat or a follow-through consequence, such as
cleaning up that wasn't done (or that the student refused to do) in class time, and
whether we should keep students back to complete work. If we keep students
back on trifling issues we will unnecessarily strain our relationship with them.

3 Briefly acknowledge how the student might be feeling 'at this point' (when they
have to stay back after class, or complete detention time.)

■ 'You look annoyed, Jason.' (Some students may be anxious.)

■ 'I can see you're annoyed, but I need to speak to you about …'

■ 'It can be a hassle to have to miss a bit of recess, but I won't keep you long.
  I need to speak to you about …'

Many students are naturally annoyed at having to stay back after class (they are
missing recess, and they also don't know what to expect from a teacher's follow-
up, especially on Day One). It may help to follow with a question: 'Do you know
why I've asked you to stay back?' (Few students will say, 'Yes I do, actually. I was
being significantly disrespectful to you in class when I …') But at least the question invites a bit of thought. I often add – where relevant – '*You're not in trouble*,
Jason. I just need you to explain to you about what happened in class when …'

4 Focus on the student's *behaviour* – the *specific* behaviour that occurred in the
classroom when they were calling out, butting-in, wandering, avoiding a task,
being 'rude' in tone and manner, and so on. It may help to briefly 'mirror' the
student's behaviour back to them, that is model what it 'looked like' when they
were behaving disruptively. (See later)

5 Invite their feedback on what you have said, or 'mirrored', regarding their behaviour:

- 'Maybe you're having a bad day, Lisa?' (After all, students have bad days like us.)
- 'Can you think of what you can do differently if you're having a bad day in the future? How could you let me know you need my help in class without shouting out?'

We make our feelings known, raising awareness *and* acknowledging our joint humanity. This may well be enough for some students. Other students will give us feedback that gives insight into their behaviour, their learning or some idiosyncratic need. This can alert us to garner wider support from the school counsellor, home-school liaison officer or some other support colleague. Keep the focus (of the shared dialogue) on the behaviour all the time. Avoid getting sidetracked into what other students did or said, or what other teachers allow them to do, or that they don't like this subject. We need to acknowledge student comments and refocus back to the main issue or concern: 'Leigh, it sounds as though you believe Damien does a lot of calling out too. I'll be speaking to him as well. For the moment ...'

6 There are a number of basic relational skills to remember in all one-to-one settings with students however brief the amount of time spent:

- Keep the classroom door open for ethical probity. With an extended one-to-one session with male teacher and female student, it is important to have a female colleague 'sitting in' nearby ('abstractedly' doing their work-programme perhaps.)
- Calm yourself before trying to calm the student. It is important not to use a loud voice or convey sarcasm. Seek to keep the tone pleasant and invitational. Where it is appropriate, we can be firm without a hostile tone of voice, stance or body language.
- Give the student psychological and personal space. We don't crowd the student, or jab with a finger in the air to make a point. I've seen teachers jabbing students in the shoulder to make a point loudly in the corridor, so half the school hears!
- Avoid rushing the dialogue; a pause here and there will help dialogue.
- Keep the focus on the 'primary issues' that occurred; refer to the rule or right, and avoid arguing, for example:
  Student: 'Yeah, well I don't do that all the time, do I?'
  Teacher: 'I don't know. This is the first time I've had you in my class, Dean (partial acknowledgment/agreement). I do know your tone of voice was hostile when I ...' (Be specific and brief about what is meant by 'hostile', or 'rude'; the teacher then refers to the *right* regarding respect.)

Teacher: 'We've got a right in our classroom to respect. I don't speak to you like that and I don't expect you to speak like that to me. If you're uptight about something in class, even with me, and if you think I've been unfair [or whatever] then come and see me after class. Let me know so I can do something about it.' What is crucial is that our tone and manner is not petty, mean-spirited or dominating or hostile. Our tone and manner will powerfully affect what we say and what is really heard by the student.

7 Finish the after-class chat or after-class consequence with a *brief* reminder of what you expect next time in class and separate amicably: 'I appreciate you staying back, Damien. I just wanted to make sure you were aware of … We've got to work together for a whole year in 7C.' Here the teacher smiles and adds a 'goodbye.' Most students give a wry smile in return. They – mostly – realize we do care, and that what we are addressing (with regard to their behaviour) is a 'fair brief.' It is really important not to hold grudges with students. Most students want to know that their teachers basically like them, that they are fair, and that they won't play favourites or have a 'downer' on them for the next day, week or term.

8 It is important to 'track' these students beyond the early after-class chats to see if their behaviour is more than 'bad-day syndrome.' If there is some pattern to the behaviour we will need to look at a more whole-school approach to the address the student's behaviour (see Chapter 7).

Mirroring behaviour

When discussing a distracting and disruptive student's behaviour (one-to-one) it can help to 'mirror' their behaviour to them. It recreates (as it were) the 'concrete' features of a student's repeated calling out; silly noises; rolling on the carpet; talking while the teacher is talking; overly enthusiastic and repetitive seat leaning; overly loud voice in class; hiding under tables; pushing in line … 'Mirroring' is a way of briefly recreating an emotional-behavioural moment.

Whenever we use this approach, it is important to do so only to 'illustrate' the child's behaviour to them; to clarify what it 'looks', or 'sounds', like when they behave in distracting and disruptive ways. It

Tracking students

is crucial we do so respectfully, briefly, and then physically step away as if to say 'well – that's what it looks (or sounds) like when ...' The 'stepping away', after having mirrored the behaviour, is important in 'separating' out the adult/child roles.

Often students will laugh when we mirror their behaviour in this way (after all it does look funny to see a teacher rolling on the floor 'just like me!' Particularly me at 58 years of age ...!)

- Only mirror a student's behaviour if it is within your comfort zone. If you're not comfortable with mirroring back to a student their tone of voice and behaviours (such as calling out, butting-in, seat wandering or pushing in line) it may be better to just use action phrases and descriptive phrases: 'Nazim, when you had your feet up in class – you know, on the desk and leaning back – can you remember what you said and how you said it?' Here the teacher repeats the words instead of mirroring the sarcastic and insouciant tone of voice used by the student. The teacher describes how the voice sounded, 'It sounded really sarcastic, Nazim – as though you couldn't have cared less about having your feet up and also as though you didn't care about me either.'

- We should always ask the student's permission. If the student says 'no' (this is rare) it is enough to carefully – specifically – describe his behaviour and its 'effect on others in our class.' It may help to have a drawing or cartoon that can pictorially image the student's behaviour (Rogers 2003a). When describing the student's behaviour it is important to show concern and support. Our confident follow-up is saying, 'I'm concerned and I'm serious; I'm inviting your understanding and seeking to raise your awareness of your behaviour.'

- Mirroring is illustrative, designed to raise behaviour awareness in students. Keep it brief. We should never use it to embarrass students or to make students feel bad about themselves.

■ After we have mirrored the student's behaviour, we step back physically and become the calm (and caring) adult again. Point to the now vacated emotional space and say, '*That's* what it looks like, Craig, when you ...' Some students may genuinely not know what their behaviour looks like, and how 'rude' or 'sarcastic' their tone of voice characteristically sounds. A lot of students will involuntarily laugh at their 're-created behaviour' (either from anxiety or because it does actually look silly, even 'stupid', in retrospect). Acknowledge, 'Yes, it does look a bit funny, but in class, Craig, it's really annoying because ...'

One of my colleagues 'mirrored' to a rather challenging Year 9 girl how she often entered the classroom (*dramatis personae*). Apparently the normal after-class chats had not been 'taken up' by this student and so my colleague, in the *one-to-one* setting, 'became' Lisa for 30 seconds. Mirroring Lisa's typical behaviour, the teacher entered the room with a flamboyant 'notice-me' look as the teacher scanned the imaginary 20 pair of eyes alighting on her as she came in late – again. This teacher was a dab hand at drama. She imitated the way Lisa gave a 'snort' and said, (in a 'Lisa voice') 'What are we doing today then?', and the final sitting down with an extravagant leg-cross. This seemed to do the trick! 'Gees,' said Lisa, 'I don't cross my legs like *that*!' The teacher replied, 'You do, Lisa, well, pretty close to that.' The teacher pointed back to the now vacated 'kinaesthetic space'. The word *that* (as used by Lisa) now had meaning and specificity. Lisa responded with an 'I-know-you-know' grin and from here they had a productive chat about 'attention' and – together – made a plan for a considered, thoughtful, way to enter the classroom.

The 4W Form

Rather than have a student writing lines as a punishment or consequence it can be more constructive to direct students to write about their behaviour (I still meet teachers who 'give out lines'). The following approach is appropriate for those behaviour disruptions that are not serious but have a degree of frequency that is annoying. The 4W Form (Appendix 2) can be useful as a basic right of reply:

1 What I did against our class or school rules (my behaviour).
2 What rules (or rights) I broke or infringed.
3 What is my explanation?
4 What I think I should do to fix things up or work things out.

Have a place for the student and teacher to sign (name, date etc).

The value of the 4W approach is:

■ It gives the student a fair, and workable, right of reply.
■ It provides the student with an opportunity to think through what happened.

- It refocuses the student's attention back to the right or rule affected by *their* behaviour.
- It gives a basis for further teacher–student (or even student–teacher) dialogue.
- Most of all, it concentrates on what the restitutional outcome ought to be (what I think I should do, or can do, to fix things up or make things better).

It is not helpful to force students to write, or to ask them to do it when they are really uptight, or upset. After some cool-off time, the 'form' can be used to help students clarify their thinking, refocus on what happened regarding their behaviour, and work with their teacher towards a solution …

If the answers to the question on the form lack basic thought ('I was bad' or 'I was naughty') we will need to help the student to extend or refocus. For example, say, 'In what way were you naughty? What did you do that was against our rules?' Students who really struggle with writing should not be forced or embarrassed by having to write out a reasonable response. We can instead ask the questions and record their answers for them: 'So, is that what you mean?' or 'Are you saying that …?' Young children can draw responses (to the questions) and the teacher can dialogue within that framework. The 4W Form is also a record of the student's attempt to come to terms with their behaviour. If there is no significant change using such an approach, an individual behaviour plan might be an appropriate next step (p 132*f*).

Managing a crisis situation: Time-out

In hard to manage classes there are often students who are catalysts for significant group inattention and disturbance: tantrums, running around the room, persistent refusal to respond to reasonable teacher requests, and so on. Most teachers in challenging schools can recount examples of students standing on desks shouting, 'You can't do nothing to me!' or that back-to-back disruptive pattern that just goes on and on and on with the persistent attention seeker or powerbroker desperate for an audience or a contest of wills. (I've had my share over the years!)

No teacher should ever be left in the invidious position of having a student hold a class to ransom. Such behaviour not only stresses the teacher but also affirms – even confirms – that pattern of behaviour when it is allowed to continue on … ('I can do what I like and say what I like').

Time-out practices

Students learn about behaviour in many ways but one of the more powerful ways is by association. If time-out is consistently associated with repeatedly disruptive or any dangerous behaviour then students will at least learn the following:

- Certain behaviours will never be tolerated in our classroom (corridors or playgrounds).
- Refusal to respond to fair guidelines and fair discipline will result in temporary exclusion (time-out).
- 'As night follows day, time-out *will* happen here *when* you repeatedly behave in unacceptable and unsafe ways.'
- All time-out occurs within the concept of 'behaviour choice' and occurs within known, fair rules and understandings about expected behaviours.
- The *whole* class is protected from extremes of behaviour, and time-out is seen as a just, *short-term*, solution. The rights of all students are protected. This psychological protection gives the other students an assurance that something is being done for their benefit (as well as for the disruptive student).
- The disruptive student always has a chance to work through a right-of-reply *after* time-out.

'Time-out' is probably the most intrusive short-term consequence a school will employ for disruptive behaviour. Time-out can occur in the classroom as a formal, even semiformal, cool-off time or it can involve temporary exclusion from the classroom. It is often used as a formal discipline 'mechanism' across the school to temporarily exclude students from the classroom where their behaviour is significantly affecting the fundamental safety, treatment and learning of others. Students should be supervised during time-out especially at primary level.

It is essential, especially in hard classes, that teachers have the assurance they will always be backed up by colleagues and administration in crisis situations. This is especially so where students blatantly refuse to leave a class. It's very distressing to see a teacher screaming at a recalcitrant student, 'Get out! Get out now!', and the student standing there laughing and saying, effectively (or really), 'You can't make me!' No matter how ineffective a teacher's management may be no teacher deserves that.

The practical question concerns the issue of *how* we get such students out of the room in a heated situation? It may be more effective, in the longer term, to direct the student to leave (or arrange for the student to leave) *before* serious verbal conflict ensues! How can we do this on a whole-school basis?

In the first place, it is important that all teachers have a general consequential plan that is part of their establishment phase (rights/rules/responsibility/consequences – see p 49f). For example, if a student makes it difficult for other students to learn or feel safe, one of the following consequential 'steps' will occur:

- Students will be reminded of the class rule.
- Students may be directed to work somewhere else in the room (away from the students they are affecting by their disruptive behaviour) ie: relocation.

■ Students may be directed to take cool-off time (COT) *within* the classroom. Some primary schools use the term 'take-five'. The students take five minutes COT away from others in another area of the room watching a five-minute egg timer (Rogers 2003a). This gives a visual, referential, focus to the cool-off time.

■ Students will be asked to stay back and discuss their behaviour with their teacher, fix things up or put things right (restitution).

■ Students may be asked to leave the room or may be escorted from the room to a COT area – a time-out area or room.

A time-out room

William Glasser (1991) describes a time-out room as a place in the school (a room):

> *run by someone who has experience dealing with students who have been asked to leave class ... The student may protest that it is unfair and that you are punishing him by keeping him there, but you have to point out that it is his choice not to begin to work on the solutions. As soon as he starts working on a solution, he can go back to class ... he is always treated with courtesy ... and offered counselling. He should be constantly reminded that no-one wants him to stay in restriction: Everyone wants him to begin work on the problem and will help in any way possible. (p144f)*

Teachers need the security of a – school-wide – time-out plan for crisis situations. There should be a known, published, procedure and a workable plan to enable a teacher to direct very disruptive students from the classroom to a safe, supervised, place where they can calm down, refocus and make some plan to re-enter the classroom (at a later stage that day) in a way that considers others' rights. Some students will leave the classroom if directed aside and spoken to calmly and firmly: 'David, it's not working. I've asked you several times to settle down and ... [be *briefly* specific about the behaviour and effect on you and others in the room]. It's better that you leave now. I'll get together with you later to see how we can work things out.'

Of course this implies the following:

■ There is a place (and person) to which you can direct the student.

■ The student will actually go.

■ We will keep to our word and follow up with the student.

■ If the student refuses to leave there is a back-up plan, for example a colleague *cue* system (see below).

As Glasser (1991) points out, 'All the students, including the one who has disrupted, should hear the message that "lead-managers" do not threaten. They recognise that there are problems and they try to solve them by themselves. They need the co-operation of the student.' (Glasser contrasts teachers who 'boss' by threats and coercion and teachers who manage by leading.) If the student is unwilling to co-operate with their teacher (assuming the teacher's approach is positive) then the student will need to be directed to leave the classroom.

If the student refuses to leave the classroom to go to time-out (at any age) there will need to be a simple, workable, back-up plan. This is essential. Many schools use a simple colleague *cue* system. Each teacher in the team (or the faculty) has small laminated cards noting the classroom number (coloured, say, green for 'go', or red for 'danger' even pink for 'calm'). In one primary school, for example, the standard printed card reads:

TIME OUT: Could you please assist me as soon as possible in Room 17.
Thank you.

_____
(Teacher's name)

This card can be sent with a trusted student to a colleague (generally a senior colleague) who will come as quickly as possible to that room and escort the disruptive student to a cool-off time area. Disruptive students will almost always go with a third party (another adult) simply because that teacher is not part of the conflict cycle in that classroom. If they refuse to leave the room with the senior teacher, it is more effective if the third-party teacher stays in the room while the class teacher escorts the rest of the class out of the room, away, to another area. When the audience has gone, the supporting colleague can then escort the student to the time-out area and the class teacher escort their class back to their classroom. This is in preference to trying to drag out a kicking, yelling student who has a huge audience to 'feed on', especially at upper primary and secondary levels. I know; I've done it in years past (!).

Schools sometimes refer to this area as the 'time-out-room', 'work-it-out-room' or 'thinking room'. It is often at (or near) the administration section of the school where students can be supervised while they settle down.

In the time-out area (or room) several posters (with illustrations) can adorn the wall opposite the seat and desk where the student sits. A poster could contain the following:

Think about why you have been asked to leave your classroom. ASK YOURSELF:
1 What did I do?
2 What is my side of the story?

3 What rule did I break? What right was affected by my behaviour (this for secondary-age students)?

4 What can I do to fix things up?

5 What help will I need?

It is also helpful to have a poster on the wall with the school's rights and responsibilities for older students.

It is important that any back-up time-out plans are well thought through and published as internal school policy. It is especially important that relief (supply) teachers and teachers new to school are taken through such a policy and assured that use of time-out by a teacher is not a sign of weakness, but that – rather – it is a positive expression of colleague support; the way we do things in our school. It will be important to explain in a policy document to parents what is meant (philosophically) by time-out, why and how the school uses it, and most of all that it is a *short-term consequence*. Countless teachers have shared how such a simple, school-wide support procedure, has given them confidence in their behaviour planning and reduced their stress levels at school.

Any teacher who institutes a time-out consequence with a student should (normally) be directly responsible for follow-up and follow-through with that student. If possible that follow-up should occur within that day. At secondary level it may be a couple of days before we can get to meet with the student to: clarify our concerns about their behaviour; give the student a right of reply and work with the student to effect some repairing and rebuilding.

By making that effort we communicate our care, our concern; emphasise the fair certainty of the consequential process and give the student a right of reply and rebuild that essential working relationship between teacher and student.

If we easily (or only) pass on a 'problem student' to a senior colleague we also unhelpfully affect our appropriate leadership role (and our working relationship) with that student.

Caveat

Some teachers will initially use (or overuse) the time-out card system for minor disruptive behaviours. It is important, therefore, to monitor (and appraise) the policy, and *purpose*, of time-out.

■ Explain the appropriate use of the time-out card: safety concerns; back-to-back disruptions; perception of a possible crisis, and persistent refusal to obey a reasonable teacher request are the sorts of situations requiring the use of time-out support. However, behaviour such as a student merely sulking or avoiding a task can be often tactically ignored, refocused in class time and followed up later, providing such behaviour is not significantly affecting other students.

■ Make sure that records are kept by the initiating teacher and the administration (in part to see which teachers may be having problems with difficult students). These records will also be required for parent notification, case conferences and simple tracking of the student to see if any future correction, mediation and behaviour plans are having any effect on the student's behaviour.

■ Time-out rarely changes disruptive patterns of behaviour in itself. It is a short-term solution to give support to the teacher, the rest of the class and the disruptive student. It is essential that a student be supported with an individual behaviour management plan if they have been in time-out several times for similar patterns of behaviour. (See Chapter 7)

One primary school lists its time-out policy this way:

Time-out

Time-out is used in the classroom or playground to help people cool down and think about what they have done wrong. Time-out only happens after someone has been reminded about a rule they have broken.*

If you are given time-out in the classroom, you go and sit on your own for a few minutes to sort out how you are going to put things right. This may be in the classroom or in another room.

If you are given time-out in the playground, you go and sit (away from others) on a seat for a few minutes to think about how you can make things right.

Hare Street Primary School, Harlow, UK

* This means, of course, reminded a few times, not just once. It implies a pattern of behaviour and refusal to respond to fair reminders of the rule.

Staff survey: Exit/Time-out policy review

1 How often do you (as a class/subject teacher) use the exit/time-out consequence (that is, directing a student away from your classroom to a colleague's class, administration or the time-out room)? Distinguish between usage of in-class and out-of-class time-out.

2 What sort of behaviour or situations do you use exit/time-out for?

3 How often do you use exit/time-out? (Once a day/several times a week/weekly/a few times a term)?

4 How do you normally follow up your exit/time-out of a student?

5 What is the school (or faculty) policy for:

■ use of time-out in the immediate short term?

■ following-up of behaviours that initiated the time-out episodes? (Time-out is a 'primary' consequence often needing 'secondary' consequences to follow through.)

■ students who refuse to leave the classroom for time-out?

■ students who have been in time-out several times (in close succession) for similar behaviours (and across several class settings)?

6 How effective do you regard the school's time-out policy?

Classroom rotation

One of the variations of time-out (largely used at primary level) is *classroom rotation*. The student is 'enrolled' in another class for at *least* one period a week to give the grade (or subject) teacher a formal break from those students with persistent patterns of disruptive behaviour. These students tend to *never* have a day off, they tend not to be school refusers and some parents will personally admit they 'cannot stand to have them at home.'

The student takes set class work from their host class and does that work in another classroom setting. It will need to be explained to the student and their parent(s) that this is not punishment. It is part of the support program for the student and the grade teacher.

Follow-up and three-way facilitation

Some follow-up may need to include a face-to-face meeting between a 'perpetrator' and a 'victim'. In some classes, because of the 'regularity' of silly (and hurtful) comments being made, some teachers do not follow up or follow through. 'It's not worth it,' some say, 'I'd be keeping back several kids each session.' It *is* always worth the effort of follow-up in the establishment phase because it says to all the students that we care; we will not tolerate put-down, or abusive, behaviour. In this case a three-way approach will often be necessary (class teacher, support teacher and students in conflict with each other).

In most cases it is desirable for the grade/subject teachers to conduct their own follow-up or follow-through as this enhances teachers' appropriate role/leadership with the students, as well as personally demonstrating care and support. In some settings with very challenging students, however, the follow-up will need mediation or, at the very least, facilitation by a support colleague (generally a senior teacher).

■ Have a school-wide due process for *supported follow-up*. This school-wide process needs to be established to address issues of concern that a teacher feels cannot be solved by teacher–student dialogue alone, or for those situations where teachers do not feel confident in pursuing a one-to-one dialogue on their own. For example, where a male teacher wants to pursue an extended one-to-one meeting with a female student, ethical probity (and commonsense) would see the need for a female facilitator. Staff need to be assured that there will always be facilitation support for conflict resolution and mediation, that there is a school-wide due process available to support them. There is no shame in seeking colleague assistance in resolving difficult issues with students. The initiating of a three-way facilitation is a normative feature of whole school colleague support.

- Make sure that it is genuinely 'three way', that is, the initiating teacher, the student (or students) and the support colleague who facilitates (and/or mediates) all have an appropriate opportunity to have their say. Part of the problem of facilitation is that some teachers are not able to accept that the student has a right to an 'equal voice' in conflict mediation and resolution. This needs to be clarified in the school-wide due process. Some teachers persist in butting in while the student is giving their version (or perception) of events; calling the student 'a liar'; refusing to apologize to a student when a teacher is in the wrong (it happens!) or even refusing to accept a student's apology.
  The facilitator can enable a calmer re-framing within some clear, fair, guidelines.
- Make sure, too, there has been ample cool-off time between the disruptive event(s) and the three-way facilitation.
- It can be helpful to take notes at the meeting (it says 'we take this issue very seriously'). The facilitation role is to make sure that teacher and student(s) have a fair voice. The facilitation will clarify the issues and the comments, keep the parties on track and work for an appropriate resolution. The 4W questions can be useful as a guide at this meeting (p 202).

At all times the focus is how the issue at stake affects the basic rights and responsibilities of teacher, student and the class as a whole. From this focus the meeting will proceed towards appropriate apologies; assurances of moving on and not holding grudges (a hard one!); any necessary restitution and (where required) an individual behaviour plan. A common outcome of such meetings is a recommended review meeting(s) with the facilitator over the next week or two.

Students who refuse to stay back after class

Some students will race off at the end of a class period even though the teacher has specifically directed them to stay back (this is more common at secondary level than primary). The teacher may barely get the last words in: 'If you choose not to stay back, I'll have to follow it up at …' The student mutters, while walking or running off, 'Yeah, well, it's recess. Anyway, I didn't do anything! I'm not staying back!' It doesn't take the student long to reach the exit door and perceived freedom. It will be unhelpful (though tempting) to chase the miscreant down the corridor into the playground. This will only add to the student's attentional behaviour or their incipient power struggle(!).

If a student doesn't stay back or keep an appointment (to discuss his behaviour or follow through with consequences), it is still important to follow up at a later stage. It is important to communicate the *certainty* of the follow-up, even if it is several days later (as it may well have to be at secondary level). It is important for the student in question and it is important for the 'tribal tom-toms' to know that 'in this class *the consequential chickens will come home to roost.*' This is not about 'winning'; it is all about fair, necessary, known, *reasonable and respectful certainty.*

I have at times used my off-class time to follow up students in other class settings. I've knocked on a colleague's door and asked to see a student and noticed the student's eyes look back, not believing I'd actually follow up several days later. I've never had a colleague refuse me the option of 'withdrawing' a student from class for a brief chat, outside that student's class, or in the interview room near the office. I always carry a notebook (p 108) to remind me of whom to track, and a brief note to remind me of the issue. It is easy to 'forget' in a busy teaching week.

Apologies

It was the task avoidance that annoyed the teacher. He'd gone back to Peter at least half a dozen times: 'C'mon, get working, Peter. The bell's going soon!' Peter snapped back, 'Yeah, well you're picking on me!' The teacher replied, 'Don't you speak to me like that! How dare you! I'll have you on a detention!' As the teacher walked off, Peter mumbled, 'Gees you're an a … hole!' To which the teacher said, 'Right! Get out, go on, get out! Go to the principal now!' No doubt the teacher was fed up with the boy's intransigence – he was angry. He'd taken it personally.

The principal had a chat with Peter and with the teacher (after he'd cooled down). The principal managed to encourage Peter to agree to apologise for what he'd said. Peter had actually written a short apology. They went to the teacher together and the student, frowning, looked at his teacher (whose arms were folded) and said, 'Sorry I swore and that.' The teacher looked at him and said, 'No, I'm not having that! You don't mean it. You're not *really* sorry.' Here is an adult (nearly 40 years old) speaking to a 12-year-old with an unfair (unnecessary *and* unreasonable) expectation. He had not even acknowledged the student's effort. Imagine what might have happened if the teacher had said, 'Well, Peter, it's not easy to apologise, but you made the effort. I guess we were both angry, eh? If you get uptight again, can you say it in a more helpful way?' A brief assuring handshake and a wry smile wouldn't go astray either.

Some teachers find it very difficult, even demeaning, to apologise *to* a student or work through a reconciliation. It is as if the teacher is somehow condescending to 'the minor'; conveying weakness. It is important to remember that we are the adult in this situation. We need to make reconciliation bearable and possible. If we apologise, or pursue reconciliation when it is appropriate, students are often very forgiving. It comes down to fundamental, and basic, respect.

If we've got unnecessarily angry with a class or gone 'over the top' (we know when we've done it), an apology will clear the air. It doesn't have to be sycophantic, just genuine. We clarify what we have done or said, and why we believe it happened that way. We keep the apology brief, focussed and fair. Leave it, then, to their goodwill.

Detentions

The most easily wielded and overused behaviour consequence in schools is detention, especially at secondary level. Detentions, though, can be an easy way out for the class teacher in that the behaviour problem is referred to someone else to detain and even punish the students. I've been in many schools where students from various classes sit, waiting against the clock or just doing homework, while the teacher who initiated the detention engages in no actual follow-up, follow-through and resolution. It has also been my experience that overuse of detentions in hard classes is self-defeating in the long term. The least effective detentions (of course) are class-based – keeping back the whole class for the misdemeanours of the several students. Whole-class detentions are used by some teachers to effectively punish the hard class. We will need to distinguish (for our students) between a whole-class after-class chat and a whole-class detention. Whole class *detentions* are self-defeating; they breed resentment in the very students whose support we need to effectively lead the class.

If detentions are going to be effective, in any way, there needs to be a school-wide, team-based or faculty-based framework for their use. Further, if the detention is seen as a *consequence* and not merely as a referral punishment (passing the problem student along the line) it can be used to teach students something constructive about their behaviour and encourage their understanding and responsibility.

In a survey: 'Attitudes of British secondary school teachers and pupils to rewards and punishments', Caffyn (1989) notes, 'In [this] present study the giving of detentions was rated as significantly more effective both by teachers and pupils in the school which gave them rarely and operated a well-run system. Obtain the optimum balance between "good use" and "overuse".'

It is the association in students' minds between 'sparingly used' and 'frequently used' that gives detention any useful 'currency'. If teachers are giving detentions for every kind of misdemeanour from not having equipment and lateness through to verbal abuse that currency is 'devalued'.

Detention needs to be seen within a wider framework of consequences and punishment:

- after-class chats – not really a punishment at all, more a clarification of what behaviours are affecting mutual rights and working on student understanding and restitution where necessary
- catch-up time where a student completes or continues some piece of set work
- clean-up (mess the student had left earlier in the lesson)
- the 4W Form (p 202)
- detention as a *formal* process of detaining the student: with notification to parent, a set time and a due process geared to working on the behaviour at issue and not just 'doing time'
- accountability conference (see later p 191*f*).

In other words a school needs a consequential framework that has degrees of seriousness relative to how behaviour affects fundamental rights and how significantly and repetitively it affects those rights.

Detentions can be so entrenched in usage in a school that serious whole-school reflection may not have been given to this topic.

- Is the detention *time* (and process) related to the actual behaviour for which the child is being detained? ie: It is hardly a *related* consequence for a student to be picking up a letter for 'talking in class.'
- What do we want the student to learn (if anything) from detention?
- Do we want the students to just sit there or work on a 4W-type feedback (p 202)? Work on a behaviour plan? Plan any accountability or restitution? Do set work? Do any work quietly?
- What sort of behaviours do we agree would normally 'merit' detention?
- Should detention be faculty based or year-level based? Is there a place for subject-teacher detention?

- If detention is conducted by a teacher other than the referring teacher, what is the responsibility of *both* teachers in detaining the student? It is easy for a subject or class teacher to refer the student to someone else and just leave it at that–no further responsibility is exercised by the 'initiating teacher', and no effective resolution is developed with the student.
- What 'mechanisms' can be used to track and process detention across a year group? Do several detentions in succession equal some sort of referral for an individual behaviour plan? How does that work at our school?

It is worth publishing the detention policy and framework/philosophy of use, especially for beginning teachers and those new to the school.

Suspension and expulsion

Suspension is a serious 'step' in the consequential chain within a school. It needs to be part of a school's behaviour-management policy because:

- it gives a formal cooling-off time for the student (and his teachers!)
- it indicates to the rest of the class and school that the behaviour resulting in suspension is serious and will not be tolerated at our school.
- it can also be used as a constructive step towards restitution and support.

Suspension can be utilised as 'in-school suspension' or 'at-home suspension' (not all students who are suspended will actually stay at home!). When it occurs in school, suspension is an extension of the time-out room concept. Work is set, no extra school privileges are allowed and recess times are taken separately from other students.

Suspension has to be backed up by careful follow-through, and geared to problem solving and restitution processes with those directly affected by the student's behaviour at school (teacher, student, parent(s) and facilitating senior colleague). Any student who has faced a few suspensions would normally go on to an individually supervised plan and case-supervision (Chapter 7). Obviously suspension is not a consequence to be used lightly. It is properly used for severe misbehaviours rather than the last straw in a chain of less serious behaviours that are best dealt with by effective follow-up procedures.

Suspension should also be attended by appropriate 'ceremonial formality' (*Positive Discipline*, 7, 1989):

- An appearance before senior staff and reporting teacher(s). Some schools even utilise a 'suspension committee'. Suspensions are not conducted merely at the whim of an individual teacher. It can help if the school behaviour policy outlines the sorts of behaviours that would normally occasion suspension.

- Focus on the certainty and justice of the act of suspension. It is not an occasion to berate, or villify, the student. The focus should always be directed to the student's *behaviour*; the rights affected by such behaviour; and the effect on others of that behaviour.
- Offer whatever support is possible to parents while emphasising student responsibility.
- Offer to the students the support of an individual behaviour management plan. (See Chapter 7)

Expulsion

While expulsion is a very serious step (even a traumatic step), for a school to take, a student (and sometimes their family) cannot be allowed to continue to disrupt the safety and welfare of a school. In some cases the student (through persistent harassment and bullying) may well be effectively holding a school to ransom. This cannot be allowed to continue. If a student (and their family) has continued to flout the school's reasonable code of behaviour, and refused to work with supportive measures such as counselling and behaviour plans, a school needs to consider the safety and learning rights of the rest of the students and act accordingly.

Normally a school will pursue alternative options, rather than *formal* expulsion alone. Such processes would have been developed over several case conferences with parents and school and with Education Department personnel.

There are very few options outside formal schooling for students with persistent, and extreme, patterns of challenging and recidivist behaviour. What options there are (that are available) are stretched to the limit. Notwithstanding that hard reality, expulsion still needs to be an option for schools.

Chapter 7

PATTERNS OF BEHAVIOUR AND CHANGING BEHAVIOUR

The young people of today think of nothing but them-
selves. They have no reverence for parents or old people.
They talk as if they alone know everything and what
passes for wisdom with us is foolishness to them.
Peter the Hermit (1098) (cited in Conway 1974)

First principles of behaviour management

Human behaviour is a complex phenomenon. There is no single, simple reason for people to act supportively, co-operatively, thoughtfully, carelessly, meanly, nastily and aggressively. The following understandings provide a framework within which teachers often seek to address, and support, student behaviour in schools:

1 Behaviour is *learned*. Children learn by association (both good and bad). They learn, over time, what behaviours receive approval and/or disapproval. They also learn from the modelling of significant others. Of course, if unhelpful, poor, inappropriate, inadequate, and ineffective behaviour is learned, it can be unlearned and relearned. This is the power of new association, new modelling and the development of new behaviour skills. If we do not believe this, if we believe behaviour is *totally* fixed, we will be effectively unable to support students with behaviour needs and behaviour disorders.

2 Behaviour is *conditioned*. Conditioning is another form of learning, largely from one's environment and not always reflective (especially in younger children). If a home environment is dysfunctional, with abuse, frequent yelling, put-downs, harsh nagging and frequent physical discipline, it will have an obvious effect on behaviour. Bullying, as one example, has its early 'learning' from conditioning at home – that first social laboratory where words, gestures, emotions and beliefs are tracked into often unreflective and habitual behaviours

(Rogers 2003a). When children come into a school community, teachers pick up the residue of that conditioning. The home environment is outside our significant control. Of course, we will report to relevant authorities if we believe the child is 'at risk' but we cannot change the dysfunctional home environment. This should not deter us, however, from realising the powerful effect schools can have on students from disadvantaged and dysfunctional home environments. Supportive school environments; the school curriculum; teaching style and method; learning styles; consideration of prior content knowledge of our students; working with the natural desire to learn; grouping of students; catering for a range of educational and social options to enhance access and success through school; regular encouragement and even the classroom environment can all significantly affect learning and social outcomes at school (Rutter et al 1979; O'Brien 1990; Rogers 2003a).

3 Behaviour is *purposeful* in a social setting. Children are not *just* naughty (at least not all the time). Dreikurs et al (1982) note that mistaken social goals of attention and power see students engage in disturbing classroom behaviour that enables (in the child's private logic) a sense of social belonging. All children (all people) have a fundamental need to belong in social settings. If children do not believe (or feel) they can belong in socially acceptable, reasonable, ways they 'learn' to belong through attentional, or power-seeking ways. Behaviours such as *frequent* calling out ('notice me'); clowning behaviours; overly demanding-assistance patterns of behaviour; provocative-argumentative behaviours; challenging or defiant behaviours ('come on, make me'!) – are all ways that students can gain a sense of 'belonging'. Dreikurs (1982) notes that such behaviour arises in part from a child's insecurity and in part from a 'mistaken goal' of how we can belong in a social setting. If attention seeking (a natural need) is over-serviced early, and often, children will believe that this is how they can 'belong'. The exercise of seeking attention, power or revenge in a setting such as school has to be seen in its social context in the public domain of classroom, corridor or playground. Here students have an audience that (in their private logic) they believe is acknowledging, affirming or supporting their attention-seeking or power-provoking behaviours. In the 'hard-class setting' some students frequently exhibit these 'behavioural goals'. It is a challenge to work with these students to help them identify what their behavioural/social 'goal' is, to acknowledge why they pursue such attentional, or power-seeking, behaviours and to support them in a process of behaviour change (without denying the need for appropriate consequences).

4 Behaviour is *chosen*. It is unhelpful to treat students as if they are merely the victims of an emotional or 'causative pathology' over which they have no control. When a student spits at another, swears abusively, kicks a chair over and so on,

there is an element of choice. Of course that choice is conditioned by non-school home environments; by peer-association as well as by the immediate emotional/behavioural context. A student's behaviour may well be affected by a behaviour disorder such as attention-deficit disorder (ADD). But ADD doesn't simply cause anti-social behaviour – it contributes to it. Once we say students just can't help their behaviour, we do them and their families a disservice. Far better to *teach* students how to make better choices (about their formal learning and their behaviour) and then hold them responsible and accountable for the choices they then make and the consequences that go with those choices.

5 Behaviour *communicates information about needs*. It is hard (not impossible, but hard) to behave thoughtfully and considerately. It is hard for a student to learn well at school if their school day carries significant inner turmoil from home. All of us have 'bad days' and some students' bad days are frequent (!). If their teachers are not considerate of their welfare and basic needs and do not 'read' the students' behaviour then the classroom can be a place of continued conflict. It is possible to be both considerate of a student's welfare and still be positive with necessary, and appropriate, discipline. For some students school is the significant place where they feel safe, more secure and have some caring, stable adults around them on a daily basis.

6 Distracting, and disruptive behaviour, may be the *result* of 'bad-day-syndrome' caused by tiredness, friendship hassles, hunger, sickness, transitional concerns, problems at home … Thoughtful teachers will recognise those situations and allow for them, 'Lisa, you're not normally like this – what's the problem?'. They will allow cool-off time, and a chance to explain as the case may be and (of course) if the child is willing. At the very least they will acknowledge how the student might be feeling and offer support.

7 Behaviour can be *changed*. Behaviour is not totally static and fixed. Students can learn new, different, more positive and effective ways of relating, responding and coping in social settings and with their formal schooling. They can also learn from the kind of discipline we exercise and the modelling we offer as teachers and by the kinds of repairing and rebuilding options we offer.

8 Behaviour is *taught*. In the myriad of interactions engaged in each day at school both students and teachers are learning about behaviour. At times we will be seeking to directly influence and teach students by and through our behaviour as a teacher-leader. Even deceptively simple routine-behaviours such as how we 'line them up' in the corridor (in fact we can't 'line them up'; they line up – or not as the case may be – in response to our behaviour as they perceive it). Teachers need to explain, discuss and even *teach* appropriate behaviours to the whole class (in the establishment phase of the year) and to individuals as the need arises.
Teaching of behaviour is as deceptively basic as discussing noise levels; sharing

in a class discussion (one-at-a-time, listen when others speak, take-your-turn); reasonable movement; toleration of others' differences; consideration of others' needs and feelings; even basic courtesy and manners.

At all times when we *teach* behaviour we need to give age-related reasons 'why' we *ought* to behave in these ways. We make value judgements about any 'ought-ness' based on those core rights and responsibilities of learning, safety, respect and fair-treatment of others. At other times we will be seeking to influence their behaviour indirectly through the teacher-student relationship. We cannot simply, easily or quickly *control* others. The art and skill of behaviour management is to lead and guide others, so students understand that they are making the behavioural choices. Our aim is that this guiding process will lead students to be more self-reflective and self-directed regarding behaviour that is considerate of others.

Case study

It was a science lesson in Year 7. I was team teaching. Several times throughout the introductory phase of the lesson Alex called out and made silly remarks (for example, 'What are we doing this for anyway? This is dumb! We did it in Year 5'). I *tactically* ignored most of his foray into these 'notice-me' behaviours. It wasn't easy as I had to keep the rest of the class on track as well. He tapped with his pencil, annoyingly, several times as I began whole class teaching. I motioned with my hand downwards, hardly looking at him. He'd slow down for a while and repeat it. Some of his classmates giggled (naturally); watching me as well as watching him. When he blatantly turned and started a private conversation while I was talking to the group, I paused and directed him to face the front and listen. He replied with a laconic sarcasm, 'Yeah, well, I was listening, wasn't I?' It seemed as if he wanted both attention and an opportunity to 'provoke' ('I can do what I want and you can't really stop me …').

Later in the on-task phase of the lesson he wandered aimlessly around the room and a couple of times into the laboratory presentation room. My colleague was getting frustrated – as was I. Thankfully almost all of the students were on-task and needed only encouragement with some refocusing; they were 'used to him' (as I found out later). We had the class working in groups of three. Had it not been for that fact, I would have used time-out earlier in the lesson. But at least I knew what Alex was doing in terms of his behavioural goal: 'Notice ME!' (seeking frequent attention). I suspected, too, that it was borderline power seeking: 'You can't make me settle down and work.' Apparently he was used to doing this in science. This was the first time (though) that I'd taken this Year 7 group.

I decided to direct him out of the room for some brief time-out. I suspected, though, he wouldn't go. I thought that he would set up a power struggle (a win–lose context) or he'd start a 'wasted-energy argument', typical of power-seeking students, for example 'Why do I have to go? I wasn't the only one! You're picking on me!'

I went outside the room for a few seconds (where the students bags were placed against the corridor wall) and said in a loud voice, 'I wonder if Alex has any writing paper in his bag.' I had said this because Alex said he couldn't do the work because he didn't have any paper. It was a ruse to get him out of the room for a few minutes. He came out like a shot and said, 'You're touching my bag!' I wasn't, I didn't.

Away from his immediate audience, he was more settled now. We had a 'chat'. I briefly described his behaviour and gave the immediate choice: work quietly until recess or leave for 'time-out'. He grumbled, I repeated the directed 'choice'/consequence – and we went in. He sat and sulked and did virtually nothing. At recess I directed him to stay back along with another student I needed to speak with. He yelled at me and kicked at the wall, but he stayed back. I calmly explained what had happened. I then directed both students to complete the set written work. Alex finished the diagram (roughly written) and then said, 'Can I go now!?' I said, 'I'd like to check the work first, Alex, won't keep you long'. (It's not easy staying calm when students are displaying hostile body language and tone.)

He ripped up the work in front of me, threw it up in the air and walked off – swearing under his breath. I knew now it was obviously a power-struggle, not just merely attention-seeking. I didn't chase after him (that's a waste of time) but I did follow him up, later, in another colleague's class (p 121).

Eventually we set up a year-level 'personal behaviour-plan' for Alex. It took some time and school-wide planning. Alex was one of half a dozen challenging students for whom no *school-wide* plan had been made. Teachers had (up to this point in time) been basically left to do their own thing – some were more successful than others. The problem was that Alex was clearly a catalyst for a number of other students. The plan we developed involved:

- working with Alex one to one, especially looking at reasons for his behaviour regarding attention and power seeking (p 145*f*)
- improving follow-up and follow-through procedures by all the teachers who taught Alex (p 107*f*)
- having a clear consequential chain (p 56*f*)
- following a well-organised 'tracking procedure' across all his classes
- developing a school-wide time-out plan (p 132*f*) – this was crucial in the early stages of the plan
- working one to one with Alex over several weeks (and a number of sessions) to help him come to terms with his behaviour, its effect on others and the effect on his mother at home (see below)

■ Most of all-teaching Alex new patterns of behaviour to help him in his learning and social relationships.

The elements of this individual behaviour management plan were set up by a 'case-supervisor' (or adult-mentor) who acted on behalf of all the subject teachers by:

■ developing the individual-behaviour-plan with the student
■ teaching skills to the student within the framework of 'a plan'
■ communicating with support personnel and administration, so they were clear as to the purpose and process of the 'plan'
■ giving the student ongoing feedback and evaluating the plan.

The 'case-supervisor' was a senior-teacher skilled in working with 'more-challenging students'.

Alex was withdrawn from a couple of subject areas for a few weeks (initially for safety), but in time he settled back into a reasonable school existence. He is still at school. The relative success of this approach was due to the fact that it was *whole-school* in its development and implementation. Like all such programs it was labour-intensive but we actually spent less time overall than the approaches we had been using (initially) teacher by teacher.

Developing an individual behaviour management plan with students who present with behaviour disorders

There is a small percentage of students in most school populations whose behaviour frequently and (at times) severely affects the rights of teacher(s) and students. In some schools this may be up to 5% (see Wragg 1989; Rogers 1994, 2003a). These students are often resistant, or show no significant response, to the teacher's classroom establishment of rights, responsibilities and rules. After-class chats, use of consequences, detention (and so on) may see little or no changes in the *pattern* of their disruptive behaviour.

These students are often referred to as 'behaviourally disordered' (BD), that is, their behaviour is disordered to an inappropriate degree relative to student behaviour within the 'normal range'. Very often it is necessary (and beneficial) to develop an individual behaviour management plan (IBMP) for these students.

We do so as early, as is necessary, when such behaviour is observed on a regular basis.

One of the first steps in setting up any program or plan for BD students is to have a school-wide assessment of the student's behavioural profile.

Some students may present with behaviour disorders such as Attention Deficit Spectrum Disorder (AD(H)D); Autism Spectrum Behaviour (such as Asperger's

Syndrome); Oppositional Defiance Disorder Spectrum Behaviour (ODD); Tourette's Syndrome. ... While it is crucial for schools to be consciously aware of the 'normative' symptoms and behavioural expressions of such 'disorders' (and the role of medication) it is essential to also address such disorders from an educational-therapy approach.

Behaviour profile

The issue for teachers, on a day-by-day management basis, will also include an assessment of the student's behaviour in terms of the following:

- *Frequency:* How frequently does the student call out, seat wander, push in line, butt in, avoid a task, refuse a task and so on?
- *Intensity:* Calling out, rolling on the mat, seat leaning and so on are all annoying when they are frequent; when they are *intense* in their expression they are significantly more stressful for the teacher and other students.
- *Generality:* Teachers will need to assess if a student's disruptive behaviour pattern is situation specific (associated with one teacher or subject area) or generally disruptive with all the teachers who work with that student.
- *Duration:* Is the behaviour consistently disruptive Monday to Friday, or is the behaviour worse on particular days (for example, on Mondays)? Has the student's behaviour improved with the onset of the teacher's establishment process?

This initial 'behaviour profile' forms the basis of a whole-school (grade or year-level) approach to the development of an individual behaviour-management plan for the student.

It can help if teachers keep note of frequency and durability of distracting and disruptive behaviours in their classes to give feedback to the team meeting. It is important to keep ongoing records for case conferences, departmental meetings, suspension and inquiry procedures.

If it is only one subject teacher who finds a student's behaviour 'challenging', or 'problematic' then a senior staff member would normally work with that particular teacher and student. Is it a personality issue? Is there a need to develop some conflict resolution? Is it the subject area? Does the behaviour issue with this teacher demonstrate a need for some kind of individual education plan or at least some catering for the student's differential ability?

Early intervention is essential where an unsatisfactory behaviour profile is noted across subject areas. It is important that staff work together on an individual-behaviour management plan. The emphasis with all behaviour planning for such students is to approach the issue with *colleague support*; even if just one or two teachers are struggling with a student's behaviour.

Colleague support in this area is considerate of the following:

■ No blame is attached to particular teachers because of (or for) a child's disruptive behaviour. The team takes a problem-solving approach. When developing 'case-management' there is a shared expectation of teacher professionalism; a willingness to demonstrate care, encouragement and support for the student. 'Blaming' the student, or teachers, is self-defeating.

■ Where a student's challenging and disruptive behaviour affects several teachers across the year level, it is important to have a *year-level plan* rather than an English teacher's plan or maths teacher's plan. This plan is more than a 'behaviour monitoring card' (which, of course, has its place with some students). An individual behaviour plan aims to both *track* and *teach* a student across all subject areas.

■ Any behaviour programme for the student in question must involve a year-level, faculty-supported (even school-wide), time-out plan (p 114*f*). This plan needs a crisis-management option for situations where the student is effectively 'holding a class to (psychological) ransom.' This back-up plan needs to be simple, workable and tied in with positive follow-up by any teacher who initiates time-out.

■ A year-level meeting of all the teachers who teach the student is the shared 'starting point.' Although this discussion is time consuming, it is always worthwhile. After a natural whinge from colleagues, it is important to get down to a problem-solving and action-planning approach. Discuss the student's behaviour profile (p 133). Share background information (accessible within ethical probity) that can affect an understanding of the student's current behaviour. Discuss basics such as who the student sits with; whether behaviour is better or worse on particular days and in particular subject areas; and whether behaviour is worse during on-task time or whole-class teaching/learning time. We will need to ascertain if there are any approaches being used that staff have found effective. It is also important to discuss discipline approaches with such students. Teachers who rely on confrontational/authoritarian approaches frequently struggle with the management of students who present with attentional, challenging and confronting behaviours.

Case-management (adult-mentoring)

'Case management' involves an adult mentor working with a student in a one-to-one capacity to develop an **individual behaviour plan**.

A 'case supervisor' (or adult mentor) is often a senior teacher who knows the student and is well regarded (and trusted) by colleagues to develop a workable plan with those students 'at risk'.

The role of a 'case-manager' involves:

- liaising with all the teachers who teach the student (who has been nominated for case supervision. See behaviour profile p 133).
- working directly with the student to clarify behaviour concerns and to teach, *model* and *practice* new (necessary) behaviours. The behaviours embrace both 'academic-learning skills' and core 'social-relational skills'.
- developing a workable plan with the student to enable, and teach, those skills.
- communicating that plan to all staff who teach (and work with) the student.
- assisting and encouraging teachers in monitoring 'the plan' at the classroom level.
- fine-tuning a workable time-out plan for such students. Eg. in one school I worked, a young girl from a very troubled home environment would refuse (point blank) to leave a classroom for time-out. She would often set up loud, time-consuming, arguments if a teacher tried to 'exit' her from a classroom (almost always with male teachers). My colleagues and I finally came up with a more considered time-out plan that involved two key, female, colleagues who could be called in to calmly exit the student for time-out (using the time-out card p 117). Most of my colleagues saw this as a positive approach to support colleagues and the student (rather than some 'professional sleight').
- assisting colleagues in supportive feedback to the students (and parents where appropriate).
- assisting the student (one-to-one) to reflect on their progress:
  '*What part of your plan is working well – and why? What part are you strug-gling with and why? What can we do to improve things? How?*'
- liaising with parents (for feedback, encouragement and review).

N.B. In allocating case-supervisors to one-to-one settings with students we need to be acutely aware of ethical probity. Female students would normally be allocated a female case-super-visor. There are many occasions where a male student benefits from a male case-supervisor.

At primary level such case supervision will normally be carried out by the Grade teacher, unless that teacher is so disaffected by the child's behaviour that any one-to-one work would be counterproductive. Some teachers effectively lose the emotional, and psychological, good-will to engage in developing an individual programme for behaviour with some students. In such cases another colleague can serve as a 'behaviour-tutor' to work with the child as well as supporting the teacher to work with the child in the classroom setting (see Rogers 2003a).

Context for behaviour planning

The *context* for all behaviour planning is the basic rights and responsibilities inherent in the school's behaviour policy. The *aim* of any behaviour plan is to increase the student's:

- *self-awareness* of their behaviour and how it is affecting their own learning
- *self-control and behaviour ownership* in relationship to their learning and social relationships at school.

In developing such a plan the student is encouraged to work on 'academic survival skills' and 'social survival skills' at school. (Of course, these are not the terms we use when working with the student.) Basic academic survival skills include how to get teacher attention during whole class-teaching time and on-task learning time; how to initiate and sustain a learning task; how to monitor one's (own) learning time; how to communicate frustration about a learning issue; having basic equipment; having a work schedule and doing one's best (always give the student a specific structure for the concept of 'doing one's best'). Basic social skills include how to enter and leave a classroom without causing hassles; how to find a seat and stay in it; how to keep hands and feet to oneself (particularly important for infants when sitting on 'the mat' in whole-class teaching time); how to use basic social cues such as 'please', thanks, 'excuse-me' and 'can I borrow?'; how to put things back in their place or return them to their owner; and how to move around the classroom (and when it's appropriate to move around in given subject areas) without annoying others – this is linked to the concept of staying on task, an issue that is particularly difficult for students who present with attention deficit spectrum behaviours (particularly AD(H)D).

In developing an individual behaviour plan with a student, the emphasis is not on counselling per se but on teaching the skills of behaviour ownership at school. The process emphasises an educational model: *teaching behaviour* in a way that enables students to consider *others'* rights and the specific skills necessary to that end.

An effective case-supervisor develops positive relationships quickly with such students and will be 'privy' from time to time to information from school counsellors and social workers. In the one-to-one sessions, however, the case-supervisor's role is primarily to help the student with their behaviour through 'reskilling'. Whenever a student discusses their difficult home background or life's circumstances the case-supervisor should be – naturally – empathetic while at the same time explaining that such circumstances *contribute* to ineffective and stressful behaviour (at school), but they don't *cause* that behaviour.

For example we would point out to the student that: 'No one *makes* you kick a chair in the classroom; call out frequently; come late to class frequently (with a 'loud entrance'!); argue with your teachers; swear at teachers or refuse to do work you know you can actually do. There are different things you can do when you're uptight, frustrated or even angry. I want to help you with a plan for your behaviour so you don't keep getting into hassles with your teachers and parent(s). Your behaviour is your choice. However, that doesn't mean that the choices are easy – they are often hard. There are skills you can learn.'

In all conversations about behaviour the case-supervisor is supportive and gives descriptive feedback about behaviour (rather than judging the student). The emphasis is always: 'We like you but we don't like some of your behaviours … because … [always refer to the *context* – the basic non-negotiable rights and responsibilities in our school]. Your behaviour is sometimes unacceptable [the rights-affecting behaviour], wrong or bad; not *you*.' We should never refer to the student as a bad *person*. For example, we never speak about *bad anger*, we refer, instead, to bad *anger habits*. It is the characteristic expression of our anger *behaviour* that is relatively 'good' or 'bad'. We *learn* 'good' or 'bad' anger habits. We are not bad because we get angry; anger is a *feeling* (often related to frustration). What we characteristically do *when* we are angry is learned.

Anger – in itself – is neither good nor bad. When a case-supervisor teaches anger management skills the emphasis is on teaching good anger *habits* and unlearning bad anger habits.

The process of developing a behaviour plan is much the same whatever the age of the student:

- a one-to-one context (over time) where we discuss, and *teach*, new patterns of behaviour
- an adult mentor with support mentoring (where appropriate) from the student's peers (primary-age level)
- focus on the student's present behaviour(s) but with a view to immediate and ongoing change
- starting with a few behaviours at a time
- using multiple entry points into the teaching of behaviour such as 'mirroring'; picture cues; goal disclosure; modelling; rehearsal feedback and ongoing evaluation (see later).

Sessions covering behaviour and behaviour skills

Most students will need several sessions with their case-supervisor. Session One will concentrate on the reasons for the student being in the position of needing a behaviour plan. The case-supervisor will describe (even 'mirror') the behaviours specifically affecting the student's learning (and other students' rights, including the teacher's right to teach). 'Mirroring' involves *briefly* modelling the child's distracting/disruptive behaviours (see p 111*f*).

Supplementary questions will address:

- How *often* do you think you speak like that (or call out or butt in)? This to assist children with an understanding of 'frequency' of distracting/disruptive behaviour.

- How do you think other students feel or are affected by …? When students are invited to give feedback they often (not always but often) do the following:
  –Shift blame: 'Yeah, well, I'm not the only one!' or 'What about Jason? He calls out too.'
  –Excuse their behaviour: 'Yeah, well, I don't do that all the time' or 'Well I hate this subject!'
  –Make 'global' statements: 'All the teachers here couldn't give a sh-t!' or 'I hate this school.' 'No one helps me.'
  –Adopt provocative avoidance tactics: 'Yeah, well, I don't care!' or 'So?' When students say they 'don't care!' – a brief, reasurring, 'I care' is enough.

To increase a child's sense of 'behaviour-awareness' my colleagues have found the following strategies helpful.

- Simple drawings can give another entry point into students' understanding about their behaviour (Rogers 2003a). Picture cues are particularly helpful at infant level or for students whose communication/dialogue skills are not as focused as those of other students. Such picture-cues also give the student something to look at and refer to *while* the teacher is speaking. These drawings, or picture-cues, are prepared beforehand. The picture cues portray the *off-task* (disruptive) behaviour(s); the social disapproval of student and teacher, and the on-task behaviour with corresponding social approval. Many infant teachers use simple stick-figure drawings to *represent* the teacher; the disruptive student and the class group. The social disapproval is shown on the faces of the teacher and student's peers (sad faces.) In the second picture the teacher portrays the student engaged in the appropriate (on-task) behaviour. The faces of teacher, student and peers display social approval (smiles).

The teacher converses with the student 'through' the pictures:

Teacher: 'Who do you think this person here is?' The teacher points to the student (in the picture) represented as calling out; butting in or seat wandering …
Student: 'Is that supposed to be me?' (I've heard that response a number of times.) Almost all students will nominate themselves as the student shown behaving disruptively in the first picture.
Teacher: 'Best drawing I could do.'
Teacher: 'What are you doing in the picture?' If the student says they are: 'being silly' or 'being naughty,' or 'mucking around' we need to specify *what* is meant by

'silly' or 'naughty' …

The teacher converses with the student 'through' the pictures as a form of 'social-story'. The teacher invites the student to talk about their distracting/disruptive behaviour. If they choose not to talk (or share) the teacher will quietly, calmly, clearly and briefly focus on the behaviours portrayed in the picture: '*You see here* (the teacher points to the picture). *You're calling out loudly, lots of times … Look at the faces of the teacher and the students. What do they think? …*' '*What should you do if you want to share, or ask a question?*' '*Have a look at this other picture.*' Here the teacher directs the student to a picture that portrays him putting his hand up *without* calling out (in contrast to the picture where he is calling out and his teacher and classmates are pictorially portrayed as upset). The teacher and students in this (second) picture look happy (social approval) … in relationship to his thoughtful behaviour.

Young children (at infant and middle primary level) can be encouraged to draw their 'own' plans – illustrating the aspects of behaviour they need to work on with their teacher. The 'picture plans' become the basis for student-teacher dialogue about the student's behaviour goals. They are also used (in class) as a *visual aide-memoire* to remind and encourage the student.

■ *Target a few key behaviours.* The teacher discusses with the student behaviours they will need 'to stop' (and why) and behaviours they will need 'to start' (and why). This can be developed through picture cues or written form (see appendix). It is preferable to target just two or three behaviours, keeping the language specific, simple and behaviourally focused. For example, 'If you need teacher help in work time, put up your hand and wait, and remember to check the work carefully first, or quietly check with a class mentor.' It can be helpful for more restless students if they have ancillary work task(s) to go on with while they wait for their teacher to give personal assistance. It can also help to ask the student if there is a student in their class(es) whom they would be comfortable to accept support from with their plan (primary level). Offer one or two names of students who would be willing to act as peer mentors (Rogers 2003a). The teacher would need to have checked beforehand with the students whose names are offered (as peer-mentors). It would be important to discuss with nominated mentors what their role would be, especially how to remind and to encourage (not to force) their classmate with their plan. It is helpful if the mentor sits with (or on the same table as) the student who is on the behaviour-plan.

■ *Modelling the target behaviours.* When developing the individual behaviour plan with the student it will help if the teacher *models* the behaviour 'targeted' in the student's plan.

We model: the 'partner-voice', or 'sitting on the mat appropriately'; or the 'lining up without pushing'; or the 'organised desk and task focus' ... For example, sitting on the mat appropriately is (in itself) not clear enough for a 5 year old. We need to model *how* to sit in a way that does not distract others; how to wait your turn (and why); how to put your hand up, and think first without calling out; how to listen when other students share; how to listen to the teacher with *eyes* and *ears*.

■ *Invite the student to practise (rehearse) the target behaviours.* The case-supervisor will encourage the student to practise the *behaviour* the teacher has discussed and modelled. If the student is uncomfortable we obviously should not force such practice. Most students will give it a go, several times, until they are clear in their mind what is meant by 'their plan'.

■ *Discuss the bad-day syndrome with the student.* This both reassures that teachers know students have 'bad-days' and it also prepares the student by teaching some strategies to use *when* they are having a bad-day. 'What will you do if you are having a really bad day and are feeling like ...?' A frustration–tolerance plan can help: count backwards from *10*; breathe in and out slowly five times; ask to go out for a drink; or write down 'what's hassling me' to show it to their case-supervisor later that day. If it's a particular teacher that the student perceives is 'really hassling' them, we will need to discuss how the student can approach the teacher later, after class, to make their feelings clear. We find it helpful to 'rehearse' with the student some of the things they could say – these are often written down as an aide-memoire. Some students will be helped by having some rehearsal sessions addressing anger-control behaviours (Rogers 2003a). 'On bad days let the teacher know, quietly, that you're having a bad day and remember to use your personal *plan*. Tell yourself, "I'm getting really annoyed" and then remember your plan: "I can calm myself by ..." Now, let's go over it again. I'll show you how and then we'll write it down.' Point out that, as with any new skill (or new/different way of doing things), we have slip-ups or bad days when things don't go right for us and that the students need to recognise that and learn from it, but stick with their plan. I find it helpful to talk about something the student is proficient at (say in sport or hobbies) and ask how they got better at it. The student soon realises that we only get 'better' at anything 'By practice, effort, going back over it, and doing it until it becomes sort of second nature.'

■ *Publish the plan.* The case supervisor will develop a written or pictorial plan in a user-friendly form. This can be through simple descriptions of behaviours (as goals) or off-task and on-task behaviours (Appendix 3). In may be in a picture format (p 138*f*). Some infant teachers even use digital photographs of children modelling the 'target-behaviour(s).' These photographs (and cue-phrases) then become the plan. When using digital photographs (for such a purpose) it is appropriate to seek parent permission; explain that this behaviour-plan has been developed to support their child's *learning* (as well as behaviour) in the classroom. List any idiosyncratic caveats such as: 'On my bad days I'll let my teacher know by having a quiet word on the way into class.'

Each subject teacher (or specialist teacher) receives a copy of the student's 'plan' (exactly as given to the student) so that teachers can refer to the plan with the student for both support and discipline and of any effort, and progress, made by the student. It is important that all teachers are supportive of the student's plan. I've seen positive efforts by a student damaged by a few teachers who won't make the effort to be supportive with the student and quietly referring to the plan when disciplining the student who is off-task (and off-plan). For example, 'David, what's your plan for …?', or 'What should you be doing according to your plan? How can I help?' As obvious as it sounds there ought to be a normative expectation that all teachers will give the student regular descriptive feedback and encouragement (p 101*f*).

It is important to stress to all teachers that the student in question is not being granted special privileges by being on an individual behaviour plan. Rather, the student is being given individual *support* (in much the same way as a student with any special needs has a plan, for example an individual education plan).

Students with behaviour disorders are subject to the same discipline (and consequences) that any student has to face when overly disruptive.

The consistent support of subject teachers is essential to the success of any IBMP.

If the student refuses any one-to-one assistance from a case-supervising teacher, it is pointless pushing the concept of an individual behaviour plan. Even if it is written up the student won't 'own' it, and ownership is an important part of the program.

The case-supervisor will point out that, if the student continues to behave in the ways noted (revisit, *specifically*, the disruptive behaviours at issue), there is a chain of consequences the school will have to undertake: 'This is not because we dislike you, it's because we can't allow you to continually call out (wander, push in and so on)'. We always add, 'However, my door is always open to work on a plan to help you with your behaviour.' If the student responds with another, 'I don't give a …!' We clearly, and calmly, point out, 'But I do and so do your parent(s).' (At least we hope they do.)

By outlining the consequences (continued time-out, possible suspension, continued parent contact and so on), the case-supervisor is putting the responsibility back where it belongs – on the student – but always with the genuine caveat that support – long-term support – is available for behaviour change. It is also important for the student to get the message that their behaviour is their choice. The case-supervisor's role is to support the student with the skills to make better behavioural choices.

Evaluating the program – a case study

Some students respond quickly to the concept of a personal behaviour plan. Chris, a young lad with diagnosed AD(H)D (in Year 3) was constantly rolling on the mat and making silly noises during whole-class teaching time. He also found it difficult to stay in his seat during on-task learning time.

His grade-teacher set up some 'special' one-to-one meetings with Chris. The teacher also received support from a behaviour-tutor colleague.

In the first session the grade teacher used picture cues (p 138) and some gentle mirroring (p 111) to clarify his current, and typical, disruptive behaviour. She asked Chris how many times he thought he called out and rolled around; she referred to the mirroring she had just done ('just like that') and the picture displaying Chris rolling on the carpet while the teacher and students looked upset. It was a basic, stick-figured *representation* of Chris's typical disruptive behaviour. The student was pretty close to the mark when he said, 'About 10 times?', to which the teacher replied, 'Actually 15, Chris; it's a *lot* of times Chris.'

The teacher didn't waste any time with exploring 'why' he rolled on the mat and called out. She invited Chris to work on a plan to help him sit on the mat (like the other students), and put up his hand without calling out. She explained why these behaviours were important and referred to the effect of his (present) behaviour on other children. Using the picture cues of the student engaging in off-task behaviour, she referred to the sad faces of the children near him.

Chris responded by saying they were sad because he was 'not listening to the teacher' and 'moving around too much'. His teacher then showed Chris a second picture with him behaving appropriately (sitting on the mat with his hand up) with corresponding social approval on the faces on his peers. One of the naturally

occurring benefits of such a plan is that it can increase social/peer approval. This is especially important with children diagnosed with AD(H)D who are often alienated from positive peer approval (though of course they may often receive inappropriate and negative peer attention). The concept of social approval can be discussed with children of any age.

After modelling the new behaviour (twice), the teacher invited Chris to practise the plan with her (twice). She gave him feedback and encouragement during the practice/rehearsal session. She also gave him a small copy of the 'plan' they had been using in the session (reduced from A4 size). She asked him where he'd like to keep his copy. He replied, 'In my work tray.' Younger students sometimes request to keep their copy on their class table (it is always their choice). Over the first few days Chris increased his 'on-task' behaviours (sitting on the mat without rolling around or calling out, and putting up his hand without calling out when he wanted to ask a question or make a comment). The approximations of his behaviour to what he had practised in the one-to-one sessions were noted as a tick in the boxes at the bottom of his *reminder plan*. When he left the mat to work at his table the teacher quietly called him aside from the other students and asked him to get his copy of his 'plan'. She encouraged him by saying (with a smile), 'You remembered your plan. You sat on the mat quietly and safely. You remembered to listen with *eyes* and ears; you remembered to put your hand up without calling out – and to wait your turn. Let's put a tick on your plan and on my copy too.'

In subsequent sessions the class teacher worked on a plan to help Chris stay on task at his seat, including work-task cards for key learning times. She also worked on a simple plan to help with his loudness of voice in class and tied in this individual plan with the whole-class 'noise monitoring plan' (p 86*f*). The class teacher made sure all the specialist teachers, teacher aides and the administration had a copy of the plan. She particularly asked them to support Chris in the ways she had found helpful such as the quiet, brief, descriptive feedback eg 'You remembered to …' (followed by a brief descriptive comment of what Chris had remembered to do …)

It is important to remember that it takes students some time to develop new patterns of behaviour, and the attitude changes that go with the process of behaviour change. It is also important to see that success is *realistically* measured in a reduction in frequency and intensity of distracting/disruptive behaviour and an increase in generality of 'on-task' behaviour over time.

Teachers should be consciously considerate of the efforts students make with their plan and treat 'bad days' as 'bad days'. They should not discount progress with the plan because the student has a 'bad', or 'off' day. On those days the normal (and fair) process of discipline still needs to be exercised. If teachers want perfection they are wanting what is unrealistic – even some of the 'good' students behave in distracting ways from time to time.

Subsequent sessions

In all subsequent sessions the case-supervisor and the student will pursue the following:

- Discuss how the plan is going in respective classes: what is working well and why, what isn't working well and why, and areas where the plan needs to be finetuned or modified.
- Refine or add elements to the plan, or make new plans as necessary.
- Go over old and new skills, especially those challenging the student's beliefs: 'It's too hard!', 'It's not worth it!' or 'What does it matter anyway?'.
- Discuss teacher feedback from teachers across all classes/subjects. The student may need help dealing with what they perceive to be unfair or unsupportive teachers. It may be necessary to develop some skills of how to speak to a teacher after class and the sorts of things that could be said when wanting to make a complaint or share a concern.
- The adult mentor may well have to revisit old behaviour through 'mirroring' (p 111) and goal disclosure (p 146f) as well as set up more practice sessions.

It is also important to give feedback to the parent/s (caregiver) about how the program is going with their child. Most parents are very supportive – some are only too glad the school is 'doing something' (some parents may feel 'powerless', or feel that 'nothing they do matters'). We encourage them that everything we seek to do (thoughtfully and well) matters.

A home–school diary or a special letter to outline the positive outcomes their child is making can elicit the secondary encouragement that the home environment can provide. It is probably better to make sure that any negative feedback is given in person at a school meeting so that the principal (and adult mentor) can give such feedback in context to minimise it being misconstrued.

I have had case conferences with parents regarding their offspring where the following comments were made:

- 'He was all right at the last fifteen schools!'
- 'Just do what I do – give him a good smack! Never did me any harm!'
- 'You're just picking on my son!'

Giving feedback to authoritarian/hostile/suspicious or jaded parents is not easy. Keeping them focused on the child's present behaviour and taking a *supportive* approach that allows for corrective consequential discipline is the purpose of a parent/teacher meeting. The meeting is not an opportunity to blame the parents (tempting as that may be on some occasions). We emphasise what we've found helpful and why, and what the school is seeking to do to give support with respect to their child's learning and behaviour and why. Then we invite parental support.

'Goal-directed behaviours'

According to Rudolf Dreikurs, behaviour is *purposeful and goal-directed* in a social setting like a classroom (or a school.) These behaviour 'goals' enable students to feel that they 'belong' to the social group. When students are disruptive they may well be pursuing goals within the social context. When a boy *repeatedly* calls out instead of putting up his hand, his need for attention is met – this is his *goal* ('I belong when my teacher and/or the class is frequently noticing and attending to me'). In the student's 'private logic', he perceives that this is how to gain attention. This does not mean the student is fully aware of what is happening (especially with infant-aged children), but, if a teacher or parent constantly reinforces inappropriate attention seeking, the association still confirms (in the child's perception) that this is how the need for attention (belonging) is met.

Dreikurs et al (1982) have identified four, common, patterns of behaviour associated with mistaken 'goals of belonging':

- *Attention* seeking may take the form of frequent clowning, or frequent, and silly, nuisance behaviours. Teachers may 'over-service', over-remind or coax some students regarding such behaviours, but at the same time become irritated and frustrated, and resent the amount of time taken up by these students.
- *Power* seeking may take the form of stubborn, often argumentative, and challenging behaviour and disobedience. Teachers may feel threatened and even angry at the pressure this puts on their leadership (and status position) – particularly as they perceive their leadership in the eyes of the wider student 'audience'.
- *Revenge* seeking may take the form of surreptitious, or openly, destructive behaviour while – at the same time – accusing or blaming others of unfairness. Teachers may feel hurt and may even want to 'hurt back' when students behave in these ways. They may well feel like engaging in 'emotional payback'.
- Feelings of *inadequacy* may take the form of students giving up easily and not participating. Teachers will often feel discouraged in their difficulty in reaching the student.

Dreikurs proposes that teachers can assist a child's awareness of their behaviour by 'disclosing' their 'behaviour goal'. In a one-to-one setting the teacher will sensitively pursue several questions to enable the child's awareness, and understanding, of their distracting and disruptive behaviour. (See below)

It is important to plan these questions ahead of time and to consider the likely reactions from the student.

The tone – in such a meeting – is supportive and invitational.

It is, in effect, part of the repairing and rebuilding process. This 'goal disclosure' process is another way of raising the child's self-awareness of their behaviour. It is another step in enabling ownership of their behaviour through the case-supervision approach. 'Goal disclosure' should also consider a child's age and ability to comprehend such questions.

It can help to use picture cues or some gentle mirroring (p 111) to set the scene (Rogers 2003a).

Key questions

The key questions are designed to focus on what the child is trying to achieve through their behaviour. Dreikurs makes the point that these questions need to be phrased as considered 'guesses'. At no point do we say: 'I *know* why you do ...'. Rather we say '*Do you know why ...?*'

For example: '*Do you know why you call out many times during whole-class teaching time?*' The tone of the question is calm; allowing some take-up-time by the student to reflect. My colleagues and I often find it helpful to gently 'mirror' the specific behaviour under question at this point (p 111).

Most students shrug their shoulders, lean back and frown, or say 'no'. The purpose of the question 'why?' (shared respectfully, calmly, with some take-up-time) is to raise cognitive awareness in the student about 'why' they behave the way they do.

After the child has been asked to consider 'why' they behave the way they do (in class) the teacher then proposes their possible 'behaviour goal'.

Each question (see below) is prefaced with '*Could it be that ...?*', followed by a brief description of their typical distracting behaviour, followed by the suggested 'disclosure' of their goal.

'Could it be that when you call out many times in class you want the class (and me) to notice you a lot?' The phrase 'Could it be' is not an 'accusation'; it is only a thoughtful guess that may be correct or incorrect. If it is incorrect, we should 'guess' again (Dreikurs et al 1982, p 30).

The following questions have been adapted from Dreikurs et al (1982, pp 29–32):

1 *Attention:* 'Could it be that ...
   - you want to keep me busy with you and your requests?

- you want me to notice you more? Help you more?
- you want the rest of the class to notice you?/laugh at you when …?
- you want to keep the group/class busy with you?
- you want to be special to the group?'

2 *Power:* 'Could it be that …
- you want to show me that you can do what you want and that we can't stop you?
- you want to do what you want to do *when* you want to do it – and that no one can (really) stop you?
- you want to be the boss – you want to be in charge – the one calling the shots?'

Remember, the tone is questioning and 'guessing', not judgmental or pejorative.

3 *Revenge:* 'Could it be that …
- you want to get back at …, pay back, get even for …?
- you want to hurt me, get even with me for …? [or] You want to hurt him (name …) or her (name …)?
- you want to show me that I cannot get away with …? [for example punishing, contacting parents, notifying the principal …]
- you want to make me (or the class or …) feel bad or feel hurt?'

4 *Display of inadequacy:* 'Could it be that …
- you want to be left alone because you feel 'you can't do anything?' You're 'afraid to fail?'
- you can't be 'the winner', 'first?'
- you want me to stop asking you questions or trying to 'make' you work? (see Dreikurs 1982: 29f.)
- you 'feel you don't know the answers in class' and 'you don't want the other students to know?'
- you feel 'insignificant' [explain] unless you 'can always succeed' … 'be the best in whatever you do' … or 'always get it right?'
- you feel you must never make mistakes (in your work, in sport, in school)?'

In pursuing the questions it is important to pace the process and go through the sequence beginning with attention onwards. If the teacher suspects borderline power, say, rather than attention, it is worth pursuing the disclosure on power. These questions form the framework for how the teacher could approach the counselling approach of 'goal-disclosure'. Dreikurs gives a wide range of examples in his helpful text (1982). For example, take passive power (what some teachers regard as 'dumb insolence'): 'Could it be that you are not talking to me now in order to frustrate me (and others) and make me feel helpless and defeated?' or 'Could it be that you are willing to do anything in order to feel as if you are the boss here; you can do what you want and I can't make you ...? or 'stop' you?' What is crucial is the 'calm'-questioning-tone; no hint of accusation.

Completing the 'goal disclosure'

In responding to the disclosure (expressed in the question: 'Could it be that ...?') the younger student may involuntarily agree with the teacher. Most students will demonstrate some acknowledgment such as a smile, embarrassed laughter or pulling a face. Dreikurs calls this the 'recognition reflex'. Older students will also give away some non-verbal agreement or recognition even if they say 'no' – their mouths often twitch, their seating posture shows discomfort or they look away and up. It's as if the student knows 'we're on to something here.'

The questioning process is designed to enable insight and recognition for the student. After the response I find it helpful with older children to partially agree with the student's private logic and goal. If we are dealing with power seeking behaviours, we can say: 'Well, I can't really *stop* you being boss ... or *make* you do the work ... or *make* you like me or any of your teachers. I need your help and co-operation to change things.'

We need to frame our language and approach relative to the age of the student. I would encourage the use of picture cues, 'mirroring' and modelling as 'entry points' into the student's understanding, especially at primary level. It is important to also point out to children that their behaviour is not simply 'accidental' – it is learned and they can relearn with our support. Goal-disclosure is a means to that support process.

Some very helpful programs for older students with behaviour-disorders have been developed by Wragg (1989). These programs and plans, he points out, need to have a voluntary commitment by the student in order to be effective. This is important with adolescents simply because without voluntary co-operation, and effort, by the student, any behaviour program will be self-defeating. Some students will tacitly agree to work on a program only to 'stay out of trouble' without working on the behaviours (and attitudes) expressed in their disruptive patterns of behaviour.

Wragg's program (1989) also offers a range of approaches designed to skill students in cognitive, and self-talk, behaviours. 'Talking sense to yourself.' He explores the link between negative self-talk and disruptive behaviours. It is important when developing behaviour plans to consider the issue of self-talk (self-guiding speech), how it affects behaviour and how teachers can teach students to challenge and 'dispute' erroneous, demanding and 'globalised' thinking. ('*All* teachers are idiots' – or worse!, 'I *hate* school', '*No one* here cares', '... *can't* change things'.) Learning to dispute, challenge and reframe negative, and global,

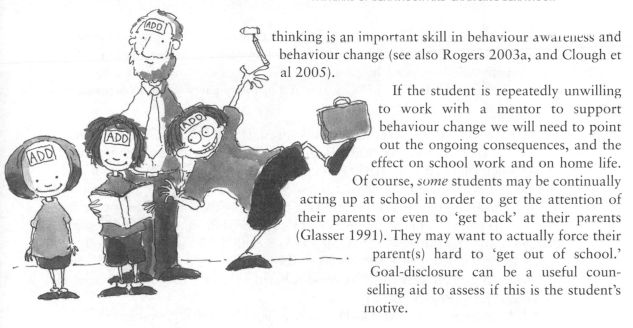

thinking is an important skill in behaviour awareness and behaviour change (see also Rogers 2003a, and Clough et al 2005).

If the student is repeatedly unwilling to work with a mentor to support behaviour change we will need to point out the ongoing consequences, and the effect on school work and on home life. Of course, *some* students may be continually acting up at school in order to get the attention of their parents or even to 'get back' at their parents (Glasser 1991). They may want to actually force their parent(s) hard to 'get out of school.' Goal-disclosure can be a useful counselling aid to assess if this is the student's motive.

Behaviours associated with attention deficit disorder

Teachers at every level of education are well familiar with the most commonly diagnosed behaviour disorder: attention deficit disorder – ADD (or ADHD where the hyperactive factor is dominant). Countless popular articles have been written about children with ADD. I have spoken with some teachers who have labelled typical physical restlessness and lack of concentration as ADD behaviour, even when the student has never been diagnosed with the disorder. It is very important that a student be correctly diagnosed before being 'labelled' as ADD. That diagnosis should only be carried out by an educational (or clinical) psychologist or a paediatrician working with the school and parent(s). I've heard some teachers comment: 'Half my class is ADD! And some of the male teachers are too!'

The symptoms of Attention Deficit Spectrum Behaviour Disorder are typically noted as:

- Frequent inattention, overactivity, physical restlessness, instability, impulsiveness, and social clumsiness (delayed social development may also be noted as symptomatic of ADD behaviour).
- ADD-diagnosed children often find it difficult to concentrate or focus on learning tasks and are very easily distracted (particularly by other children).
- A lack of task focus in ADD children is exacerbated by the fact they often appear as disorganised, and are inattentive and impulsive (at times recklessly impulsive).

- ADD-diagnosed children consequently may present with low self-esteem because they may well be shunned by their immediate class peers who get fed up with their behaviour in class (or in the playground). As *Time* magazine noted: 'They are the kids no one wants at a birthday party' *(Time*, 5 September 1994).

If you have a child/adolescent diagnosed with ADD in your classes (and odds on you will), they may be on medication, normally Ritalin or dexamphetamine (Dexetrine). Children with ADD(H) are often helped by medication (but not all). Medication assists the condition (in terms of focus, concentration and a consequent re-focusing of physical restlessness). Some parents and doctors swear by these medications and many teachers will testify the difference it makes in some (diagnosed) ADD children's behaviour (see especially Serfontein 1990; Green & Chee 1995; Clough et al 2005). What medication cannot do, however, is teach children what to do with any new-found behavioural focus; they will still need a behaviour plan (Rogers 2003a).

A behaviour plan – an individual behaviour plan – can teach the student the academic and social skills needed to cope and achieve at school. While the taking of medication may be an important support in the overall management of ADD(H) the student will also need to learn the essential basic self-coping skills he needs at school.

As part of any 'behaviour-recovery' programme (Rogers 2003a), teachers will need to consider the following aspects of the classroom environment:

- Thoughtful classroom seating organisation where students can see the whiteboard, where they are near the teacher and they are sitting with a classmate (or classmates) who is a positive and helpful role model. Some students will benefit from having a nominated student as a 'plan helper'. This is a student who is willing (and able) to support the child with their behaviour plan and their on-task learning. (See p 139)
- Basic as it sounds, it is also important that we cater for visual learners in our classes. Many children within the attention deficit spectrum of behaviour will be assisted by the kind of 'cognitive anchoring' that comes from visual cue-ing (eg the example of Nathan p 152).
- Auditory cue-ing *and* visual cue-ing are more powerful than auditory cue-ing alone. This is why my colleagues and I often use 'behaviour reminder cards' as a quiet *aide-memoire* during class work (p 142. See also Rogers 2003a).
- Assist the student with time-management tasks. Teach clock-related time-on-task to enable the student to get a sense of how long (say) a given writing, or maths, task would *normally* take. Time-task cards can also be beneficial where the child has daily task cards that outline the specific learning task and also give a time breakdown of the task. This helps to make a longer task seem more achievable.

- Students with ADD (H) do not always write quickly or correctly. It can help to have written notes or allow the student to copy from another student.
- It can help to make sure the student's desk is uncluttered and kept clear of distractions (see p 152). It will help the student to have a well-organised routine and structure to their day (even written up with simple picture cues at lower-middle primary). In Special School settings, photos and time allocations provide visual checks and 'benchmarks' for a student's daily routine. For homework tasks, a homework book is utilised so the student can paste in their worksheets, or set homework tasks.
- Have a personal checklist and train the student to check through the list before going home.
- Because students with ADD(H) often exhibit natural physical restlessness it can be helpful to build the option of appropriate physical movement into the student's behaviour plan. For example, after 5–10 minutes on their work plan the student takes it over to the teacher to have a look (this quiet, and directed, movement gives a brief, purposeful release from sitting). Wherever possible give some movement/monitor role to the student. Avoid overuse of recess times as a punitive consequence for students with ADD(H) – they need the physical exercise/release that playtimes bring.
- Keep encouraging the student with descriptive feedback. Where possible give such feedback close to the effort exercised by the student.
- Wherever possible we seek to exercise positive discipline practices.

The most important point about working with students with diagnosed ADD(H) is that we have a whole-school approach to supporting them. If necessary there will need to be a common school-wide individual behaviour plan. Even if a student is not diagnosed with ADD, the practices noted here are relevant for children with symptomatic ADD behaviour – these children too will benefit from individual behaviour management plans/programmes.

While it may seem like a lot of work at the outset it is worth it over the long term.

Staff will need to be reminded that individual behaviour programmes with such children are not 'excusing' their behaviour – these are supporting positive behaviour change. These students do have special needs that schools have to cater for. This does not mean they are excused normative discipline, but it does mean that any discipline is exercised within a *known behaviour plan*, making disruptive and off-task behaviour easier to manage for all teachers.

Case example

Nathan, Year 8, was struggling with his class work. He was very disorganised: several class books on the desk at a time and a *huge* – distracting – pencil case (full mostly of broken biros and felt-tip pens, and toys, and a can of soft drink, and a broken watch and …). He found it hard to focus on any *one* thing; he was (not untypically) easily distracted during on-task learning time. He often ended up with one or two sentences on a page; one or two algorithms in a Maths class …

Nathan was often quite distracting to other students; some teachers suggesting he would rather be seen as a difficult student than a 'dumb' student. These teachers were not being unkind. They believed that while much of his behaviour was 'task-avoiding' it was also compensatory behaviour for his struggle with classwork.

We decided to teach Nathan several basic 'academic survival behaviours' (relevant to any of his classes).

In the one-to-one sessions the case-supervisor:

1 Discussed his concerns about (the student's) characteristic distracting or disruptive behaviours. In Nathan's case we also 'mirrored' the typical disorganised desk (the teacher also put his head into Nathan's pencil case to 'mirror' what he had seen Nathan do in class). Nathan thought this was quite funny. '*Well, I've seen you do that Nathan – quite a few times*' It's a very big pencil case!

2 They **discussed** *what* a reasonably organised desk looks like and *why* an organised desk helps a student to focus on a learning activity.

3 The teacher then **modelled** how to organise a desk: one class book, a *small* pencil case (containing one red and one blue pen, one ruler, one eraser, one pencil, no sharpener – the big pencil case stays in the locker) and a text book or worksheet (as necessary).

4 The teacher then clarified how to come to a learning task and focus on a task: – **read carefully** ('*If you're struggling with your reading we can organise a 'reading buddy' who will help you in a way that doesn't embarrass you … have you got any suggestions? Or we can arrange for you to quietly read your work through with the teacher before you start?*')

It is crucial the case-supervisor comes up with a *supportive plan* to help this student read through the work (whether it is the board work, worksheet, or text book). A plan that will not embarrass the student.

– 'Ask yourself WHAT AM I ASKED TO DO NOW?' (with board work, work-sheets, text-book exercise …). Many students rush into their work without asking themselves this fundamental question.

5 '*Start and give it your best shot (bit by bit) – avoid comparing yourself to your classmates. I know this isn't easy. You do your best with the work for **that subject, that day** …*'

6 '*When you need teacher assistance this is how you get it …*' Many students are used to calling out or demanding teacher assistance. With Nathan we *taught him* how to fairly (and reasonably) get teacher assistance. As with all such 'teaching' the key elements are *modelling, rehearsal* (practice) and *feedback* in the one-to-one setting. The key skills taught in this plan were noted on a small (postcard sized) reminder card. Each subject teacher was given a copy of the card and Nathan was encouraged to use it as a *personal* reminder (kept in his school diary).

Each teacher – in each subject-class – was encouraged to give some regular, quiet, brief, *descriptive* and non-judgemental feedback.

In class his teachers would come alongside him (as he settled to his work) briefly (and quietly – so as not to embarrass him) and note: '*Hi Nathan – your desk is well organised. You started quickly. I see you've got your table pencil case today. Hang in there*', (check your plan).

Later the teacher comes over and *quietly* acknowledges the student's effort. '*You read through carefully. I can see by your writing you've understood the main point*' (be specific).

It is important in giving descriptive, encouraging, feedback not to qualify the feedback (in a negative sense) eg: '*Why* can't you do that *all* the time …?'; or '*If you were organised like that every day you would get much more work done …*'

Nathan's learning skills developed within (and because of) this plan; because teachers cared enough to make the effort. His general self-esteem also improved as his confidence increased and his teachers began (more consciously *and* purposefully) to encourage and support him. Of course there were days when the 'plan' did not work as well as other days – this is normal (sometimes it's three steps forward and one step back) – but his teachers didn't give up or give in.

Chapter 8

RELIEF TEACHERS AND THE HARD CLASS

A winner
Seeks for the goodness in a bad man and works with that
part of him.
A loser
Looks only for the badness in a good man, and therefore
finds it hard to work with anyone.
Sydney Harris, Winners and Losers, 1973

'Who are you? You're not our normal teacher.' I have had that question/comment many, many times when I have worked with a class as a mentor-teacher. My standard answer is a quiet: *'There are no **normal** teachers'* (delivered with a wink and a wry smile).

Challenges facing relief teachers

It is very common for relief teachers to be challenged by students about issues of routine, work requirements and management generally. *'Anyway, she lets us sit with whoever we want; chew gum; wear our hats in class; listen to our "I-Pods" when we work; dance on the tables in an east wind and; and...'* My standard reply is, *'I can check that with Ms F. (or the principal). In our class the rule is ...'* It is pointless 'debating', 'cajoling' or arguing. Respectfully, clearly, re-affirm the rule and convey the expectation of co-operation. Most schools have clear rules/routines for chewing gum/hats etc. It will help to know this in advance of course. It's a waste of time arguing with the student about the veracity of what their regular teacher does or doesn't do. That is why it is helpful for relief teachers to bring a set of key rule reminder posters into the class with them. These rule reminders will cover areas such as:

- the fair learning rule
- the fair communication rule
  - movement around the room
  - respect in our classroom.

You're not our normal teacher!

Relief or supply teaching has its own unique challenges where students test out, waste time and have fun with this new teacher. As one child notes, 'Children who muck up for the relief teachers usually muck up for our own teacher but not as bad' (Wood & Knight 1994).

A relief teacher has to go through what all teachers go through in their first encounters with a new group – the 'establishment phase', that important 'first meeting'. This is the testing out of boundaries, relationships, responses, and comparisons with other teachers.

It is important that relief teachers define the teaching situation for themselves and not just assume they walk into a set pattern that will automatically occasion a co-operative class group; the pattern changes because they are there with a new teacher. In their study on relief teachers and their initial encounters with a class, Wood and Knight (1994, p 390) note that students were able to find out (through having 'fun' and 'fooling around' or 'loud mouthing') 'how much noise or lack of manners (for example, calling out) individual supply/relief teachers would tolerate and how much or how little work they would have to do'.

Colleague support

A common observation (and complaint) of relief teachers is that they believe other staff do not take them seriously, and that they are not always treated as 'real teachers'. We feel that we're 'sort of baby-sitters', 'second-class citizens' and 'not a colleague'. Students, too, may see the relief teacher merely as a supervising adult, who is there for controlling classes or revising work – not really there to teach. 'Unless the supply/relief teacher has his or her job viewed by pupils, their parents and teachers as a valuable part of teaching, not just for baby-sitting (control) purposes, then pupil expectations will remain low, as status of teachers is communicated to pupils by others' (Wood & Knight 1994, p 392: see also Rogers, 2003b).

The relief teacher walks into a staffroom full of strangers – yet these people are his 'colleagues'. He reaches for a cup (he's been looking forward to a cuppa). He'll take it out with him on playground duty. (Relief teachers *always* get playground duty!) Someone says, 'That's my cup!' I've even seen teachers challenge supply teachers about the rights to particular chairs or seating places in the staffroom! I have observed countless staffrooms over the years and have seen a 'teaching stranger' walk in (loaded with the bits and pieces common to relief teaching) and no one has moved across to their colleague to even say 'Hi'. In some cases the body language of the regular staff indicates they don't even acknowledge the existence of their visiting colleague. When you have just had a hard to manage Year 8 class the last thing you need is this ill-considered, dismissive, thoughtless behaviour from your peers.

What a difference it would make if the visiting teacher were to be:

- introduced by a senior colleague (briefly) to the staff at morning briefing and/or morning tea-break
- given a cup (some relief teachers take their own just in case)
- personally introduced to a few teachers (some people are not 'self-starters').

If there is a 'teaching buddy' for the day this teacher will often do these things on behalf of a senior colleague. I'm not talking about shepherding relief teachers all day – just a little bit of understanding by colleagues of how they might be feeling as newcomers.

Supporting relief teachers

Imagine the relief teacher covering 8D for several days or a relief teacher coming in to cover a challenging Year 2 class. They may not know anyone at the school and may have got this job via a phone call. They get to the school early (most do) and go to the office to find out exactly what's on for that day: *where* the classroom is; the particular class or year level. Class routines such as seating plans; noise level [routines]; the class register; *specific* bell/recess times; the *core routines* that may be relevant in a classroom, even 'leave for the toilet' routine etc…; the school's *basic* discipline code – particularly any time-out procedures. This is all critical information when you are new to a school. Sometimes the office doesn't know what class(es) this teacher will be taking. The time is ticking away and the relief teacher is thinking, 'I need the photocopier. I don't know my way around the school. What year (or class) have I got? Can I get there early enough to set up…?' They may well be at school to cover that hard class (the possible reason for the regular teacher taking a few days off). This preys not a little on the mind of relief teachers!

It is important that the office staff demonstrate basic professional courtesy to the relief teacher, not some dismissive: 'Oh, go down to so and so – he'll know where you are today.' Basic as it sounds, a 'relief teacher guide to our school' would be a helpful start. It needs to be a simple, user-friendly document (one or two pages) outlining the following information:

- Bell (recess) times should be given. This may sound basic, but it is, in fact, essential to the smooth running of a teaching day. It should not be left to the relief teacher to merely find these things out for themselves, or (sometimes worse!) asking the students.

- Having a 'teacher buddy' available (a colleague in the grade/faculty team nearby) can give a sense of moral, as well as professional, support. Such support is highly valued when one is covering a known, challenging, class.

- Essential rules for that class or group being taken by the relief teacher should be supplied. Children do tend to test out any new teacher, especially a relief teacher who is *only* there for a day or two. It can help enormously at primary age level if the relief teacher is made aware of any special routines for 'lining up', 'sitting on the mat', 'quiet reading', 'lunch monitors' (published by the grade teacher) and so on. It can also help at secondary level to know how the 'home'/tutor group session is normally conducted.

- The key people within the grade (or faculty) team are also noted so the relief colleague can enlist their support quickly (as is needed). It can help, for example, to use their regular teacher's name when referring to class rules and routines – it makes it sound as though the relief teacher knows what is going on. The list will also include support teachers (and teacher aides) and, of course, the teaching buddy for the day. Having a teacher buddy (a colleague, in the team, teaching nearby) gives an immediate sense of emotional, moral and professional support – particularly with a known hard-to-manage class.

- Notification should be provided of any students on special behaviour plans or 'daily report cards'. Note down the normal routine for checking such 'contracts' with the student. This would normally be done privately, one to one (rather than saying out loud, 'I know that three students in this room are on daily report cards').

- Notification should also be provided of any students who are on special medication or first-aid regimes plus the name of the referral person. Basic, I know, but easy to overlook.

- The exit/time-out plan should be outlined, with special reference to any particular students. (It can even help to know, in advance, some key phrases used by the regular grade (or class) teacher for example: 'I normally direct Jason to time-out in this way ...') I've seen this preventative caveat used successfully in many schools. It provides another link between the regular teacher and the supply/relief teacher. Managing a crisis situation is probably the most important structural and emotional assurance we can provide for a relief teacher – the assurance that with a hard class, back-up can and will be provided. Relief teachers will need to know how to exercise the school's time-out plan, who the reference colleague is and what written reporting is necessary. It is also crucial to let the relief teacher know that the exit time-out card can be used if the teacher senses the class is becoming extremely difficult to manage (p 117). It will also help to notify them of the 'colleague safety-valve option' (p 23).

In schools with challenging classes the calm, clear, whole-school use of time-out is a critical factor in communicating calmness to both individually challenging students and to their peer audience.

Many teachers (at primary) have a file box with these essentials written out for use by relief teachers. The supervising teacher can then refer the relief teacher to this as soon as practicable that day.

- It can help (especially at primary level) to have a 4W Form available for use as the preferred option as a consequence. The 4W Form can be a link between the regular and the supply teacher (p 202).
- If the school has a particular discipline plan, common to all teachers, then the relief teacher will need a user-friendly summary of such a 'plan'.

Schools can assist the welfare of their relief teacher colleagues by creating a welcoming, collegial, environment. The senior colleagues enable such support in deceptively small ways:

- invite the relief teacher to have a cup of tea/coffee
- show the teacher the photocopier (often the first 'port of call' for the day!)
- introduce the teaching buddy for the day
- give the teacher a user-friendly (clear) map of the school and shade in the classroom(s) where the teacher will be that day (remember how confusing the geographical layout of your school was the first week?)
- provide a timetable (especially important if the students have a specialist teacher that day) and a playground-duty roster.

If at all possible it will be extremely helpful if the supervising colleague introduces the relief teacher to the class (or classes) that day. This is a little difficult at secondary level but with a hard class it can be helpful because it can 'validate' the 'supply colleague' as *the* teacher in front of the class (the 'relief' teacher is not merely a 'baby-sitter'!). The supervisor could say, 'Good morning, everyone. This is Ms L who will be teaching here while Mr M is away for a few days ('having a nervous breakdown' – leave that bit out!)'. The supervisor may even stay for a while if the class is particularly difficult, and constructively team teach until the class is settled. It will be important that the senior colleague does not then leave with the parting words: 'And you know who to send them to *if you have any trouble* Mrs. Smith!'

A brief word to supply/relief teachers

If you are a relief teacher reading this you have probably been depending (in the short term) on relief teaching for your bread and butter. It is money hard earned. As one of my colleagues (Michelle) wrote in a letter: 'A new casual teacher on an upper primary class can be subject to a "baptism of bulldust." Children delight in getting up to high jinks and the day can quickly degenerate into a "dump on the casual teacher" day. What the children perceive as an uplifting fix of fun the casual teacher may find a dose of insanity.'

There are a few basic things worth remembering:

- Get to school early enough. The last-minute haste and rush of students arriving at (or in) the class room is not a helpful start to the day or session. If you can get into the room early enough it can help to check out the chalkboard, whiteboard, materials, room layout and so on. This is especially important at primary level. At secondary level be sure to take your own supply of chalk (in case they're still using chalkboards); whiteboard markers; (replenish if from the office later); duster and so on. It's not worth the hassle of sending students to look for the basics.
- Make sure also that you have a key to the room, especially at secondary level (if it's a 'lock-in' school).
- Avoid big discussions with students regarding: who you are or why you are there. When I take demonstration classes (and mentor-teaching classes) some students initially perceive (or suspect) I 'might' be a 'relief' teacher. When lining up, several students call out loudly, 'Ay, you're not our normal teacher!' I think, 'Here we go again', as I usher them into class. I give a brief and positive good morning, with no extended discussions at the door. A brief, clear, intro to the group before we are to go in (p 76*f*), 'My name is Mr Rogers. I'll be taking you for English today. Sit in your normal seat everyone.' There is no guarantee they will, and so later in the lesson I am prepared to relocate students. If you are with the class for a few weeks a class relocation seat plan my be helpful. It would be worth developing this with a colleague well known by the class (p 30).
- Check in advance (where possible) normative routines for the school or even for the year teacher (primary) for such procedures as 'lining up', 'sitting on the mat', 'toilet passes' and so on.
- Have a separate tray to receive the returned notes for 'swimming', 'the excursion' and so on. They'll easily get lost on the teacher's desk. I also find it helpful to have a tray for completed work to be marked. You may also find it helpful

to direct students to do their work (if there for just one day) on paper rather than in their set workbooks ('I've lost my book Miss!'). Take in A4 paper with you, plus a box with all the writing implements including rulers (p 84) required for classwork. Photocopy key pages of any set textbooks (half a dozen for those without textbooks). In other words, be prepared.

- At upper primary and secondary level ask a trustworthy-looking student to do a 'seat-name-map'. The nominated student can draw this simple plan of the class seats/names as they are on *that* day. They do this – unobtrusively – while the relief teacher settles the class, introduces herself and welcomes the class to their teaching and learning day/period ... (p 81).

- Know where the monitor list is at primary level.

- Have your own rules poster with you, just in case. Many of my colleagues who do relief teaching point out that this is a very helpful management device. Begin on a positive note to the day or session and introduce the rule reminder sheet. for example you could say, 'Good morning, everyone. My name is ... [write it up]. I'll be taking this class today for English. Your regular teacher, Ms T, is not able to be here today. I'm aware that you have some class rules and routines to help us co-operate and learn well here.' (Get that brief acknowledgment in early.) However, you have checked the room, and there are no published rules anyway. It won't be helpful, especially with a difficult or reputation class, to ask, 'What rules do you have in this class?' Just acknowledge there *are some rules* and then add, 'Just to make life easier for us all I've brought the rules we'll be using today. You can see they're not much different from those you use with Ms T.' At lower primary it can help to have these rules in picture format. For example, the noise meter at lower and middle primary is a valuable novelty device that relief teachers can use (p 86). It is a simple way to remind students of what their regular teacher would expect for 'the hands-up rule' and 'working noise' during class time.

- From the outset manage behaviour decisively and positively. Give rule reminders early to the group (when students are calling out or are engaged in private chatter). This is not easy when the relief teacher does not yet know students by name. Eyeball the disruptive student. Ask the student's name. If a false name is given and class members laugh, avoid pressing the name, just focus on the behaviour and the specific rule: 'We've got a class rule for asking questions. Remember to use it thanks.' If the student argues, refocus firmly and calmly. Avoid arguing or overly raising the voice (difficult as this is!) (p 19). If the student continues to repeatedly disrupt it is important to clearly, firmly, calmly clarify the consequence (p 91*f*). Avoid pointless power-struggles. I had a student one day, on receipt of the invitation to give his name, reply, 'I've forgotten' in a sulky, clownish voice. I replied, as calmly as I could, 'Well, when you've remembered, let me know. In the meantime if you want to ask a question or make a point put your hand up without calling out or finger clicking. Thanks.' I then resumed the flow of the lesson. I've had many students play this 'game' on our first meeting.

■ Set behaviour standards early by not talking over student chatter or noise or accepting students who call out or butt in. Remind them of the fair rule. Acknowledge positive behaviours. This is not easy, it needs conscious focus. Be prepared to do some brief follow-up even if only there for the one day. A note-book is helpful to record the names of students you believe need a follow-up chat or a class consequence. Avoid any whole-class detentions (p 123*f*).

■ Be prepared to do playground duty (you're bound to score it).

■ Avoid power struggles over teacher comparison: 'You're not as nice as our normal teacher!' The tempting reply to often sulkily delivered and attentional comments is: '*You mean the teacher who is taking a week off with a nervous breakdown!*' or '*I don't care whether you like me. I'm your teacher today – get it!*' Instead – of course – we avoid defensive comparisons. It is enough to acknowledge what they have said and calmly, and clearly, refocus them to the work at hand, or the rule in question, and offer support. '*I'm glad you like your teacher; I'm your teacher today. This is the work we're doing today. How can I help?*'

■ Avoid arguments over what their regular teacher allows them to do in class. This can be dealt with in part by knowing the routines (at least the essential routines) and by not arguing with the student.

■ If the lesson material left for you is going to prove too taxing (in terms of com-municating it to the students) it might be better to run with some 'tested and true' lesson material (activities) of your own. It is not worth the stress of having to run a difficult lesson topic or activity that will overly stress (and confuse) you at the outset. *If* the class was a normally co-operative group it wouldn't matter of course. You might (however) enjoy the risk of 'teaching' way outside your comfort zone! Explain: 'The regular activity on … will be resumed when your teacher returns. Today we'll be doing …' It might even provide some cur-riculum relief for the class. Leave an explanatory note for the regular teacher.

■ It won't hurt the class to have some busy work early in the day (at primary level) to get an understanding of classroom dynamics. I've often begun the day with some games – get-to-know-you games or communication games. The point is to work within your comfort zone.

■ Be aware (very aware) of the exit and time-out plan and how to use it. If any-thing, use it earlier in the cycle of disruptive behaviour rather than later, especially if you sense 'this is going to get very hairy *if he keeps on behaving like this*'.

- Have a notebook with you, especially on playground duty, to note students' names and behaviours that need following up (p 108).
- Follow up students who have left a mess, who were particularly rude or who were persistently disruptive (p 107*f*). After all, you may be coming back to work with them again and it is worth setting good habits in train early.
- Finish the day as positively as possible (p 96*f*).
- Leave the students' work marked (some teachers get a bit annoyed at having to mark other teachers' work).
- Make sure the room is tidy (even tidier than when you came).
- Leave relevant notes about any follow-up you have done or any 4W Forms (p 202).

You'll probably be asked to come back (make sure you return the cup!).

When your class has given a relief teacher a hard time

If a relief teacher has been given a hard time by your class it is important to convey appropriate displeasure; even anger. Do not give a 15-minute (pacing) lecture, 'Who the hell do you think you are, eh? You pack of animals!' Rather, give a firm, clear message about how their behaviour has affected both the relief teacher and you (their regular grade/class teacher.) We need to convey our strong feeling but geared to resolution not revenge.

We could say, 'I was really upset when I heard that this class, *our* class, had really given Ms S a rotten day yesterday. I was particularly upset that she had to hear comments like [here be specific], and put up with behaviour like [here give the worst, specific, examples]. OK, maybe it isn't all of you [pause] but you all let it happen. I was upset for her [pause] and also that you would behave that way. I think better of you than that! I'm going to ask you to think about:

- how you can put this right
- what you can *reasonably* do now (after all Ms S had gone) and the *next* time you have a relief teacher.'

This exercise can be carried out as a class discussion or written activity. Most students suggest they write an apology and suggest a list of things they can do to make the situation with the next relief teacher better: monitors to assist with work distribution; a nominated student welcomes the relief teacher; students stay in 'regular' seats; the class works by fair rules and so on. Of course, this approach works best when the regular grade teacher (or co-ordinator) has a positive working relationship with the class.

Thoughts of three relief teachers

NOTES FROM A RELIEF TEACHER

A student may continually nag you to change seats. A confident, decisive, relaxed 'icy' stare is the best rebuttal although you ache to scorch the recalcitrant with a terse, 'I said "no". Which part of no don't you understand?'

Once the students are seated I state that these are our five rules for the day:

1   Hands up – no calling out.
2   Hands up – no coming out.
3   Speak and behave courteously and pleasantly at all times.
4   Today we do lessons Mrs Q—'s way.
5   Do your best work – neat writing, lines to be ruled with a ruler and no textas (ie no felt-tipped pens)

Students calling out comments and questions or moving out of their seat at whim rarely works when a relief teacher is in the class. This freedom may be possible with the usual class teacher, but students may exploit this 'privilege' with a relief teacher.

Once the students are seated, remind them that it is required courtesy to let the teacher know if they want to leave the room. Despite this request students may leave the room without explanation during the day. When the relief teacher inquires about their absence they may give an abrupt reply, 'I needed a drink.' Remind the students privately, politely and quietly that they must put their hand up and ask next time. These days most students bring bottled water so it's less of an issue.

Michelle

BEHAVIOUR MANAGEMENT ACTION PLAN FOR RELIEF TEACHING

Before going
Things to prepare and take:
■   materials for lesson, including extras for early finishers
■   box of equipment and materials to deal with 'I haven't got a pen' and so on
■   rule posters/noise meter/help board
■   4W Forms
■   notebook for jotting down names and so on to enable follow-up (p 108)
■   labels and ideas for games to help in learning names
■   plan language/actions for discipline, including entry–exit procedures

At the school
■   Check rules/routines/procedures with staff.
■   Find out if time-out exists and *how* it operates (if not, ask – in advance – to whom students may be sent *if necessary*).

In the classroom
■   Explain cues, routines and rules to the class.
■   Use discipline plan consistently.
■   Note anything needing follow-up.

After the lesson
■   Follow up if necessary and/or report back to school staff.
■   Leave a note of work covered and so on for the normal teacher.

Ros

REFLECTIONS ON ACTION PLANNING FOR RELIEF TEACHING

Rule posters were helpful in making expectations clear. In secondary music classes I put up some rules before pupils entered the room. My equipment rule – 'Hands off unless you have permission' – was then clearly visible and could be pointed out straight away. This is essential when using Casio keyboards which (for practical reasons), needed to be set out on tables before the lessons. It also gave rise to some good-humoured interactions with the bright sparks who decided to interpret it as meaning they couldn't touch tables and chairs either!

Having name labels and making an effort to learn names was perhaps one of the most important things. I've only used labels with primary children. They seem to enjoy them and it makes it very easy to refer to everyone by name. I also found that seeing the names all the time helped learn them (I must be a visual learner too). After one afternoon in a reception class, I went back the following week and managed to remember several names without badges. I particularly remember the pleased 'glow' of a five-year-old girl when I asked her to collect the register and managed to use the right name.

In secondary classes, I made a point of calling a register and trying to put names and faces together. I always asked pupils to remind me of their names when they answered questions or when I was working with them, and apologised if I forgot their name. I'm sure this was appreciated and it certainly made me feel better. (Doesn't it feel awful standing at the front and wanting to address a pupil, but not knowing the correct name?)

It was helpful to know the rules and so on *already in place* in the schools. Teaching secondary music, I was particularly grateful to be able to 'remove' one or two individuals on occasions and knowing *reward* routines was good too. In one primary school the children could be given tokens in their group colour to store in a class treasure chest, which was counted up each week. It was a pleasure to give a token to one student, who I later heard very rarely got any. He had worked very well; I think this was as a result of my knowing him (and remembering his name) from a holiday club at church that he had attended. I found that children who had met me outside school like this (at primary level anyway) were very keen to be acknowledged in school.

Following up after lessons made an impression on both pupils and staff. It also helped me to focus on *individuals rather than classes* in difficult lessons at secondary level, and to remember that not all of the pupils were behaving badly. I wrote lots of notes to form tutors asking for help in chasing up missing books, homework and so on. Some of them did not appreciate this, but I did get good support from others which, in turn, made a difference to the behaviour of pupils in lessons (they know I know that the form teacher knows and so on).

Jo

Ros   Jo   Michelle

Chapter 9

SUPPORTING COLLEAGUES

*'... from this point of view one might indeed consider that the
appropriate form of address between man and man ought
not to be "monsieur, sir", but fellow sufferer, "compagnon de
miseres". However strange this may sound it corresponds to
the nature of the case, makes us see other men in a true light
and reminds us of what are the most necessary of all things:
tolerance, patience, forbearance and charity, which each of
us needs and which each of us therefore owes ...'*
Arthur Schopenhauer (1788-1860): Essays and Aphorisms (p 50)

John was a new teacher at this school. It was his first day. John entered the staffroom looking jaded and disoriented. Several staff were sitting down, talking animatedly. Teachers walked in, some acknowledging each other with a nod or smile. No one came up to him to say 'Hi' or 'How'd it go today then?' He felt like a stranger – out of place. It was his first day of 'proper' teaching. He'd had a really difficult Year 9 maths class. The class at one stage had almost rioted. He thought, 'They didn't prepare me for this at uni – no way.' He sighed as he reflected on the miserable day. He was not sure where to sit down in the staffroom: 'Should I sit near that group – there's the head of department?' No one came up to him. He didn't feel as if he was really 'one of them.'

Still bemused, he saw a fellow teacher walk across. The teacher said, 'Hi, my name is David. I haven't seen you around before. First day here?'

'Yeah,' John sighed in return.

'Sounds as if it wasn't the best?'

'I couldn't believe how 'off' they were! I just lost it with them. I tried being friendly, but they just didn't seem to care ...' John's voice trailed off in another sigh.

'You had Year 9? For maths?'

'How did you know?'

'I guessed. If it was 9D I can see why you'd feel out of it!'

The first-year teacher smiled, somewhat jaded, but not defeated. He felt a little better. David said, 'There's a few of us working on a team approach with 9D. If you're interested, we're having a short lunch meeting tomorrow. Fancy a cuppa?'

The first-year teacher felt better. He'd found a colleague. The small act of acknowledgment, and value, as a fellow professional had cheered him. Support from a colleague makes a difference.

Colleague support varies significantly from school to school. As one secondary colleague succinctly put it, '*I worked in a school where I dreaded walking in the gate because of the lack of colleague support – and I've worked in other schools where I enjoyed spending my days there **because** of the staff ...*'

Teaching can (strangely) in some schools be a 'lonely' profession. Yet we teach 'next door' to the very people who experience, know and understand our common concerns and struggles. Research has shown that the *degree of consciousness* in a school – regarding colleague support – can significantly affect the wellbeing of an individual or a group of individuals. Moral support; professional support; structures; processes and supportive plans (within a school system) can all affect how an individual copes in a naturally stressful profession like teaching (Rogers, 2002b).

Colleague support is fundamentally concerned with meeting colleague needs as realistically and as meaningfully as possible. We best do this by *consciously* seeking to be aware of colleagues' espoused – rather than assumed – needs. In a consciously supportive school culture senior staff work within, and across, grade (and faculty) teams to 'factor in' colleague support; it is not left to mere chance. Most teachers, in most schools, can find some level of *ad hoc* moral support from one or two colleagues who can give that moral support, that 'coping edge' to the day. It may be a word of assurance; a chance to whinge (or 'moan-bond' as some of my colleagues call it); it may be a chance to sit and gain a bit of transitional perspective over a cup of tea ...

Moral support, though, is not enough by itself. Schools need to 'factor-in' opportunities, plans, processes, policies that seek to realistically meet colleagues' espoused needs. To do that we need to be aware of, and give a voice to, those needs.

For example, in some schools supposedly 'small' issues like flickering neon lights; doors that jam; inadequate furniture (ever had to 'scrounge' for chairs for a classroom?); poor staff toilets; poor organisational and communication processes are just some of the 'structural stressors' that staff face. Many of these structural/organisational stressors can (and should) be dealt with quickly. Letting them drag on (unattended) can be a daily irritant in an already stressful profession when we are seeking to teach (and manage) hard classes.

Where a school *consciously* affirms the value of a supportive colleague culture, staff know they are not 'battling on alone'. Most of all staff need to know that they will receive support when they ask, and are listened to (with respect), when conveying their needs. (See Appendix 1)

Offering support

How can we offer meaningful support – early – in the cycle of a teacher's struggle with a hard class? How can we approach the issue in a way that does not imply censure, or blame?

In some schools teachers will go for weeks, many weeks, struggling (even suffering) with a hard to manage class and only get any support when they finally break down at the end of term one. I have seen this many times in less consciously supportive schools.

Support may not be offered by senior staff because they believe that in such an offer they are implying that the teacher cannot cope, is ineffective or (worse) incompetent. Conversely, support may not be asked for by a teacher because they may think that they are perceived (by others) as ineffective or incompetent.

Supporting colleagues who struggle with a hard class

My colleagues and I have found the following approaches helpful in enhancing and enabling a supportive colleague culture:

1 A school-wide survey on colleague support is always helpful (Appendix 1). Focus questions enable a school-wide colleague response on the 'protocols of approach regarding teacher welfare and professional support'. In this way the issue is raised school-wide and everyone gets a chance to comment on this difficult issue. For example, we can preface the questions with the following: 'From time to time teachers struggle with a class well beyond the bad-day-syndrome. Support is available at our school from the confidential chat through to mentoring and teaming approaches. The problem is that some teachers will not ask for support because they feel that other teachers may think they are ineffective, or – conversley – they may not be aware or believe they have a problem. In these cases it is important that senior colleagues approach their fellow teachers to ascertain what the problem is, and offer appropriate support. We don't want to unnecessarily hurt a colleague's self-esteem. We want to give support and assistance for the welfare of both teacher and student.'

Question: If it was believed that a colleague had concerns or problems with their teaching and management, and there was evidence that a colleague is finding it very difficult to cope:
- How do you think that colleagues should be approached?
- What basic guidelines do we need to enable a support process to occur?

The responses normally cover issues such as:
- maintain confidentiality (Don't call out to the colleague in the staffroom, 'Can I see you in my office Period 6 for an interview about 8C?')
- provide an opportunity to share their perceptions, feelings and concerns about that class.
- put their problems in perspective or in context.
- show me – don't just tell me.

■ give me *time* to develop a plan with a supportive colleague.

2 Approaching a colleague when you know they are experiencing significant behaviour issues with a class is not easy:

■ Set up a meeting (pigeon hole note? private word?).

■ Tune in (briefly) to how colleagues might be thinking or feeling: 'You may be thinking ... or feeling ... about this meeting.' (They'll be anxious; they may even be feeling angry.)

■ Briefly share your concerns as you see them or know them from *reliable* feedback (avoid the overuse of 'it seems' or 'I think'). The person conducting the meeting will need to be sure of the facts of their colleague's situation and their 'struggle' (the ongoing rowdy classes, and the complaints from parents and even other teachers and students).

■ It is essential to be supportive and invitational in this feedback process and, above all, stay calm! This is the really hard point. *Some* colleagues can be annoying, infuriating even, with their avoidance behaviour, laziness, ineptitude, and avoidance behaviours. It will help to plan questions thoughtfully beforehand; especially with colleagues who 'go silent', who procrastinate or who get angry quickly. (See particularly Rogers 2002b)

As senior teachers, my colleagues and I are well aware that our colleague's sense of professional esteem is vulnerable when under daily, weekly, stress of a hard-to-manage class.

We need to be aware that they may have lost confidence in their ability to manage the class. One of the most unpleasant, even stressful, emotions for a teacher is that steady loss of confidence; that things will not, or cannot, get better.

Any offer of support seeks to reassure (not judge); 'allow' our colleagues to share their perspective; i.e. offer some immediate support but also factor-in some longer-term support that will enable the teacher to rebuild professional confidence and that goodwill essential to enabling a fresh start with a difficult to manage class.

Basic as it sounds (on paper), being prepared to listen is essential when we offer support. Perspective-taking is important. We can all probably remember a time when we lost some sense of 'control', or leadership, of a difficult class. It can be very dispiriting. It is important to acknowledge and affirm how it affects one's ability to cope at school.

Some colleagues will also raise issues outside of school which may be affecting their stress in the daily, professional, role. We need to be sensitive to such concerns but bring their focus back (supportively) to the issues at hand with the class group (or individual students) in question:

■ '*How do you see the situation ...?*'

■ '*How long has this been going on?*' (be specific wherever possible)

■   '*What have you sought to do so far? Has anything, at all, been helpful?*'
It is also crucial to be aware of any concerns about students who have been bullying the teacher. Harassment/bullying of a teacher needs to be addressed as
soon as other colleagues are aware it is occurring in a fellow colleague's class.
This is addressed at length later (p 185*f*).

■   Seek agreement with the colleague that what has been identified is what is
actually happening. Offer a *supportive* process as a means of assisting the
teacher longer-term to address their issue of concern.

3 One of the most helpful approaches (longer-term) is to set up a supportive mentorship of a fellow colleague. A colleague mentor is (normally) a fellow teacher
(within the school) who makes time to work with a teacher in the hard-to-
manage class. Using *team*-teaching approaches and non-judgmental
(descriptive) feedback a mentor can help raise perspective-taking with the hard-
to-manage class (or the 'catalytic student element'). They also act as a
supportive 'coach'; modelling and teaching behaviour leadership skills.

Of course such an approach needs to be elective and invitational. 'Forcing' a
mentor-option on a colleague will almost always be counter-productive. Senior
staff need to select such mentors thoughtfully: colleagues held in high regard
(by their collegial peers); skilled in behaviour leadership; effective and positive
communicators able to demonstrate empathy, focus, meaningful problem-
solving and supportive feedback.

Often a mentor-colleague will work with the colleague over several weeks
(even a whole term) one or two periods a week.

The mentor's role includes:

■   discussing the issues of concern about the hard class and helping the teacher
with perspective-taking.

■   working directly with the teacher in the classroom in a team-teaching
capacity. Often finding the timetable slots to do this is a challenge.
Mentoring is a labour-intensive approach to colleague support but *worth it
in the long run*.

■   Through team-teaching there is the heightened opportunity to observe a
fellow-teacher. These 'observations' are an initial feature of the *professional
self-awareness* that occurs in shared feedback after classroom teaching times.

■   The mentor, and 'mentee', use their shared observations to plan goals for
their own personal behaviour leadership; their discipline of the class group
(and individuals) and their teaching and management practices.

■   There is a conscious *coaching element* in this model of mentoring.
Sometimes a teacher cannot always ascertain – and emotionally comprehend – a given teaching or discipline practice, approach, or skill until they
see it *in the natural setting of the classroom*.

Nowhere is this more relevant than in behaviour leadership skills. I have sat with many colleagues, over tea or coffee, who have said (after a shared teaching session) '*Now I know what you mean!*' (relative to a given skill or practice).

Giving this level of support is labour-intensive, it is also naturally tiring for the colleague giving the support. If we have developed an invitational, supportive, trusting and professional relationship a lot can be learned – and gained through colleague-mentoring. The earlier such support is offered the more effective it is likely to be.

Shared struggle: case study

It is worth noting that *as a mentor* (in team-teaching) we too will naturally struggle with hard classes and challenging students (particularly in those critical first meetings).

Scott

In one such class I had a Year 7 student persistently calling out and making irritating (attentional) comments while I was engaged in whole-class teaching and learning. Mostly I *tactically* ignored such behaviour; a few times (when his comments were more excessive) I reminded him of our class rule about contributing and asking questions. He tried to argue with me several times. I refused to argue back. It wasn't easy! I reminded him of our class rule and continued (as calmly as I could) with the ebb and flow of whole-class teaching time. He leaned back in his chair, arms folded, sulking and muttering ('*Can't say nothing here …!*')

Later in the lesson, just as my colleague and I were moving around the room, Scott dragged his chair (past several other students) and plonked it in the middle of the U-shaped seating arrangement.

He then rocked backwards and forwards on his chair – 'notice me everyone'. I directed him back to his table. He refused and started rocking – more precociously now and singing, '*I'm not f—ing doing it! I'm not f—ing doing it!*'

I looked across at my colleague, she looked back with the pained eyes I had seen a few times during whole-class teaching time. I am sure she was saying, '*It's not just me is it Bill?!*'

I decided to direct him to time-out (the school has a well-developed time-out policy). He continued 'singing', making no eye-contact, '*I'm not f—ing going! I'm not f—ing going!*'

Power struggles are never easy but I have learned that I cannot simply control others. I can use my power (as an adult in a professional role) *for* and *with* others. All through the lesson I was well aware of the audience of peers and never more so than now (pp 4–5).

I walked across to my colleague and quietly asked her to calmly exit the whole class (row by row). If we cannot get a disruptive child away from his audience we direct the peer audience away from the child (p 115*f*).

I stood by the door (in case he did 'a runner' – that, too, has happened to me in the past). Even when the class (and teacher) had left, he paced around the room swearing, muttering *sotto voce* 'oaths and incantations'. Eventually he went under the computer table and started to cry. I crouched near him, and calmly, quietly, started to chat …

'A very damaged young lad' was how his teachers described him.

Talking with my colleague later (over a cup of tea) she said aloud what I had sensed, '*That class … Scott, David, Craig, Hayley … it's not just me is it?*'

'*No way is it "just you" – you saw how I struggled with the class. No way …*'

That admission (it not difficult to make at all!) was a boost to my colleague's professional esteem. We then worked together on a number of fronts to address the concerns we both had with the students she had mentioned.

Developing skills of confidence

Without in any way wanting to suggest that some teachers 'invite' a hard time from students, there is no question that within the dynamics of teacher–class behaviours some teachers portray indecisive and non-assertive behaviours that can significantly affect class dynamics and student behaviour. This is no new phenomenon in schools either. Back in the late 1950s I can recall a couple of teachers (both male) who had enormous problems managing the classes in which I was a student.

One of these teachers would walk into class sighing. He had unusually baggy pants and his shirt was often hanging out. His face looked a cross between weariness, puzzlement, confusion and anxiety. He couldn't find the chalk and he'd ask us in a 'wimpish' kind of voice: 'Where's the chalk, the chalk?' He'd often mutter, seemingly to himself. His voice wasn't clear – either in diction or range (and I'm not talking about loud). At times he seemed oblivious to us as he talked over or through the residual chatter. He was also very, very, boring. He'd shuffle a lot and seemed unprepared – at least as we compared him with other teachers. Students are very 'knowing' and practised at comparing and evaluating their teachers in terms of 'control', sense of humour, fairness (any favourites?), knowledge of their subject and provision of help, and also whether they embarrass you in front of your class mates. Will they follow up with their stated consequences? When this teacher got angry he really lost the plot. In fact some of the students worked out schemes to set him up and start him off. We gave him a hard time – from memory (1959). That practice hasn't changed either. Of course he didn't *deserve* it, but we didn't lose any sleep over it. That phenomenon is a hard *reality* of the teaching profession.

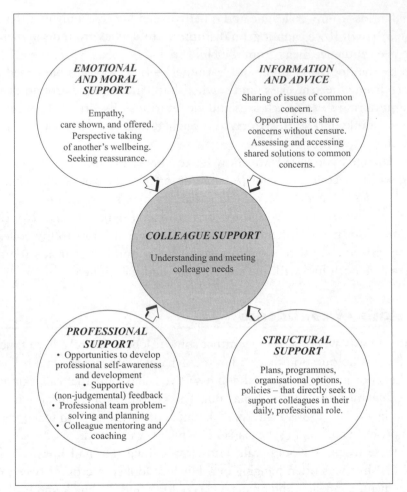

Figure 9.1

And that's the point. In the social reality of a school environment some students will pick up on a teacher's dress, non-verbal behaviour, patterns of speech; in fact *any* idiosyncrasies, especially confidence and assertion level. I'm not referring to aggression or loudness but the skill of assertion: the ability to convey one's needs and rights, the needs of the situation, or the needs of others, firmly, clearly and confidently.

When consciously addressing confidence in behaviour-leadership there are fundamental attributes and skills we need to develop. These skills are noted (earlier) in Chapter 5.

Teachers who are characteristically non-assertive and indecisive and lack confidence may well be in the wrong profession. However, if they wish to stay in teaching because they have a love of teaching and generally like working with children, they will need to develop skills of assertion and confidence.

They will also need to be able to convey some enthusiasm for their 'teaching subject' and be able to engage and sustain student interest and motivation. None of this is easy but *most* teachers learn the skills that enable confident teaching and behaviour leadership.

They will need, at times, to be able to convey and communicate frustration, and even anger, in assertive ways when managing student behaviour. These are skills a teacher can learn in terms of confident (not arrogant) teaching practice. The ability to fairly, appropriately and firmly communicate one's anger is not merely dependant on one's personality. One can learn to:

- differentiate; to get angry on issues that matter not on trifling matters. The skill, too, is knowing the difference between them: eg we would not normally say to a student *'I'm angry that you haven't done your homework'*, *'I'm angry that you haven't got the right school uniform on today ...'* (etc). We might be concerned about such issues as homework not done (or even irritated) but not angry. Anger is a 'big-league' emotion: it has significant 'emotional weight'. We need to be careful not to lose its 'moral and emotional currency' (Rogers 2002a).
- focus one's anger *briefly* (and assertively) to the behaviour, or issue, addressed.
- address the issue or behaviour without attacking the child.
- be aware of the peer audience when communicating anger to an individual.
- develop 'degrees' of assertion according to the context (particularly with threatening and abusive students).
- de-escalate emotional arousal (in the emotional moment when anger is present). We do this mostly by using a calm voice (without rushing the words) and calm, controlled, body language (see p 78). We may also need to calmly, firmly, direct a child to formal time-out.
- most of all *we* (as the adult) need to repair and rebuild with an individual (or a class group) where we have been angry.
  Even when our anger has been justified. We will still need to work with the child (or class) to repair and rebuild.

If a teacher has been bullied by students, it may not be enough to deal with and even punish the bullies. We also need to support our colleagues by enabling their skill development in the assertion of their rights to fair treatment. We need to skill teachers to confidently, assertively, confront 'bullying' students. We do this with children who are frequently cast in the role of victims, so why not with adults? Part of our natural hesitancy in giving this kind of assistance is any imputation of 'inadequacy' in our colleagues. If we can move the focus on to developing skills of confident behaviour leadership we are more likely to make positive change meaningful and possible.

Confidence is both an attitude and a 'composite' of certain skills and behaviours, each reinforcing the other. The key question to consider is: what do confident people look and sound like? For example, if I stand in front of a class with shoulders heavily bowed and uncertain eye contact, shuffling my feet, smiling nervously and speaking with an overly hesitant voice, I communicate what the non-verbal behaviour is modelling.

Students will – naturally – make inferences directly from our characteristic behaviour in the classroom. Our non-verbal behaviour is a significant variable in how our level, and degree, of confidence is communicated to others.

Some teachers are not aware of what their characteristic non-verbal behaviour is like; how they 'come across' as a teacher-leader. It can help to model to a colleague *characteristic* aspects of their non-verbal behaviour (eg non-assertive, unconfident, body language, or tone of voice). This is, of course, a very sensitive area of peer-coaching. It is essential (therefore) to ask permission beforehand, and explain the purpose of such 'modelling'. Often there is good-willed humour when colleagues become behaviourally aware of how they may be perceived by their students.

A key aspect of behaviour change is feedback – supportive (descriptive) feedback. Both the positive and the ineffective aspects of behaviour have to be addressed if successful change is going to occur. If colleagues are not aware of where their behaviour is ineffective, they may not be able to see a need for particular skills, or finetune the change process. For example, I've worked with colleagues whose posture, movement, and stance (during whole-class teaching time) actually 'contribute' to class entertainment. For example, pacing 'to and fro' at the front of the room during whole-class teaching time; or rocking up and down on one's heels in (perhaps) unconscious nervousness. Such behaviour in a classroom often 'telegraphs' kinaesthetic energy to the more restless students in the class. When I have modelled such behaviour to a colleague (one-to-one) they are almost always unaware of such unhelpful kinaesthetic energy and how it 'stirs up' their more restless students. The skills redolent in communicating calmness enable a teacher to be more consciously aware of their 'positional place' and whole-group communication, during whole-class teaching time (see p 77*f*). If colleagues are unaware that the way they stand, move and gesture is a factor in their management it will need to be gently pointed out (within the professional one-to-one mentoring relationship). Even where teachers stand – or sit – can have an effect on student behaviour. I've worked with secondary teachers who sit down and do all their teaching from the 'sitting position'. This is less than helpful with more physically restless students whose behaviour and general motivation is enhanced by a teacher *standing up* and visually scanning the room, using a blend of visual teaching (on the whiteboard) and thoughtful class questioning and dialogue. In other words, *engage* the students! When I've gently mirrored one-to-one features of a teacher's characteristic behaviour that is adversely affecting student behaviour they are often surprised – even unaware: 'do I really do that?' In peer-coaching this enables professional self-awareness.

There is little point in observational team-teaching if there is not a clear, shared, understanding about the feedback and coaching elements of mentoring. If, for example, a colleague observes a 'successful' lesson they may not realise why it was 'successful'.

- *what* made it so positive in tone and feel? (Beyond teacher personality?)
- *how*, and why, were the students more responsive, more engaged?
- *how* did the teacher communicate calmness?
- *how* did the teacher *initiate, and sustain*, whole-class attention and focus in the initial first three to five minutes? What did they *actually say and do*?
- *what* did the teacher *actually* say (and do) that seemed to de-escalate conflict with the more argumentative and challenging students? (See Fig. 9:2)

In peer-mentorship my colleagues and I consciously reflect on our characteristic corrective discipline language. My colleagues and I often consciously work on what we call 'cognitive scripting'. Planning key phrases so that when we are under the natural pressure to discipline we are more likely to use language constructs consistent with our aims.

Confidence comes with experience, yet experience needs to be useful and *informed*. Confidence also needs some success, as well as the learning that comes from failure. Some *key skills in confidence* include the following:

- Standing relaxed but upright, with feet apart (not astride) and not wobbling or shuffling from one foot to the other.
- Scanning the room with our eyes, confidently, when in the whole-class teaching phase of the lesson. Develop effective eye-scanning skills.
- Avoiding a 'wobbly' head. Focus and rest the gaze ahead during scanning of the class group.
- When speaking to individuals we look in their eyes, with *momentary* relief now and then – it's not a stare (both in whole-class, and on-task phase of the lesson).
- We speak clearly, using tactical pausing and a relaxed voice where possible.
- Display an open face (not deadpan) and smile when appropriate.
- Have a flow and lift to the voice tone.
- Use open body language (not tensed up with arms folded tightly or legs crossed).
- Open hand gesture (not pointing finger or gesticulating) – particularly on those occasions where we need to be assertive.

Developing skills: key questions

It can help to model these skills in the one-to-one setting as well as 'modelling' in a classroom setting. Each skill – in itself – may be 'small' but it is the 'global nature' of the skills – together – that convey a sense of confidence present in teacher leadership behaviour.

N.B. I have worked with some colleagues who have a significant lack of social skill 'across the board' – not just with children(!). Teaching is a profession that relies on our ability to relate, engage, motivate, encourage, take the perspective of others (their needs and moods) – in short, people who have a high 'emotional intelligence'.

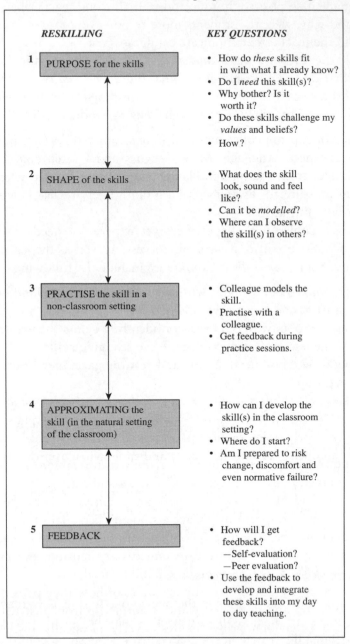

Figure 9.2

A (more) common belief is that group management skills are simply a natural gift. You either have it or you don't. Our evidence does not support this belief. Its most damaging feature is that teachers who have difficulty controlling classes tend to put this down to personal inadequacy rather than to a lack of particular skills which can be acquired through training or advice from colleagues.

The most talented, 'natural' teachers may need little training or advice because they learn so quickly from experience. At the other extreme, there are a few teachers for whom training and advice will not be properly effective because their personalities do not match the needs of the job. *It is clear, however, that the majority of teachers can become more effective classroom managers as a result of the right kinds of training, experience and support* (author's italics).

Teachers have tended to stay out of each other's classrooms and not to talk about their own discipline problems. Too often teachers do not seek help because it feels like an admission of incompetence, and they do not offer it because it feels like accusing a colleague of incompetence. As a result the tradition of classroom isolation persists in many schools.

The beliefs that either group management skills should not be necessary or that they cannot be learned seem to be traditional in part of the profession. Our evidence suggests that these beliefs contribute significantly towards teacher stress. This is further increased by the more widespread tradition of classroom isolation. We see these beliefs or traditions as barriers to good teaching. They should be removed as quickly as possible. From Elton et al (1989), *The Elton Report*, p 69, recommendations 13–16.

Personal, interactive, skills relate to the following:

- A teacher relates to students in particular ways, for example, by the use of first names, the use of greetings, pleasantness of tone and appropriate firmness when necessary.
- Many non-verbal skills are involved in daily relational interactions: such as use of eye contact, body language, tone of voice and clarity.
- Movement and proximity awareness are important. Some teachers are not aware of how to respectfully engage a student's personal space; especially when the student may be in potential conflict with the teacher. For example, coming 'face-on' to a student may create unnecessary tension, especially when the teacher has closed fists pressing down and a facial glare.
- Some teachers are not aware, for example, of how they pace the front of the room, 'bob' up and down, or wander during up-front instructional teaching time. Such behaviour easily 'invites' overly physically restless students to unnecessarily visually track the teacher and not really listen.

- It is important to keep the flow of the lesson smooth and not jerky, as when the teacher is over-addressing discipline issues (Kounin 1970; Rogers 1998). One of the more important behaviours that signal confidence is the ability to 'regain composure' quickly when one has made a mistake or briefly lost one's train of thought, or even composure. It is the ability not to be easily flummoxed. It can be as basic as the annoying tenth announcement on the intercom, something highly exciting happening outside, or the five students who came into the room (without knocking) asking if they can talk with the class about the coming school fete.
- Non-verbal behaviour such as *tactical* ignoring (as distinct from blind ignorance) should be used when necessary (pp 180/183*f*). I've worked with teachers who appear not to know what to tactically ignore in a student's behaviour and what to attend to. They often attend to behaviours that can be tactically ignored and then ignore behaviours they should address. Knowing the difference is a skill.
- It will also help to conduct school-wide professional development in this area with *all* staff.

Organisational factors

It is often necessary to address organisational and management factors such a physical seating and grouping of students; how the teacher *actually* sustains the whole-class teaching time; organisation and pacing of the lesson and *transitions* between whole-class teaching time and on-task learning time (Chapter 5).

Without overwhelming our colleagues too much, too soon, we can help them sharpen their professional self-awareness, and focus, in these areas. We can help them to see the value of particular approaches and skills, and with practice and feedback our colleagues learn to approximate those skills in the natural setting of their classrooms.

One of the challenges inherent in any new learning is the *natural discomfort*, even stress, of new learning: how we approximate and contextualise skills in the normative, natural, setting. This is where the on-going support of a mentor coach can be invaluable. It is important to point out that in all new learning, or relearning, there is natural discomfort until what is 'consciously less effective' becomes *consciously* effective and even (at times) 'unconsciously effective'.

Teacher beliefs, attitudes and change

Teacher A: Mr Smith has just 'picked up' a challenging class. It has been his first lesson with them. He is new to this school. He feels nervous but is determined to 'start strong'. He sensed this was a 'challenging class' as soon as he saw them sauntering outside Room 15. There was the initial play-punching, several students with hats on, several students chewing gum. 'Can he hear music? Walkman? I-pod?'

'*Right, get that chewy in the bin, and those hats off.*' Before he 'lets' them into class he asks a boy if he has a Walkman. '*Have you got a Walkman?*' – '*No!*' Mr Smith is annoyed by the response, the tone, the manner of this student. '*Don't talk to me like that!*' '*Like what?!*' (The student takes umbrage.) '*I haven't got a Walkman, alright?!*' The teacher is clearly, visibly annoyed by the boy's manner. '*Don't you speak to me like that! Right – get into class all of you …*'

As the class enters he notices a couple of girls rearrange the class seating. He marches (yes marches) over. '*What's your name?*' he says to one of the girls.

'*I don't need to tell you my name!*' She frowns, leans back in her seat, looks at her classmates, and then grins.

'*Who do you think you're talking to!*' He is *really* annoyed now; in fact, he is angry. This is only the first few minutes of class time. It does not get any better …

Teacher B. A similar class grouping: Mrs Brown notices the hats, chewy and *hears* a Walkman. As the students shuffle together outside their English class (day one), she waits for some natural settling. She quickly, calmly, reminds the restless boys (playfully, and annoyingly testosteronically bonding): '*Fellas, fellas (…) playtime is over.*' One of them calls back, '*We're just mates.*' '*I'm sure you are,*' she replies, '*Playtime's over and we're going into a classroom.*' They grin; a last punch. She goes to the door and says to the group, '*Good morning. Before we go in I notice a few hats on, and some chewy and a Walkman or 'I-pod'.*' Her *descriptive reminder* is enough for a Year 8 class to work out what is meant.

She has been pleasant, confident, firm (without sounding 'bossy'). The brief corridor settling has not taken long. It has been worth it.

The class are quite restless as they enter and settle (of a sort) in their preferred seating. Melissa and Kayla try moving the furniture – again – in this class.

Mrs Brown moves around the room to create a sense of calmness before *formally* beginning the lesson from the front of the room (pp 21 and 78).

She name-checks first as she comes alongside the two girls. '*Good morning … what's your name please?*' Melissa replies 'playfully', '*What's your name?*' Mrs Brown *tactically* ignores the attentional poseur (at this point) and replies, '*My name is Mrs Brown. I'm your English teacher. What's your name please?*' '*I don't have to tell you my name.*' The student mutters this quite loudly (without eye contact) as she looks around for peer-approval.

'*I'm not speaking to you in a rude tone of voice.*' Mrs Brown is calm, polite, clear, respectful. Not easy.

'*What's rude?*' (Melissa mutters, and grins again to her friends.)

'*I'm not speaking to you in a disrespectful tone of voice, I don't expect you to speak to me disrespectfully.*' She tactically ignores Melissa's sighing, pouting, raised eyes, and folded arms.

She keeps the focus of this brief engagement on the *primary* rather than the 'secondary' non-verbal behaviour of the student. She asks again, '*What's your name please?*' '*Melissa,*' she adds – in a muttered aside – 'if you have to know.' [If the girl had refused to give her name a second time Mrs. Brown would have focussed on the behaviour of moving the furniture and followed the student up later (p 107).]

Mrs Brown *tactically* ignores this muttered aside, and refocuses the two girls to the issue at hand – the changing of the seating arrangement. She could have chosen to ignore it but has made the judgment that loudly dragging chairs and tables across the back of the room is inappropriate (even on day one).

'*I want you both to move the furniture back over there.*' Her tone, and manner, is quietly assertive, confident – yet pleasant.

'*But we want to sit here with our friends.*'

'*I'm sure you do.*' The teacher briefly tunes-in (*partial* agreement) '*However the seating arrangement stays in the rows.*' She points to the vacated row.

'*Yeah, well other teachers don't care where we sit anyway.*' Mrs. Brown does not argue, or seek to verify this. She quietly adds:

'*I can check that with the other teachers and the principal. In this class the seating arrangement is in rows.*'

Melissa gets up, pushes her chair back noisily. '*Alright … we'll sit there if you want*!' They drag their chairs off huffily. Mrs Brown walks away giving them take-up-time. Again, she *tactically* ignores the huffing and puffing (the 'secondary behaviours'). She is well aware that the audience of peers has watched, and heard, this brief exchange. She is also aware that the class is making early inferences about her leadership behaviour.

Mrs Brown has learned not to argue with students about their behaviour (tempting though it is). She is aware of the attentional power-play here and the audience of peers. If the girls refuse a second time to co-operate, she will clarify the (deferred) consequence and leave the girls with the clear understanding that 'if they chose not to move the furniture back they will need to stay back at the close of the lesson.'

N.B. When giving *deferred* consequences it is important to avoid making it sound like a 'threat': '*If you don't move that furniture now I'll …!!*'

When we *clarify a consequence* (a deferred consequence) we are actually putting the responsibility directly onto the student to own (and be responsible for) their 'choice' of behaviour within the fair, school, rules.

Many, many times I have said to students with mobile phones, Walkmans, I-pods (etc) in class; to '*put them away in their bag or on my table*' (directed choice). Most respond with moans and sighs! Some will say '*No – why should I, other teachers don't care if we ...*' At this point I will *clarify* the consequence (a deferred consequence). '*If you choose not to put it away I'll have to follow it up with you later.*' In response to such a direction I have had some students sulkily respond with folded arms and an: '*I don't care!*' It is enough (at this point) to calmly add, '*I care*' and walk away leaving the student with the 'consequential choice'. If they continue on listening to the Walkman (or whatever they are playing with) it will be important to carry through with the fair, *reasonable* and respectful certainty later. Fiddling with Walkmans; 'I-pods'; mobile phones is annoying. Most students – when reminded of the rule, or given a directed 'choice' – will put them away. If they do not the deferred consequential choice is more effective, in the long run, than forcing the student to hand it over, eg:

Teacher: '*Right, give that to me now. Come on, give it to me.*'
Student: '*No, I'll put it away if I **have** to!*'
Teacher: '*You won't put it away, you will give it to me – now!*'
Student: '*I **said** I'll put it away – alright!*'
Teacher: '*If you don't give it to me now you can get out of my class!*'

Student pushes chair back – marches off, out of the door, calling back to the teacher, '*I'm going – anyway. This is a sh-t class!*'

If you tune into this teacher's self-talk (relative to this incident) you may well hear: '*Children **should not** be rude!*', '*Children **should do what I say** – without arguing!*', '*Good teachers **must be able to control** their students!*'

Our self-talk is part of our overall behaviour and has a significant effect on both our emotional state and our coping abilities.

If we tune into Mrs Brown's characteristic self-talk we may hear something like: '*Well, I'm annoyed by their rudeness and their behaviour, I don't like it ... but I'll avoid unnecessary confrontation and clarify the choices to these girls ...*'

Of course we are not always aware of our *characteristic* self-talk. It can have a significant effect on how we perceive, feel, and respond in situations where we are under stress.

Mr Smith, in contrast, has very demanding self-guiding speech:
- '*Children **should not** be rude!*' (they are; it is annoying, unpleasant, but; sometimes they are ...)
- '*Children should not answer back!*' (they do).
- '*Children should do what I say the first time!*' (they do not – well, not always).

Mr Smith may be unaware that his characteristic explanatory style, how he *explains* stressful situations, is often couched in demands ... '*Children must...*', '*I should be able to control these children ...'*

When social reality behaves differently to what we demand, the cognitive demand can be as stressful as the event itself and sap the psychological energy essential when working with challenging students.

As Martin Seligman (1990) has observed (in his studies on *learned helplessness* and *learned optimism*) one's characteristic explanatory style has a significant effect on one's emotional state and consequent behaviour under stress. He notes that 'habits of thinking' about setbacks, difficult and stressful events and personal failure actually *affect the events themselves.* 'Our thoughts are not merely reactions to events; they change what ensues ... the very thought "Nothing I do matters" prevents us from acting' (1990 p 7). Such thinking critically affects how we cope – for example – with failure.

I work with some teachers who – in stressful situations – will latch onto the most *permanent and pervasive* explanations for their struggle or 'failure'. '*It's all my fault.*' '*I'll never get it right.*' '*I'll never turn this around.*' Or '*It's all the kid's fault.*' '*They're all animals ...*'. '*They never listen ...*'. (Forgetting, of course, the 60% of students who are reasonably co-operative if given the chance.)

Such self-talk has a self-directing function as well as 'explanatory effect'. It discounts all the positive aspects of our teaching, our effort, (or it discounts the behaviour of the 60% of students and over-focuses on the 40% of difficult students *as if it were all the class who were horrible ...*)

Instead of failure being seen as an isolated event, a *temporary* setback (even a very stressful, temporary, setback), some teachers will 'globalise' their experience as '*It's all my fault, it will never change ...*' Reality, of course, is rarely that fixed. When we *over-focus* on a negative, stressful, event, or make *unreasonable* demands about social reality (eg: '*These children must do what I say ... they shouldn't answer back!*'), we allow 'bad' events, and experiences, undue influence because they do not match our cognitive demands.

When we look for *temporary* and *specific* causes for stressful events we limit the pervasive effect that those stressful events can have on our life. If we perceive that normative reality (of 8D, 9E, 10E) as redolent of *all* teaching, it will contribute to general feelings of jadedness and pessimism. This often (in turn) affects our professional self-esteem.

We are not always aware of the damaging effect of 'psychological junk mail' (Rogers 1992). We can, however, learn to tune-in to our characteristic self-talk, our internal speech; we can learn to be aware of our characteristic 'explanatory style' for stressful events (Seligman 1990). That awareness can then enable us to dispute unrealistic, and negative, self-talk and refocus our thinking and behaviour. As we do this we begin to cope more realistically, and less stressfully, under pressure.

In mentorship settings we often discuss the *skills* of disputing negative thinking where it is *overly demanding* of self or others.

As we learn to dispute inflexible aspects of self-talk (those inconsistent with social reality) we can learn to approach challenging classes less stressfully, more realistically and optimistically. This is more than mere positive thinking, it is 'non-negative thinking' (Seligman, Ibid. p 221).

We do not simply deny, or explain away, stressful reality (that is foolish); we reframe it by the way we think about and explain it. This has significant implications for developing new skills and behaviour change. Changing (our) behaviour is not merely changing belief before we change behaviour – it is working with both aspects of (our) behaviour; cognition and action.

Skills and self-talk

Some teachers will have poor take-up of behaviours skills if their *characteristic, explanatory style is overly demanding or self-defeating*.

A skill like *tactical* ignoring (for example) is a difficult skill. '*What sorts of behaviour ought I to tactically ignore?*' '*How?*' '*What do I do if the behaviour persists?*'

We often use *tactical* ignoring for attentional behaviours (such as when a student pouts, sighs, rolls their eyes or 'tut-tuts' or mutters and moans) because we have asked them to do something terribly difficult like go back to their seat when they are wandering aimlessly and task-avoiding.

We will often *tactically* ignore the low-level whingeing, and *sotto voce* moaning of the student en route …

Like most behaviour leadership skills, *tactically* ignoring is a context dependent skill. We would never ignore blatant rudeness, but we could consciously – and purposefully – ignore the 'rolling of eyes' in response to what we say when we address the 'primary' behaviour (the rudeness). We often *tactically* ignore attentional, non-verbal, 'secondary' behaviours because such 'ignoring' enables the teacher to keep a clearer, calmer, focus (in discipline) on the main, 'primary', behaviour. This will be difficult, however, with teachers who believe that '*Children should not be rude*', they '*should not answer back*' or that good teachers '*Must control the students at all times*!'

Such 'beliefs' (expressed in *characteristic* internal speech) will be in conflict (emotionally and cognitively) with 'ignoring' of a child's behaviour. The teacher may well believe he has to control *every aspect* of the behaviour transaction and *should not* 'ignore' 'sighing', 'pouting' (etc) because children *should not* be rude.

Such beliefs have more than an 'explanatory' function, they create stress – in concert – with *perceived* needs to control all aspects of the situation.

It is important, therefore, to be aware of, and 'tune-in' to, one's self-talk. It is also important to dispute and to challenge, untenable and *unreasonable* explanations and self-talk. This is a skill that can be learned. Self-talk, after all, is behaviour – cognitive behaviour. Realistic, re-appraised, self-talk is a way of remapping our stressful reality. It is not the only way but it is an important way.

The process of change often follows a familiar pattern:

1 *Awareness of a need.* This may even include some awareness or natural hesitancy about change; about what it might necessitate. I have even had teachers say, '*It's easier, "more comfortable", to shout. At least I don't have to **think** about what I ought to say!*'

   Typical questions teachers will ask about skills (presented in mentorship programmes) are: 'Why do I need this skill?', 'Who says this way of doing things is better, 'right', necessary …?', 'Why?', 'How will these skills actually help me in 8D, 9C?'

   This last question is not always based in utility – some teachers want to see the values attached to particular practices and skills (see Fig: 9:2).

2 *Awareness of the skills and practices* (in the natural context of the classroom). Questions raised have included '*What does the skill/approach look, sound and feel like?*' In the mentor/'mentee' relationship, colleagues observe the target skills in the context where we seek to develop them, the classroom itself. Peer-coaching allows a colleague to see; hear; sense and feel behaviour leadership skills – 'in-situ' and in context. We can then consciously discuss (later; one-to-one) what *tactical* ignoring really involves; how effective is the 'language of discipline' we are seeking to develop; how effectively are we managing tense and conflictual situations? When colleagues see these skills 'in operation', in the classroom, they more fully comprehend and appreciate why these skills are the focus of the mentorship journey.

3 *Willingness to experiment, to take risks, with behaviour change.* If a teacher is half-hearted, unwilling, unconcerned about their need to (and for) change then the effort applied to new practices will create resentment. '*I knew it wouldn't work.*' Any meaningful (and purposeful) change obviously takes time and reflective effort. With practice, and support, colleagues can overcome normative struggle (and failure) when pursuing change. We rarely get anything right the first time. In the cycle of change we need to *de*habituate as well as *re*habituate. This is why *on-going* practice and supportive colleague feedback is crucial to mentor-coaching.

It is important that the mentor affirms, and encourages, positive changes in their colleague's behaviour leadership practice. It is also important that the 'mentee' acknowledges and affirms 'things are different now, better, because I have changed in these ways ...' Professional self-awareness and reflection need to become habit. There is no question that effective teachers are reflective teachers.

N.B. Colleague-mentoring can become a normative feature of a school's on-going professional development. It should not be merely seen as a supportive option for 'struggling teachers'. Teaching is one of the few professions (these days) that does not include mentoring, and mentor-coaching, as a *normative* feature of professional development.

Bullying (students who bully teachers)

Case study

It was the ghastly note that finally pushed her 'over the edge'. For many weeks she had been bottling up her anxiety and her frustration – she had hoped it would go away. It didn't. A Year 9 student was bullying her – almost 'stalking' her. The way he stared at her and eyeballed her, and the 'accidental look' as he walked past her. Then it was the comments – the snide *sotto voce* comments about her clothes and her physical appearance. At other times it was the comments he made in class, out loud, that could garner the pathetic laughter of his little collusive peer–coterie. Most of his comments were made in the classroom when others were around so that the teacher (who was already clearly flustered and unfocused when this student was in the room) couldn't always be sure who said it.

Like most bullies he perceived in the teacher a weakness of character or personality that he could manipulate to his advantage. He had it in his head that this teacher was 'fair game' and even deserved it.

He even 'legitimised' his behaviour as 'having a bit of fun' (the typical, gutless, mitigation of the bully).

He watched – each class period – to see the effect of his 'look', his words, his manipulation of members of the class to join in with his bullying. Like a 'gun' firing psychological bullets he could – effectively – sabotage a lesson by sending out non-verbal cues, and signals, to classmates who would collude with him in disrupting a lesson; refuse to comply with teacher requests; laugh at the teacher when she got upset or angry. He felt the 'power' of *control*. That is the awful nature of bullying behaviour; the abuse of relational power.

The teacher had allowed his bullying to continue: the insidious comments; the non-verbal, suggestive, simulations; the 'whispered' corridor comments; the group 'going quiet' and then laughing as she walked past.

She had hope it would go away – it did not.

She blamed herself. It was not her fault.

No one *deserves* to be bullied.

But the note was the culmination. She was sure she had seen him pass it. It was disgusting. She had found the note (by accident?) on the floor after class. She'd recognised his writing though he hadn't signed it.

She took it to the co-ordinator after weeks of personal torment. Finally something was done. The student was confronted and suspended. By then the psychological damage had been done.

Individual and group bullying

Bullying is not accidental. It is not the occasional funny, ill-thought or stupid (if hurtful) comment about other people; their appearance; their voice; their mannerisms and so on. Bullying is the calculated and intentional desire to hurt someone else. It is the *repetitive* nature of bullying that makes it so insidious and damaging. The purposeful selective desire to psychologically control a situation so that another person is hurt in the process.

The bully finds (and looks for) a 'target' and then finds something about the victim they can exploit. Bullies will assess, through the responses of the victim, whether they have found a 'target' to bully; to harass. If there is a non-assertive response to bullying comments or gestures (the victim looks pained, upset, confused, worried, anxious or fearful), the bullies know they have succeeded. Bullies may even believe they are justified in what they do because they believe the victim is weak, stupid and 'different' – not like them. When a teacher appears to accept, or 'ignore', the comment, the taunt, the suggestive body language, then the teacher is perceived as powerless. The bullying will 'most often' continue.

I've seen male teachers put up with appalling comments about their clothes, their person, their perceived life preferences ('You're a poofter') and laugh it off nervously in the hope it will go away or (worse) try to get on the side of the students. All that happens is that the bully repeats their behaviour because the effect, and response, they seek is confirmed by the victim's response. Bullying has to be confronted if it is going to stop. The earlier this is done the better it is for all.

Group bullying occurs when a significant number in the class emotionally support, collude, or play 'patsy', to the bully's comments or behaviour. A bully who is allowed to become a key powerbroker and 'work the group', can make life 'hell' for a teacher:

- Rumours are often spread about the teacher.
- The class laughs when missiles are thrown.
- The collusive bullies laugh at verbal put-downs of a teacher by a student, and will even laugh at verbal abuse.

Bullies need the collusive support of other class members in order to 'validate' or 'excuse' their bullying behaviour. They seek the confirmatory laughter; the acquiescence and perceived 'approval' of class peers. If there is no 'approval', no peer-acceptance, a bully would rarely choose to behave the way they do.

Bullies, of course, 'select' their target (a teacher who they believe will not fight back or assert the right to respect or follow it up with senior teacher support). They make sure their bullying behaviour is indirect so that they can plead ignorance ('Me? Me? What did I do?').

The picture I have painted is bleak, but it happens in some schools. It happens for the following reasons:

- Some teachers tolerate it. Even some senior teachers!
- Some teachers do not know what to do.
- Some teachers are not supported, because there is no direct 'evidence'.

The worst comment I've heard from some teachers is, 'They [the bullied colleagues] bring it on themselves.' To suffer implied collegial blame, or 'fault', only adds indignity to the degrading survivalism of teachers who are being bullied.

No one deserves to be bullied. Teacher bullying, like any bullying, is wrong because it affects the fundamental rights of safety (physical and emotional safety) and fair treatment.

Dealing with the bullying of teachers

Preventative measures

Bullying should never be tolerated, excused, or played down. It is crucial that a school has a clear policy framework within which any bullying is addressed. *The central aim is that we seek to create (and sustain) a safe environment for staff and students; not just physical safety but psychological safety.*

Policy and practice will need to address what constitutes bullying, what the due processes are for addressing bullying and how we support victims of bullying.

- *Bullying.* The school policy needs to state exactly what bullying is, especially in its most common form – psychological harassment. Students will need to recognise that they are responsible – and accountable – for behaviours that are *calculated* to hurt (the snide comments; the ambiguous non-verbal behaviours; the missile throwing; the pretence to spit or vomit when a teacher walks past; the holding of the nose; the 'passive power struggles'; the stirring-up of the other students; the spreading of rumours about the teacher and so on).
- *Due process.* Any policy should outline clearly the sorts of unacceptable behav-

iours that constitute harassment (bullying), encourage the reporting of what is really happening, and give the assurance of a supportive hearing and the setting-up of procedures to confront the perpetrator(s). Due process should also outline the sorts of consequences that bullying will entail, including (in serious cases) suspension or expulsion. Many schools use the term *harassment* in their policies rather than 'bullying' alone to highlight the more common psychological aspects of bullying behaviour. One of the more difficult aspects of due process with bullies is confirming these behaviours as fact and, more importantly, establishing that the student's motivation is designed to calculatedly hurt rather than seeing it as 'having fun'.

One of the more effective ways to address the issue of harassment is to *empower the victim* (in a bullying situation) by confronting the bully(ies) directly (in a one-to-one setting with a senior colleague facilitating). The victim explains specifically what it is the student is doing that is hurtful; how such behaviour is affecting the teaching and learning (and welfare) of the class and the teacher; why it is unacceptable and that it must stop. This assertive clarification of how student behaviour is affecting teacher–class dynamics is a very powerful way to remove power from bullies by exposing the hidden reality of the behavioural dynamics. Bullying students trade in secrecy from other adults who they know will make their behaviour stop. The facilitation of such a meeting is crucial. A senior teacher will facilitate this process, keep records and evaluate outcomes. The earlier this process is established the more effective it will be. Where bullying is left unchecked for weeks or even months, the victim is so traumatised that they have lost any psychological will or courage to confront the perpetrators.

Addressing bullying/harassment: a whole-school approach

The school can do the following:

■ Address bullying from a school-wide rights/responsibility focus. The clear policy perspective has to be the right to safety and fair treatment. A published anti-harassment policy puts bullying into its proper perspective. Bullying is not the occasional stoush between a student and a teacher; it is not the task avoidance or task refusal that comes from bad-day syndrome, or the occasional power struggles that exist in classrooms; it is not the bad-day muttered swear word from students with low-frustration tolerance; nor is it students clowning around from time to time. It is the selective and *repeated* harassment – the repeated unpleasantness to those who find it hard to address such behaviour or to defend them-selves. If bullies are not confronted early, decisively and assertively, they reconfirm their bullying status by a continuation of hurtful behaviour.

- Raise general awareness about the nature and behaviour of harassment and the role of the 'peer-audience' (and their responsibility). Schools often include the issue of harassment (bullying) as part of their human relations curriculum, raising key questions with students such as: What do we really mean by bullying? (This is to bring the more common definition of bullying into its more general expression of intimidation, threat and harassment rather than physical hurt alone.) Why do people bully? What do they get out of it (what are they trying to achieve)? Who has ever been bullied? How do people feel when they are bullied? How does it affect their life and their time at school? How do you think bullies feel? What can we do to stop bullying? What consequences are appropriate for bullying? How can we support victims of bullying?

- Hold class meetings on bullying. It can be helpful for a senior teacher to run a classroom meeting on the topic with a class 'suspected' of bullying a teacher. By raising the issue of bullying/harassment *generally* and inviting genuine responses across a grade/class a teacher can point out that 'having fun like this' (be specific about the harassing behaviours) is not a game; it is not funny for the person on the receiving end; and it has to stop and why it has to stop. It is also important to discuss the issue of harassment and the law with older students.

- Students, too, need a due process to address poor teaching; unfair marking; inconsistent and unfair management practices; especially students who have been unfairly targeted by some teachers. Before a class gets into some kind of perceived moral payback (class sabotage), it will help in such classes to pursue a class-meeting approach to give a voice to teacher and students alike to clarify and refocus their purpose for being together as a class group (p 33f). Giving a lecture alone is not enough. A class meeting combined with individual student conferences can see a halt in any *suspected* harassment behaviour in the class.

- Bullying is a *learned* behaviour; a matter of choice. Of course, such behaviour choices are the results of twisted logic. By having an education programme that explores the issue through values, beliefs and behaviour, the majority ethic is heard and upheld, and the bully's world view becomes the minority. Many schools run general classroom meetings on the issue of bullying as part of an overall 'human-relations education programme.' I recall having a classroom meeting last year where I spoke to a high school class about how they had per-sistently mistreated their teacher. I said that 'no teacher deserved this and that their teacher had a life – she could have been their sister, aunt or mum. She was a person who had a right to be treated with basic respect and basic dignity'. Because I had a good working relationship with the class I felt (and came to see) their behaviour was more than inappropriate – it was wrong. Full stop. I had given the class a chance to explain how they had perceived the situation and, together, we worked to bring restitution to their behaviour. They wrote an apology, and representative class members took the apology (on behalf of the class) to share with the teacher in question. She was gracious enough to accept it in good faith; it was a key factor in a fresh-start with that class.

■ *Always* report suspected bullying behaviour. An essential feature of due process is reporting suspected bullying behaviour. Bullying flourishes in a climate of secrecy or ambiguity of intent; as far as adults might perceive it. It is not a secret from a student's peers however – peer 'approval' is needed for the bully to retain their peer status. Research on schools that are described as 'high' and 'low' in bullying incidents indicates that a key factor in low incidences of bullying is a climate of safe reporting and the belief that one will be taken seriously and that something will be done (see Smith & Thompson 1991, and Rogers 2006). I have worked with teachers who believe (sometimes mistakenly) that if they report their experiences of harassment they won't be taken seriously. Because of the apparent ambiguity of aspects of student-to-teacher bullying it may merely be taken as the teacher being unable to manage a class well; having poor classroom control; or being weak or inefficient or (worse) incompetent. I have known some colleagues put up with continual harassment by an individual or a class for months until they break down in the staff room or the office ('I didn't want to cause any trouble!'). If we suspect harassment of *any kind* is occurring within a colleague's class (or even outside in the playground environment), we have a moral obligation to offer support and to assure the colleague that it can be addressed decisively and supportively. By allowing suspected (or known) harassment to continue we confirm its 'social legitimacy'.

Victim–perpetrator conference

One of the effective processes noted earlier is that of confronting the perpetrator, or suspected perpetrator, directly:

■ Having discussed the issue of student harassment/bullying with a senior colleague, the victim identifies the perpetrator(s) or suspected perpetrator(s). The *specific* bullying is noted down before the meeting (in writing) – what the student has been saying, doing and 'suggesting'; its frequency; its effect on the class.

■ The senior colleague sets up a formal meeting for each student named by the colleague.

■ It can help (with teachers who lack confidence) to rehearse what to say to the student(s) at the meetings and even write it down. It can also help to consider (beforehand) whether the facilitator might 'mirror' some of the bully's non-verbal behaviour; to emphasise exactly what is meant by *bullying behaviour*. Many bullies do not regard their non-verbal behaviour as 'bullying'.

A senior colleague can add moral authority to the conference process and indicate how serious the issue is being treated by the school administration. This approach is particularly suited to situations where students' behaviour is ambiguous or where they discount their behaviour saying what they are doing is 'just having fun'; that they weren't the only one (diminished responsibility); that they were bored in that class; that they don't like the subject or that they think the teacher is a lousy teacher.

When setting up an interview/conference it is important to meet with the perpetrators one at a time. If there are several perpetrators in a class group, they will shift blame, 'laugh it off' and even back up each other. In short they have diminished responsibility *as a group*. This is why such behaviour can be difficult to address with a whole class of students.

The accountability-conference is normally conducted as follows:

1 The senior colleague, as facilitator, sits facing the student and explains that they are very concerned about a number of behaviours in class such as … The facilitator – at this point – refers to the written account of what the bully has been specifically saying and doing (about their teacher).

  The tone of this meeting is serious and formal; but conducted with conscious respect. This is no place for tempting vilification of the student. We are there to address his behaviour – not simply to 'attack' him.

2 The class teacher (who has been the victim of the bullying) then faces their perpetrator, personally, and directly, making clear to them how the student's behaviour has affected their teaching and their ability to work effectively, and fairly, with the class group. Most of all the teacher refers to the basic right we all have to respect and fair treatment. This is the most emotional part of the conference as the teacher, looking their perpetrator in the eye, relives the emotions of the taunt, the back-handed comment, the hurtful laughter and the student's demeaning body language. It can help if the facilitator also makes some comment that relates to the behaviour in question. What is difficult in such a recounting is the avoiding of verbal hostility, or aggression. The student needs to hear the emotion without destroying the teacher-student relationship. By describing their feelings, the teacher is describing the effect of the offending behaviour. In some cases the student may not realise how hurtful their behaviour has been. By having to face their victim directly, the facilitator enables the personalising of this social transaction for the bully. The bully can see, and feel, the effect of his behaviour, and be called to account for that behaviour. The

facilitator will then direct the bully to make clear that this specific bullying behaviour has to stop. The bully is directly asked how he will do this.

3 The teacher completes the recounting of events by looking at the student and directing them to stop these behaviours. The teacher can say, '… [name the student] I want you to stop doing … [specify the key behaviours without going over the whole list again] so I can get on with the job of teaching here. I don't expect you to treat me in these ways. I don't dislike you but I cannot allow you to continually upset learning in our classroom and my teaching.' It is important that these points are made briefly, clearly and firmly without hostility and aggression. Avoid a lecture!

4 The student is invited to respond to what the teacher has said. The teacher and the facilitator will listen to the explanations, but always keeping the focus on the fundamental right or rule, and also the school's policy on harassment. It can help to re-emphasise, through a question, how the student imagines the teacher feels when the harassing students do what they do. If the student argues, 'I'm not the only one who says stuff and laughs and all that!', the teacher replies, 'Maybe you're not. I'll be speaking to the other students who have been behaving in these ways …. For the moment I'm reminding you that we have a school right about safety and fair treatment and that we don't harass others here.' If the student continues to protest we re-emphasise the point: 'Maybe you didn't see it that way … but when you frequently make gestures like … and say things like … then that is harassment. We cannot, ever, allow that at our school, it has to stop. What will you do to make it stop?'

5 If the student refuses to talk and sits there obdurate, it is enough to point out specifically that what the student has been doing or saying is against school policy and, more important, against fair rights, and that the student:
   –has a right of reply.
   –is expected to change their behaviours. Although we can hardly force an apology, it may be enough at this stage to let the student know that we expect an apology. It is right; it is proper; it is necessary.
   –gives an assurance that this behaviour will stop (particularly the winding up of other students to harass their teacher).
   –will have to face the consequences … if they choose not to change the behaviour (this should be said without threat).

6 The student is then invited by the facilitator to make amends: 'What will you now do to assure [name the teacher] that she can teach in 8D without having to put up with these sorts of behaviours? What can you do (what do you need to do) to repair the damage and help put things right?' Most students (not all) will apologise. An apology should be accepted, even if delivered sulkily. The facilitator can then ask what the student will actually do (not just stop doing)

next time in class. This is written down.

7 The conference finishes with the facilitator saying: '..., we'll meet together in a week's time to see how things are going back in class.' This, in effect, puts the student 'on notice'. The teacher(s) and student separate amicably (at least on the teacher's part).

The whole process can occur without the teacher being present. If the teacher is too upset or traumatised by the harassing student(s), then the senior colleague will go through these steps with each student one to one, although it is desirable that the affected teacher be actively present.

Suspected perpetrator

Where the teacher suspects that a student is involved in some class harassment, in a collusive ('indirect') way, the teacher and facilitator can pursue the 'no blame' approach. I have adapted this from Pikas (1989), and Rogers (2002a). For example, there are students in the group who will engage in excluding behaviours that effectively lock the teacher out of the class group so that the teacher cannot effectively exercise their relational and role authority with the group. My colleagues and I have found the following approach helpful:

1 Outline what has been happening: 'Carly, I'd like to talk with you for a moment about what's been going on in our class.' Of course, the facilitator can pursue these issues on behalf of the class teacher, for example 'Ms G has been hearing a lot of comments such as … [be specific].' Let the student know that you are interviewing a number of students in class, not just one student.

2 Invite comment/feedback: 'What do you know about this, Carly?' Again the process is both a genuine attempt to elicit information as well as letting the student know you are 'on her case' (even if you have no 'direct proof').

3 It can be helpful to outline how the teacher feels when this behaviour is going on, or ask the students how they think their teacher might feel. I pursued this approach once with several students who merely thought they were having fun (with a non-assertive teacher). Several of the students had shed some involuntary tears (tears I hadn't intended). They all apologised to him (as a small group), though they asked if I'd be present at the formal apology (I suspect to convince me they were serious about making amends).

4 Note down the student's observations and feedback, even if the student suggests that the teacher's behaviour may be 'contributing' to some of the behaviours we are now addressing in this meeting. Some teachers will benefit by being aware of behaviours that easily elicit student hassling in a group (in terms of group dynamics). The way some teachers dress; speak (those idiosyncratic behaviours that look unusual or funny); mannerisms and so on can affect student percep-

tion and give easy rise to comments, gestures and laughter. This is not to excuse the way some students behave, just to explain and come to terms with social reality and classroom dynamics. If the harassing behaviour in question is particularly offensive it will be important to add: 'No one deserves this kind of behaviour because they look or sound different, or act in a way you don't like. If you've got a legitimate complaint about a teacher, you know we'll speak with that teacher or even have a class meeting.' Finish by saying: 'I've made a note of your observations/comments. I think we've talked long enough.'

5 Reaffirm the school's behaviour code/rights (briefly) and let the student know we will convene second meeting to review with this student 'how things are going back in 8D'. (Again this puts the student 'on notice'.)

With a suspected perpetrator the teacher/facilitator does not apportion blame. They describe and acknowledge what is happening, ask questions and leave the student with the responsibility to, in effect, let the grapevine/tribal 'tom-toms' do the rest.

If the bullying behaviour is very serious, or continues on after such a meeting, the school will need to pursue full due process via the anti-harassment policy. This will involve parent conference, suspension and (in some cases) exclusion.

The key to dealing with bullying is to build a school climate and ethos that make it difficult for such behaviours to get a foothold. This will occur if the school has a climate of safe disclosure and a supportive colleague (no blame) colleague support where people look out for one another.

As Smith and Thompson (1991) note, 'If you get it out in the open, you have a better chance of dealing with it.'

Chapter 10

CONCLUSION

*Does practice ever square with theory? Is it not in the
nature of things that, whatever people think, practice
should come less close to truth than theory?
Do you agree or not? I agree.*
Plato, The Republic, Book 5, p 472
Penguin Classics, 1980. (Lee, D.)

This has not been an easy book to write. Constantly reflecting on the hard classes
I have had, and those I've worked in with my colleagues, has brought back some
tough, and, even, painful memories. I can recall the stress and strain and the hurt
that some students inflict on their teachers. Trying to put that reality into perspective, and then into print, has concerned me a little – mainly that the reader
might gain the impression that this is the way *schools* are. It isn't. Most students
and most classes in most schools do get on well with their teachers (bad-day-not
withstanding). The hard-class syndrome is, however, a reality and it has been my
attempt to address the issue *as a teacher*.

You will need to read other books if you want to explore socioeconomic or
sociocultural perspectives on the behaviourally disordered preconditions affecting
schools. That is not my brief. I'm concerned here with how my colleagues and I
can realistically cope with hard classes and how we can make a positive, supportive, difference. Genuine colleague support can always help put the hard-class
syndrome back into some perspective.

Teaching is a job that can 'eat up' your life: beyond our daily teaching there is
the ever present marking; following up students; planning units of work; fiddling
around on the computer to get the right 'feel' to that worksheet; developing individual education plans to help a student cope; more marking; meetings; more
meetings; taking work home; designing posters; organising the room; and more
meetings … This is the profession we chose. It's the normality of our teaching life.

When we get a hard class, however, it seems to dominate our perceptive; we
don't look forward to the day or that timetable slot. We may easily allow that

class an unrealistic, and inordinate, place in the overall scheme of things. What I mean is that we may be overfocusing on the behaviour of the class (or key individuals) and not seeing all the other positive aspects of the group or even all the other positive aspects of our teaching: our contribution to the school, the times when things have gone well; our successful classes.

It's like looking at a white square that has a dot in the centre. If we are not careful, thoughtful and aware, we may see only the 'black' dot – the worse elements of our stressful situation – at the expense of the many (often much more) positive aspects of our teaching, the students and even of life itself!

That is not to deny the reality of the 'black dot' (the presence of stress, produced by difficult and demanding students, hard classes, pressure and tiredness, and emotional pain). Denial is, itself, unhealthy – even dangerous. See the 'black dot' for what it is – it is there, and it is demanding. I have to cope with it and come to terms with it; and I can. What I won't do is let it dominate my teaching and my life, so it is the only thing I see in the square.

I remember when my daughters, and I, swam with wild dolphins in Port Phillip Bay (actually they were very civil). We left the pier at Sorrento (Victoria, Australia) in a largish boat equipped with wetsuits, snorkels and flippers. There were about 20 intrepid dolphin lovers on board.

As the boat cruised the bay, our professional dolphin tour leader explained that when a pod of dolphins was sighted we were to get into the water quickly and hang on to a line running back off the stern. We would be gently towed through the water and, if we looked below us, we would see the dolphins swimming around and underneath us. He also explained that we were there to entertain them, not vice versa. 'What do you mean?' I asked. 'Well, sing to them; they like singing.' I thought of my singing voice and reflected it would be more likely that I'd scare them away. But no, I was assured dolphins like 'happy noises' (not loud but happy singing).

Eventually, as the boat slowly trudged the bay, a pod of dolphins was sighted. Several dolphins were leaping, with flashing tails, in the late afternoon sun. We even saw a baby dolphin. 'In the water, quickly!' – our guide beckoned us to drop off the back of the boat and swim off onto the two trailing lines on the water, held up by buoys at the stern. My oldest daughter and I swam out. There were about ten of us along the two lines stretching from the stern. Our leader said, 'They're coming – now, underneath you!' and then said in a loud whisper 'Sing, sing!'

No one sang; their heads were under water trying to glimpse what we'd all come for. I thought I'd better kick off a song or two. For some reason I could only think of the Italian song 'O Sole Mio!' And it's hard to sing under water through a snorkel! Worse, I couldn't remember the Italian words, so I sang (in pitch, with bubbles, in the cold, green water of the bay): 'Oh sole mio, I've come to see you. I only paid 50 dollars but I know it's worth it … Oh sole mio; I'm here to see you …' You understand that I sang the refrain with a snorkel and Italian accent (no offence) and so I raved on. And they came! Two huge grey and scarred bodies, bottle-nosed with that unique smile dolphins have. They slid underneath me as I held a line. My daughter called out (under water), 'They're coming, Dad!' The two bodies rolled over each other, smoothly and gracefully as they swam a metre underneath us. It was fantastic. Everything else, for a few moments, paled into the background. One of the dolphins looked up at me; its eye seemed to lock on me. I smiled and said, 'Hi.' I don't know if the dolphin registered that I was an underwater teacher also scarred by life's vicissitudes! But as I looked at my fellow creature it helped to put back a bit of perspective in my life. It was a great day, a great experience. We've since repeated this wonderful experience (I recommend it highly!)

It is important to have a significant life outside teaching; to find healthy and creative ways to put our stressed lives back into perspective. It may be a film, a long walk in the countryside, music, a night with friends, hobbies, a book, a relaxing drink and chat or even a swim with dolphins in the bay.

It is important to keep our perspective so that we don't overfocus on the 'black dot' in an otherwise 'white square'. The 'black dot' can (if we're not careful) overly affect (even infect) the positive areas of our life.

■ Avoid letting a bad day (or bad days) affect all the other areas of your life, especially your life outside school. Our partners, children and friends don't deserve the entrails of 8D replayed unthinkingly in our home or elsewhere.

- Avoid the easy blaming of yourself when things are going wrong and you can't seem to get the class focused or on track. If you have honestly tried and have sought (and utilised) colleague support, you have done your best. Failure, bad days and genuine mistakes (that result from tiredness and work overload) usually have only a temporary effect (Seligman 1990) and if we're aware of that reality we can learn from it. As Noel Coward succinctly put it, 'The secret of success is the ability to survive failure.'

- Avoid the unthinking rating of self, 'I'm not as good a teacher as so and so.' *All* teachers struggle at times with their teaching and management role, but not all teachers admit it. I was conducting a workshop some years ago on colleague support and a teacher of 30 years' experience surprised his peers by sharing (publicly) that the Year 7 he was teaching had really caused him to reassess his teaching and management. This admission, in itself, was a source of encouragement to his younger colleagues – '*you* too.' (*cf*. p 170*f*)

- Above all seek the support of your colleagues (and support them in return). As the English playwright (and novelist) J. B. Priestly said, 'We don't live alone. We are members of one body. We are responsible for one another' (from 'An Inspector Calls', 1944).

I hope this book will be useful as a way of reclaiming a sense of perspective with your hard(er) class(es). Most of all, I trust it will assist in the process of giving and receiving colleague support – the support that can make all the difference.

Appendices

APPENDIX 1: Colleague Support
– Staff Questionnaire

The issues listed here provide a basic framework for developing a staff questionnaire.

Preface

This questionnaire survey forms a part of the process of reviewing colleague support in our school. Of course, the issue of colleague support can range from the relaxed conversations with a colleague through to how we plan together and communicate across the school. It can cover issues such as 'structural' support (where we support one another through time-out provisions for difficult and demanding students) as well as issues such as peer mentoring and staff appraisal.

We are concerned to ascertain how you perceive colleague support at our school – both its strengths and limitations. We also wish to define and improve areas in which colleagues have concerns or perceive a lack of support.

This questionnaire is, of course, confidential and all results will be communicated to staff at the earliest convenience. The feedback and opinions from the questionnaire will form a basis for review and action planning in future team-facility meetings and whole-staff planning sessions.

The questionnaire

1   What does colleague support mean for you – as a teacher?

2   In what areas do you believe colleague support is operating effectively at school? (tick boxes):

☐ planning of lessons; units of work; use of resources
☐ problem solving on issues of concern (such as discipline and classroom control)
☐ back-up support in difficult management situations (such as time-out)
☐ follow-up with difficult students (such as holding a behaviour conference and conflict resolution)
☐ colleague mentoring and appraisal.

	Very supportive/ confident	Supportive/ confident	Only if I really push it	Not supportive/ confident
3 a How supportive are your team leader, head of department and administration (deputy/principal)?	☐	☐	☐	☐
b How confident are you of receiving support from your team leader/year level co-ordinator, deputy or principal?	☐	☐	☐	☐

c   What sort of support do you receive from these colleagues?
d   What sort of support do you look for from these colleagues?
e   In what ways, if any, could such support be improved?

4   a   Looking back over your teaching career, what kind(s) of colleague support have you most appreciated?

_____

_____

Why? _____

b   Are there any models of colleague support – ways of working together – you have found helpful in other schools that you believe we could benefit from and apply here? Please summarise.

_____

_____

_____

5   a   If you believed you needed support in the area of behaviour management or lesson plan-ning from a team leader or senior administrator, how would you normally initiate such support?

_____

_____

b   If administration had to support a colleague whom they believed needed support and assistance in areas such as behaviour-management, classroom discipline and teaching strategies – how should such an approach be made?

_____

_____

c   What should the senior colleague consider when approaching and offering support? (This is assuming that colleagues have not initiated any support themselves or that they do not see they have any concerns or problems, or if they do they are not acknowledging those problems.) (cf p 167 particularly)

_____

6   In what areas here in our school do you believe colleague support is difficult to obtain and why?

_____

_____

7   Do you have any concerns about colleague support (or lack of it) in this school? If so, please note those concerns (it would help if you could also note why).

_____

_____

8   In what ways are your skills, abilities and contributions acknowledged here at school? Please note the ways.

_____

_____

9   To whom do you normally turn for professional guidance and advice that you can count on?

_____

10 Do you have any suggestions, beyond those you have already noted, about how we can develop a more supportive culture here in our school?

_____

_____

APPENDIX 2: The 4W Form

Student's name _____ Class _____

Teacher's name _____

Subject _____ Date _____

Student comments

What I did against our class or school rules (my behaviour)

_____
_____
_____

What rules (or rights) I broke (or infringed)

_____
_____
_____

What is my explanation?

_____
_____
_____

What I think I should do to fix things up or work things out

_____
_____
_____

Teacher's comments only

_____
_____
_____

Resolution required by initiating teacher (please tick)

☐ Total exits from this class
☐ I will work through the conflict
☐ I will arrange a time with my year level co-ordinator (home class issues)
☐ I will arrange a time with the subject co-ordinator (subject issues)
☐ I need the intervention of the year level supervisor to work with me and the student

Return to year level co-ordinator

Note that this form may have various names, for example Personal Response Sheet, Student Response Sheet or Behaviour Response Form.

APPENDIX 3: Stop/Start behaviour plan

OK,
think about it . . .
WHAT am I doing?

MY GOALS	
STOP DOING	**START DOING**
1 _____	1 _____
2 _____	2 _____
3 _____	3 _____

- Is your plan achievable?
- OK, how will you do it? Discuss this with your teacher.
- How will you handle 'bad days'?
- What support will you need from your teacher?

APPENDIX 4: The 3W Sheet

OUR CLASS!

Please record your answers on a separate sheet. Thanks!

So:

1   What's working well in our class?
    What things (activities and the way we run things) work well in our class and why?

2   What's not working well and why?
    Anything upsetting you? Why? (If personal, put it in writing.)

3   What are some things we can change? How?

    Let's discuss together.
    Let's make a plan for action:
    a   Things we can start soon
    b   Things that will take a bit longer
    c   How we'll do it.

APPENDIX 5: No put down zone

APPENDIX 6

The following 'rule posters' are typical examples of those my colleagues and I have used in re-establishing a class group. The language is positive (in expression) *focussing on the key behaviours that flow from the basic rights we all have as members of our school community*. Such posters can also be used on a year-level basis. The posters highlight the *summarised* expectations: the entailing of these expectations needs some brief classroom discussion (see Appendix 6A p 207).

See below (for example) the 'poster' for **learning in our class**: there are six basic reminders common to all classes, all students:

1 **Get to class on time** ('entry': refers to considerate entry);
2 **Settle** (settle in your seats); **Relax** (in a 'semi-comatose' state!); **Prepare** (be prepared to contribute and give it your best);
3 **Appropriate materials** (this will vary across some subject areas);
4 **Hands up** (this short clause is a reminder to put hands up *without* calling out; one-at-a-time; any questions, or contribution, is for all – not just for the teacher therefore we all listen as we would expect to be heard, and listened to); FGFA (Fair Go For All. We listen when others share/ask/contribute; when we disagree we disagree respectfully);
5 **Partner-voice/co-operative talk** (we discuss the nature of noise levels relative to our subject area);
6 **If you need TA** (if you need teacher assistance, check set work *yourself*; check with *nearest* classmate, or write name on **THB** – 'Teacher Help Board'. **OW** stands for 'go on with other work while I check the Teacher Help Board and get around to assist you …'). (See also p 83.)

APPENDIX 6(a)

WE ALL HAVE A RIGHT TO LEARN

TO LEARN WELL HERE WE :-

(1) Get to class on time, (entry);
(2) Settle / relax / prepare...;
(3) Appropriate materials;
(4) Hands up ...

FGFA

(5) Partner-voice Co-op. talk;
(6) If you need T.A. remember :-
(7) Check first → classmate → THB → OW

Ta!

Mr Rogers : English

See Appendix 6.

These key expectations (of behaviour) relate directly to the right to learn (without unfair, undue, distractions or disruption). These expectations will be discussed, and clarified, with the class group. The poster, then, serves as a visible *aide memoire* and is used in the brief (necessary) reminders when we engage in discipline. The teacher will *briefly* glance back at, or direct their hand towards, the poster reminder, eg: '*Remember our class agreement ... hands up (without calling out). Thanks.*' (See p 81*f*.)

APPENDIX 6(b)

The other rule poster (noted here) is a poster that highlights fundamental respect and fair treatment. In *this* format it would be relevant in any class/subject.

WE ALL HAVE A RIGHT TO RESPECT

To enjoy one another's respect here we remember that :

- **We all share the same place, space & reason for being *here*.**
- **We all share the same fundamental feelings** – it's all about the way we treat o/a here.
- **Safety is more than physical safety** (people's feelings, personal space, property).
- **Considered language** (no put-downs, cheap shots). Bullying is totally unacceptable in our school.
- **Courtesy, consideration and manners. Thanks.**

'Ta!'

Mr Rogers : English   **Courtesy is catching!**

---

o/a = one another

Bibliography

Amis, K 1996, *You Can't Do Both*, Flamingo, London.

Barrish, H H, Saunders, M & Wolf, M M 1969, 'Good behaviour game: Effects of individual contingencies for group consequences on disruptive behaviour in the classroom', *Journal of Applied Behaviour Analysis*, vol 2, pp 119–24.

Bernard, M 1990, *Taking the Stress out of Teaching*, Collins-Dove, Melbourne.

Biggs, J & Telfer, R 1981, *The Process of Learning*, Prentice-Hall, Melbourne.

Brown, D, Reschly, D & Sabers, D 1974, 'Using group contingencies with punishment and positive reinforcement to modify aggressive behaviours in a 'Head Start' classroom', *Psychological Record*, vol 24, pp 291–496.

Caffyn, R E 1989, 'Attitudes of British secondary school teachers and pupils to rewards and punishments', *Educational Research*, vol 13, no 3, Nov, pp 210–20.

Clough, P, Garner, P, Pardeck, J T & Yuen, F 2005, *Handbook of Emotional and Behavioural Difficulties*, Sage Publications: London.

Conway, R 1974, *The Land of the Long Weekend*, Sun Books, Melbourne.

Dalton, J 1985, *Adventures in Thinking: Creative Thinking and Co-operative Talk in Small Groups*, Nelson, Melbourne.

De Bono, E 1985, *Conflicts: A Better Way to Resolve Them*, Penguin Books, Harmondsworth, UK.

Dempster, M & Raff, D 1992, *Class Discussions: A Powerful Classroom Strategy*, Hawker Brownlow Education, Cheltenham, Vic.

Department of Education and the Arts, Tasmania 1990, *Positive Discipline: Improving Behaviour in Your Classroom*, Hobart.

Doyle, W 1986, 'Classroom organisation and management', in *Handbook of Research on Teaching*, ed M C Whitrock, Macmillan, New York.

Dreikurs, R, Grunwald, B & Pepper, F 1982, *Maintaining Sanity in the Classroom*, Harper and Row, New York.

Elton, et al 1989, *The Elton Report: Discipline in Schools*, Report of the Committee of Inquiry, Her Majesty's Stationery Office, London.

Embling, J 1987, 'Dark and bloody side to young life today', *the Age*, 2 June, p 22.

Glasser, W 1991, *The Quality School: Managing Students Without Coercion*, Harper and Row, New York.

Goffman, E 1972, *The Presentation of Self in Everyday Life*, Penguin, Harmondsworth, UK.

Gossen, D 1992, *Restitution*, New View Publications, North Carolina.

Green, C & Chee, K 1995, *Understanding ADD*, Doubleday, Sydney.

Harris, S J 1973, *Winners and Losers*, Argus Communications, Niles, Illinois.

Hill, S & Hill, T 1990, *The Collaborative Classroom*, Eleanor Curtin Publishing, South Yarra, Vic.

Hobfoll, S E 1998, *Stress, Culture and Community: The Psychology and Philosophy of Stress*, Plenum Press, N.Y.

Johnson, D W & Johnson B T 1989, *Leading the Co-operative School*, Interaction Books Co, Minnesota.

Johnson, L 1992, *My Posse Don't Do Homework*, St Martin's Press, New York.

Jones, P & Tucker, P (eds) 1990, *Mixed Ability Teaching: Classroom Experiences in English, ESL, Mathematics and Science*, St Clair Press, Rozelle, NSW.

Kounin, J 1970, *Discipline and Group Management in the Classroom*, Holt, Rinehart and Winston, New York.

Kyriacou, C 1986, *Effective Teaching in Schools*, Basil Blackwell, Oxford.

Kyriacou, C 1991, *Essential Teaching Skills*, Basil Blackwell, Oxford.

Lewis, C S 1943, *The Abolition of Man*, Collins/Fount, Glasgow.

McCarthy, P, Freeman, L, Rothwell, C & Arnheim, B 1983, 'Is there life after 8D? Group reinforcement at the postprimary level', *Interview*, no 11, Ministry of Education, Victoria.

McGrath, H & Francey, S 1993, *Friendly Kids, Friendly Classrooms*, Longman, Melbourne.

McInerney, D & McInerney, V 1994, *Educational Psychology: Constructing Learning*, Prentice-Hall, Sydney.

McNeil, C 1994, *AD/HD Classroom Kit – An Inclusive Approach to Behaviour Management Instruction Manual*, Centre for Applied Psychology, PO Box 61586, PA 19406.

Morgan, D P & Jenson, W R 1988, *Teaching Behaviourally Disordered Students: Preferred Practices*, Merrill Publishing Co, Toronto.

Nelson, J 1987, *Positive Discipline*, Ballantyne Books, New York.

Olweus, D 1978, *Aggression in School: Bullies and Whipping Boys*, Hemisphere, Washington, DC.

Pearce, H 1995, *Groupwork in the Classroom*, Cambridge, (unpublished notes).

Pikas, A 1989, 'A pure concept of mobbing gives the best results for treatment', *School Psychology International*, 10, pp 95–104.

Potter, S 1950, Our Language: *The English Language: Its Sources, Its History, Its Peculiar Genius*, Pelican Books, London.

Robertson, J 1995, *Effective Classroom Control: Understanding Teacher–Pupil Relationships*, 3rd edn, Hodder & Stoughton, London.

Rogers, B 1992, *Supporting Teachers in the Workplace: Teacher Stress and Collegial Support*, Jacaranda Press, Milton, Qld. In the U.K. Published as *Managing Teacher Stress*, Pearson Education,1996.

Rogers, B 1995, *Behaviour Management: A Whole-School Approach*, Scholastic, Gosford, NSW. (2nd Edition: 2006). In the U.K., second edition published by Paul Chapman, London, 2006.

Rogers, B 1998, *You Know the Fair Rule, and Much More*, ACER Press, Melbourne. In the U.K. published by Pearson Education, London, 1998.

Rogers, B 2002a, *Classroom Behaviour: A Practical Guide to Effective Teaching, Behaviour Management, and Colleague Support*, Paul Chapman Publishing, London. Second Edition, 2006.

Rogers, B 2002b, *I Get by with a Little Help: Colleague Support in Schools*, ACER Press, Melbourne. In the U.K. published by Paul Chapman, London, 2006.

Rogers, B 2003a, *Behaviour Recovery: A Whole-School Programme for Mainstream Schools*,

ACER, Camberwell, Vic. In the U.K. published by Paul Chapman, London, 2004.

Rogers, B 2003b, *Effective Supply Teaching*, Paul Chapman Publishing, London.

Russell, D W, Altmaier, E & Van Velzen, D 1987, 'Job related stress: Social support and burnout among classroom teachers', *Journal of Applied Psychology*, vol 72, no 2, May, pp 269–74.

Rutter, M, Maughan, B, Mortimer, P & Ouston, J 1979, *Fifteen Thousand Hours: Secondary Schools and Their Effects on Children*, Open Books, London.

Schopenhauer, A 1976, *Essays and Aphorisms* translated by R J Hollingdale, Penguin, London.

Seligman, M 1990, *Learned Optimism*, Random House, Sydney.

Serfontein, G 1990, *The Hidden Handicap: How to Help Children Who Suffer from Dyslexia, Hyperactivity and Learning Difficulties*, Simon & Schuster, Sydney.

Smith, P K & Thompson, P 1991, *Practical Approaches to Bullying*, David Fulton, London.

Tobias, S 1989, 'Tracked to Fail', *Psychology Today*, Sept, pp 54–60.

Tournier, P 1957, *The Meaning of Persons*, SCM Press, London.

Wilkes, R 1981, 'Fly me to the moon: A classroom behaviour management programme to enhance learning', *Interview*, no. 3, Ministry of Education, Victoria.

Wood, E & Knight, J 1994, 'I feel sorry for supply teachers: An ethnographic study', in *Introduction to Research Methods*, ed R C Burns, Longman, Melbourne.

Wragg, J 1989, *Talk Sense to Yourself: A Program for Children and Adolescents*, ACER, Camberwell, Vic.

Index